THE MAKING OF MODERN ETHIOPIA
1896-1974

The Making of Modern Ethiopia 1896-1974

Teshale Tibebu, Ph.D.

RSP THE RED SEA PRESS INC.
Publishers and Distributors of Third World Books
11-D Princess Road,
Lawrenceville, NJ 08648

The Red Sea Press, Inc.
11-D Princess Rd.
Lawrenceville, NJ 08648

First Printing 1995

Book design: Jonathan Gullery
Book Cover Design: Carles J. Juzang

Library of Congress Cataloging-in-Publication Data

Teshale Tibebu
The making of modern Ethiopia : 1896-1974 / Teshale Tibebu.
p. cm.
Includes bibliographical references (p.) and index.
ISBN 1-56902-000-0 -- ISBN 1-56902-001-9 (pbk.)
1. Ethiopia--History--1896-1974. I. Title.
DT387.T47 1995
963--dc20 94-42814
CIP

This book is composed in Life Roman and Veljovic Bold

Contents

Dedication

To my Godson, Noah;
and to my late father,
Merigeta Tibebu Beyene Gebre-Medhin

Acronyms

AEH	African Economic History
AHS	African Historical Studies
ASR	African Studies Review
BUPA	Boston University Papers on Africa
CEA	Cahiers d'Etudes Africaines
CEF	Conference on Ethiopian Feudalism
CJAS	Canadian Journal of African Studies
CSSH	Comparative Studies on Society and History
IJAHS	International Journal of African Historical Studies
IJSP	International Journal of Social Psychiatry
JAH	Journal of African History
JAS	Journal of African Studies
JAL	Journal of African Law
JES	Journal of Ethiopian Studies
JMAS	Journal of Modern African Studies
JRGS	Journal of the Royal Geographical Society
JSS	Journal of Semitic Studies
NEAS	North East African Studies
PEICES	Proceedings of the Eighth International Conference on Ethiopian Studies
PFICES	Proceedings of the Fifth International Conference on Ethiopian Studies
PFUSCES	Proceedings of the First United States Conference on Ethiopian Studies
PSICES	Proceedings of the Seventh International Conference on Ethiopian Studies
PTICES	Proceedings of the Tenth International Conference on Ethiopian Studies
RAPE	Review of African Political Economy
TAJH	Trans-African Journal of History

Preface

This work is, in any sense, an Amharic social history of modern Ethiopia written in English. It reflects my graduate training in historical social science at Binghamton University with Immanuel Wallerstein and his "world-system perspective." A good part of this work is taken from my 1989 Ph.D. dissertation of the same title.

Thanks to my exposure to "world-system perspective," I have discussed Ethiopia's modern social history from a comparative perspective, that the processes of "modernization" of Ethiopia in the twentieth century be seen as interaction of global forces and that of the Ethiopian polity. The Ethiopian concept of Ethiopia as *tafrana takabra yanorach agar* (a country that lived feared and respected by others) is let rest in historical archives. Ethiopia in the twentieth century was anything but "feared and respected," especially by Western powers.

Many people have helped me at various steps in the making of the manuscript. As it grew out of my dissertation, my first thanks go to my dissertation advisors, Professors Giovanni Arrighi, Terence K. Hopkins, and Immanuel Wallerstein. I would also like to thank the person who was responsible for my coming to Binghamton University from Addis Ababa University, Professor Samir Amin. Dr. Mohammed Hassen took time from his very busy schedule to go through my manuscript. His comments and suggestions were very helpful. Dr. Mohammed Hassen is a scholar whom I respect. I thank him very much for his help. I am grateful to Temple University for offering me Summer Research Grant in 1993 which helped me polish my manuscript.

Finally, I thank my publisher, Kassahun Checole, for the speed and professionalism in which he processed the manuscript into a book form.

Introduction

I

Ethiopia, with close to sixty million people, is the third most populous country in Africa, after Nigeria and Egypt, and the second in the so-called sub-Saharan Africa. In culture and religious composition, it is a microcosm of Africa. Besides some "traditional" African religions, Ethiopia is the second oldest Christian polity in Africa, after Coptic Egypt, and one of the first places Islam gained ground. It contains some of the highest mountain ranges in Africa, with Ras Dashan over fifteen thousand feet above sea level, and the lowest depression on earth, the Dallol depression (see Mesfin Wolde Mariam 1972). It is one of the oldest places in the world to practice agriculture (Ehret, *JAH*, 20, 2, 1979) and still has a considerable number of nomads and pastoralists. Ethiopia is a museum of cultures, religions, and modes of production. And yet, a theoretically-framed social history of Ethiopia has not yet been written. This work is an attempt to fill that gap. Richard Pankhurst's *A Social History of Ethiopia* (1992), is descriptive and loose.[1] As Pankhurst noted: "[The book] is intended to present a survey on available sources, and thereby to lay groundwork for other writers to develop more ambitious, comprehensive and interpretive, studies of old-time [in this case, modern] Ethiopian life" (*Ibid*, p. xi). My work here is a "reply" to Pankhurst's "call" for a theoretical, interpretive, and interdisciplinary social history of modern Ethiopia.

One of the first questions historians ask is the question of periodization. How old is Ethiopian history? We might answer by stating that Ethiopian history is as old as one wants it to be.

If one wanted to take an extremely long view, one could say that Ethiopian history is as old as the history of the human species itself. After all, in the beginning was Dinqinesh (How Wonderful You Are), best known to the West by the name of the Beatles song "Lucy." Her remains were found at Hadar, Afarland in eastern Ethiopia on November 30, 1974 (Johanson and Edey 1981). With the scientific name of *Australopithecus Afarensis*, Dinqinesh is the oldest human ancestor, by a good 3.5 million years. Ethiopia is thus the birthplace of humankind. The problem is that Dinqinesh did not have an Ethiopian passport.

It is, however, more customary to cite three possible timescales for Ethiopian history: (1) Ethiopian history is 3,000 years old; (2) it is 100 years old; and (3) it is 40 years old.

The first scale is that of Ethiopia's self-declared 3,000-year history of independence; the second is that of Ethiopia's modern form given by Emperor Menelik; and the third is Eritrea's incorporation with Ethiopia as a federal unit under the imperial crown in 1952.

Some historians take the coronation of Emperor Tewodros II in 1855 as the beginning of modern Ethiopian history, which can be further periodized into three 40-year eras: from Tewodros's coronation to the Battle of Adwa (1855–1896); from the Battle of Adwa to the Italian occupation (1896–1936); and from the Italian occupation to the revolution of 1974–76.

The massive outpouring of support for Ethiopia during the Italian fascist aggression in 1935—36, the ignominious failure of the League of Nations to come to Ethiopia's defense, Ethiopia's being the object of Western appeasement (Schaefer ed. 1961), the five-year continuous Ethiopian resistance against Mussolini's war machine, Haile Selassie's famous speech at the League of Nations in 1936 imploring the League, "What do I have to take back to my people?", the liberation of the country in 1941, Haile Selassie's role in the Non-Aligned movement and the formation of the Organization of African Unity in 1963 at Addis Ababa, have all created a lasting image of Ethiopia as a unique country in Africa, a country that was Christian when the Anglo Saxons were prostrating themselves in front of pagan idols. It is the modern history of this Ethiopia that is discussed here.

II

The scholarly literature on Ethiopia can be classified into three broad categories: what I call the Aksumite paradigm, the Orientalist Semiticist paradigm, and the Radical Left paradigm.

The Aksumite paradigm has been elaborated by the Ethiopian Orthodox Monophysite Church and its patrons among the notables, first and foremost the *negusa nagast* (king of kings). The Aksumite paradigm defines the self-consciousness of the ruling class of

Ethiopian civilization. I prefer to call it Ge'ez civilization. (It is discussed in detail in Chapter 1.)

The Orientalist Semiticist paradigm in Ethiopian studies was formulated by European Ethiopic-Semitic philologists well versed in the Ethiopic language. It produced the systematic discourse of "Ethiopianist Studies" based in part on the Ethiopian literate tradition. Ethiopianist Studies is a child of Orientalism, or, to be more precise, of Orientalist Semiticism. As a discipline, it started as an offshoot of Semitic philology, a branch of Orientalism.[2] Some of the outstanding names include the Germans Hiob Ludlof, the founder of Ethiopianist Studies in Europe in the 17th century (Haberland in *PTICES*, 1969),[3] and August Dillman, "the re-founder of Abyssinian studies, the Ludolf of the 19th century" (Ullendorff 1960, p. 20), the Britishers, Sir E. A. Wallis Budge — Orientalist, Egyptologist, Ethiopic-Semiticist — C. F. Beckingham, G. W. B. Huntingford, the Swiss-born Edward Ullendorf,[4] and the Italian sage Carlo Conti Rossini. And then there is Wolf Leslau, undoubtedly the most learned Ethiopic-Semiticist scholar of the twentieth century.[5] All were formidable scholars who laid the groundwork for modern Ethiopian Studies.

There are also Orientalist sociologists like the American Donald Levine of the University of Chicago. And then there were traveller adventurers like the English novelists Evelyn Waugh and Herbert Vivian, whose views on Ethiopia were benighted by racial prejudice.[6]

The modern educated Ethiopian intelligentsia forms the bridge that links the Aksumite and Orientalist Semiticist paradigms. Some were trained in Orientalist institutions like the School of Oriental and African Studies. This coterie of Ethiopian scholars, mostly historians, combined the Aksumite and Orientalist Semiticist paradigms in their study of Ethiopian history. The prominent names on this bridge of intelligentsia include Taddesse Tamrat, Tekle Tsadik Mekouria, Zewde Gebre Selassie, Merid Wolde Aregay, and Sergew Hable Selassie.

On the radical left side of the scholarly divide are those critical of the two hegemonic paradigms. Radicalized by the global events in the 1960s, this group of scholars questioned the legitimacy of the Ethiopian imperial establishment and the scholarship that rationalized the legitimacy.

On the Ethiopian side of the radical left is the celebrated Ethiopian Students Movement (see Balsuik 1985). In the last five years alone, three excellent works on Ethiopian history were published by this coterie of scholars: Mohammed Hassen's *The Oromo of Ethiopia* (1990), Gebru Tareke's *Ethiopia: Power and Protest* (1991), and Bahru Zewde's *A History of Modern Ethiopia* (1991). These works, written by scholars baptized by the radical holy water of the Ethiopian Student Movement, open a new era of young, energetic Ethiopian scholarship. Their work is testimony that the student movement intelligentsia has come of age.

In the prefaces to their books, Mohammed Hassen and Gebru Tareke said that their works focus on nationality and class, respectively. Mine is an attempt to deal with both. I happen to believe that there is no objective standard by which the Gada system, an accomplishment of Oromo genius in social organization, can be seen as inferior to that of *qene,* an undertaking of Amhara genius in literary imagination. The scriptocentric bias of literary cultures is such that a dubious written work is given more credence than a reliable oral tradition. We should not forget that the scriptocentrism against the Oromo and other "non-literate" peoples of Ethiopia includes the overwhelming majority of Christian Ethiopians, including many notables, as well as peasants, who were illiterate.

On the non-Ethiopian side of the same line of divide are the works of John Markakis, Donald Crummey, Charles McClellan, Richard Caulk, and Donald Donham, to mention but few. The grey areas include Richard Pankhurst, whose immense contribution to Ethiopian economic history and Ethiopian history at large, is without equal. Without him, Ethiopian history would still be in its infancy.

III

In the scholarly tradition, Ethiopia is depicted with multiple personalities. For the Aksumite paradigm, Ethiopia is a Christian island surrounded by a heathen sea. For the Orientalist Semiticist paradigm, Ethiopia is Abyssinia, the Black-Caucasian, Semitic-Christian land of Prester John (Sanceau 1944; Beckingham and Huntingford eds. 1961). It is the living land of the Bible, "Canaan in the age of transistors" (Dugan and Lafore 1973, pp. 11-12). And for people like Herbert Vivian, Ethiopia was simply a "nation of niggers" (Vivian 1969, p. 248).

For pan-African nationalists, Ethiopia was the "shrine enclosing the last sacred spark of African political freedom, the impregnable rock of black resistance against white invasion, a living symbol, an incarnation of African independence" (Thwaite quoted in S. K. Asante 1977, pp. 16-17). Jomo Kenyatta said Ethiopia was the "sole remaining pride of Africans and Negroes in all parts of the world" (quoted in *Ibid*, p. 16). Thomas Hodgkin called Ethiopia "the living exemplar of an unconquered, historical African people" (1957, p. 181). Mussolini's invasion of Ethiopia became a turning point in the history of pan-African consciousness and made Ethiopia the metaphor for Africa wronged by the West.[7] Ethiopia became the jewel and pride of Africa and people of African descent. The pan-African construction of Ethiopian identity made Ethiopia the concentrated expression of Africa. Ethiopia carried the burden and suffering that was Africa. Ethiopia symbolized the hope and pride of Africa. It was the feeling that the pride of Adwa, the pride of Africa, was to be erased by the Fascist Italian aggression that galvanized the passionate pan-Africanist defense of Ethiopia.

The UNESCO *General History of Africa* takes the 1935 Italian invasion of Ethiopia as the beginning of the last eight-volume series, as a turning point in modern African history, as the beginning of African nationalism. Never since Marcus Garvey have so many people in Africa and the diaspora been mobilized as during the Italian invasion of Ethiopia.

If such was Ethiopia's image among pan-Africanists, it was otherwise for the ethnonationalists and regionalist nationalists in the Horn of Africa, including Greater Somalia nationalism. Eritrean, Oromo, Somali, etc., nationalisms defined Ethiopia as a Black African colonial power against whom the subject peoples have been fighting to attain their right to self-determination (I. M. Lewis ed. 1983; Markakis 1987). Following Western scholarship, Ethiopia is seen as the anomaly of Africa, but the anomaly lies not in Ethiopia being the only success story of Black triumph over White invaders, but that Ethiopia was the only Black African power that effectively participated in the European Scramble for Africa. The Organization of African Unity has its headquarters in Addis Ababa, the capital city of the only Black African colonial country. Alas!

For Ali Mazrui's analysis of Africa, Ethiopia is depicted as having its own triple heritage: Indigenous, Semitic, and Greco-Roman. Nay more, "The whole cultural history of Africa is captured in the transition from the triple ancient personality of Ethiopia to the triple modern personality of Nigeria" (*Issue*, 13, 1984, p. 3).[8]

In some Marxist as well as non-Marxist circles, Ethiopia is seen as a feudal or feudal-like polity akin to medieval Europe (Addis

Hiwet, *RAPE*, 1, 1975; Cohen, *CJAS*, 8, 1, 1974; Clapham in *CEF*, 1976; Crummey, *Past and Present*, 89, 1980; Ellis, *JMAS*, 14, 2, 1976; Hoben, in Marcus ed. *PFUSCES*, 1975; Markakis, *JMAS*, 11, 3, 1973). For European feudalism see (Bloch 1961; 1966; Brown 1973; Aston ed. 1985; Doyle 1986; Herlihy ed. 1971; Hilton ed. 1978; Duby 1980; Coulborn ed. 1965; Critchley 1978; for non-European feudalism, see Byres ed. 1985).

What a cumbersome load to carry for such a poor nation.

IV

In the Orientalist Semiticist intellectual tradition, which dominated Ethiopianist Studies until recently, Ethiopia is seen as being unique in and outlandish to Africa. In Czeslaw Jesman's words, "Ethiopia is the oldest African country, yet in many respects it is *in* rather than *of* Africa" (1963, p. 10). Ethiopia is a land of majestic ruin, civilized inertia, and barbarous splendor. Ethiopians are seen as being fiercely independent and xenophobic, Christian and yet too Judaic, black and yet Semitic, with written culture and yet with no literature, deeply religious and yet superstition-ridden.

In this paradigm, Ethiopians, or what Ullendorff called "The Abyssinians proper, the carriers of the historical civilization of Semitized Ethiopia" (1960, p. 32), are seen as being superior to Black Africans, including the many peoples inside Ethiopia itself, like the Oromo (*Ibid*, p. 76). For they are Christian, literate, civilized, handsome, and sovereign for millennia. "Abyssinia" is pictured as an outpost of civilization, the south western end of the Semitic world in Africa, the Christian Orient of Black Africa, the dim lamp on the mountain top that lighted on the ever-dark night that was Africa. It is quite revealing that more is written on Ethiopia in the *Journal of Semitic Studies* than in the *Journal of African History*.

Three ideas are central to the Orientalist Semiticist discourse of Ethiopianist studies: its views on Ethiopian history; its geographical isolation paradigm in understanding Ethiopian history; and its "discourse of manners and customs" (Pratt in Gates ed. 1986, p. 140), the so-called national character of "Abyssinians."

Ethiopian History

In the beginning was darkness. Then came the light of Sabaean civilization from the Asian side of the Red Sea. Sometime during the first millennium B. C., a group of Sabaeans crossed from Yemen to Africa through the narrow passway at Bab el-Mandab and made their way to Northern Ethiopia. They brought with them civilization, script, and the knowledge of agriculture (Murdock 1959, pp. 183, 183-4; Bent 1893, p. 175; Muller in Bent 1893, p. 231; Kobishanov in Mokhtar ed. 1981, pp. 398-9; Budge 1932, p. ix).[9] The Agaws and Bejas, who were among the indigenous peoples of Northern Ethiopia, were primitive by comparison. The Sabaeans belong to the Caucasian race, who mixed with the indigenous Negroid peoples, producing a society of "racial and religious confusion" (Seligman 1959, p. 103). The Sabaeans were the distant ancestors of Semitic-speaking Ethiopians like the Amhara and Tigrayans, while the Agaws were Cushitic speakers (Bender 1976a; 1976b).

Thus starts Ethiopian history, with the Sabaean conquest, with the triumph of Semitic-Hamitic civilization over the primitive Agaws and Bejas (Huntingford 1993, pp. 2-3). This is the premise of the Orientalist Semiticist paradigm in the study of Ethiopian history.

The Sabaean origin of Aksumite civilization (and of Ethiopian history) has been the accepted wisdom among the chief proponents of the Orientalist Semiticist paradigm, as well as the Western-educated Ethiopian scholars, with few exceptions like Getachew Haile, Hailu Habtu, and the playwright Tsegaye Gebre Medhin (see Tekle Tsadik Mekouria in Mokhtar ed. 1981, p. 411).

To say that Ethiopian history starts with the Sabaeans, and not with the Agaw, Beja, etc., is tantamount to starting with the invaders. If we take the liberty of analogy with Indian history, *mutatis mutandis*, the Sabaeans correspond to the Aryans, and the Agaw, Beja, etc., to the Dravidians. But the *Kebra Nagast* is no Vedas.

It is quite significant to emphasize that the Aksumite paradigm disagrees with the Orientalist Semiticist paradigm on two fundamental issues: (1) the "racial" identity of Ethiopians, and (2) the Sabaean origin thesis. "Racially," Ethiopians are referred to as *yakam ledjotch* (children of Kam or Ham), as opposed to Shem and Japhet. And Kam was Black African. As to the Sabaean thesis, with its "Sabaean Man's Burden," all the *Kebra Nagast*, the canon of the Aksumite paradigm, relates is the story of Queen Saba's adventure in Jerusalem, no Sabaeans crossing to Ethiopia, carrying the burden of civilization on their backs.

The Geographical Isolation Thesis

The geographical-isolation-of-Ethiopia thesis has been one of the most influential in Western Ethiopianist discourse. In the famous words of Edward Gibbon: "Encompassed on all sides by the enemies of their religion, Ethiopians slept near a thousand years, forgetful of the world by whom they were forgotten."[10] The Gibbon statement has served to preface some of the influential works written on Ethiopia (Toynbee 1965, vol. 2, p. 365; Budge 1970, vol. 1, pp. 126-7; Rey 1923, p. 9; Buxton 1967, p. 20; Tonkin 1972, p. 13; Jones and Monroe 1969, p. 6; Portal 1892, p. iv; Connah 1991, p. 95; July 1992, p. 82). During Mussolini's invasion of Ethiopia in 1935, geography was declared to be Ethiopia's only ally (Scaetta, *Foreign Affairs*, 14, 1, 1935). And recently, David Lewis called Ethiopia "Mysterious, isolated, diminished but unconquered" (1987, p. 99). In the geographical isolation paradigm, the dictatorship of geography over history is so suffocating as to caricaturize what Fernand Braudel called the "dialectics of geography and history."

It is through the geographical isolation paradigm that the so-called Ethiopian psychological make-up, allegedly marked by xenophobia and siege mentality, is explained. That Ethiopians live in a desert-and-sea-locked plateau, encircled by the enemies of their religion, explains their social psychology. So goes the argument. The geographical paradigm of Western Ethiopianism was a common stock-in-trade of Orientalism (Said 1979, p. 216).

In the geographical isolation paradigm, "isolation" meant to refer to the domain of what Immanuel Wallerstein calls the "external arena," those regions not yet incorporated into the capitalist world economy. The "outside world," whom Ethiopia is isolated from, is the metaphor for the capitalist world economy or the West.

The geographical isolation thesis has been cited *ad nauseam* to explain almost anything Ethiopian, including the millennial independence and uniqueness of civilization of the country. This geographical determinism ignores a number of historical events that defy explanation within its terms of reference. To mention just a few: In the nineteenth century, the British expeditionary force led by General Napier reached Maqdala, the heartland of the geographically "inaccessible" plateau, fought Emperor Tewodros II, defeated him, and pulled out. The Egyptians repeatedly sent invading forces to take over Ethiopia, but were defeated. Sudanese Ansars set fire to Gondar. In the twentieth century, The Italians crossed the merciless heat of the Ogaden and the "impenetrable" Northern plateau on their march to Addis Ababa. For many an invader, Ethiopia's geography was no insurmountable hurdle. And yet, Western scholars have repeatedly explained Ethiopia's continued independence in extra-human terms.[11] When Ethiopians defeated Italians at Adwa in 1896, it was attributed to the hostile Ethiopian terrain. The long history of Ethiopian independence, the intensely proud nationalism of the people, the fighting skill and numerical superiority of the warriors, and their parity of firepower with the Italians were simply ignored.

Perhaps the best case against the geographical isolation paradigm is the centuries-old slave trade from Ethiopia to the Arab world and beyond carried out by the *jabarti* merchants, alongside with the long-distance trade that linked Ethiopia with the outside world (Abir in Hess ed. *PFICES*, 1979; Pankhurst, *Ethiopia Observer*, 8, 1, 1964; *Ethiopia Observer*, 11, 2, 1967; *CEA*, 14, 3, 1974; *JES*, 2, 1 & 2, 1964; *JES*, 3, 2, 1965; *JES*, 12, 1, 1974; Beke 1852). And then there were Ethiopia's diplomatic relations with the outside world (Donzel ed. 1979; Oriental Documents IX, 1985).

Besides the slave trade, ever since her adoption of Christianity as state religion in the fourth century A. D. until 1959, for 16 centuries, the head of the Ethiopian Orthodox Church was a Coptic Egyptian.[12] Moreover, there was the pilgrimage of Ethiopian Christians to Jerusalem, which was not interrupted even during the Crusades, and Muslims' Hajji to Mecca. How do proponents of the geographical isolation paradigm explain all this? It is time that the geographical isolation paradigm in explaining Ethiopian history be given a decent burial. Ethiopia was hardly isolated from the outside world.

National Character

Ethiopia is the "Land of Prester John," with the seductive "charm of traditional Amhara life" (Levine 1967, pp. vii-viii). Travellers' accounts and scholarly treatises on Ethiopia have made numerous remarks about the "manners and customs" of the people, their "national character." Herbert Vivian (1969, p. 218), Evelyn Waugh (1984, p. 27), and Walter Plowden (1976, pp. 91, 95), to mention a few, made negative judgements on the national character of "Abyssinians." Gerald Portal called them "a savage race, innately bloodthirsty" (1892, p. 150). He recognized their "desperate bravery," but also saw them as being "thieves and liars, brutal, savage, and untrustworthy they are by nature" (*Ibid*, p. 240). For Henry Dufton "Abyssinians" are "deceitful, lying, insincere; their breasts are seldom stirred by generosity towards others, or in gratitude for benefits received" (1967, p. 92). For Gleichen (1898, p. 152), Vivian (1969, p. 248), Waugh (1984, p. 35), Lipsky (1967, p. 5), and I. M. Lewis (1987, p. 262), "Abyssinians" are seen as arrogant. Dervla Murphy calls this supposed "Abyssinian" arrogance a "pathetic national superiority complex [that] tends to run wild" (1968, p. 5). For Donald Levine, "The Amhara is a master at *deception*. With straight face and convincing manner he will relate the most preposterous fictions" (1967, pp. 250-51). Furthermore, "Perhaps the most characteristic form of interaction among the Amhara is that of *domination*. The Amhara is at his happiest when he is in a position to order someone about" (*Ibid*, p. 253). Alas, Nietzsche must have been Amhara; he simply did not know it! "The Amhara assume that it is improper to reveal oneself fully, to disclose one's *mistir* [secrecy], to anyone but a very close friend; and that, in fact, rarely happens" (*Ibid*, p. 253),[13] added Levine.

There is a "consolation" in the national character discourse though: that Ethiopians are seen as handsome people. Chris Prouty Rosenfeld wrote thus: "Beautiful the Ethiopians are — distinct on the continent of Africa for their straight noses, thin lips, attenuated body structure, and olive skin" (1986, p. xii). Accordingly, the contrasting flat nose, thick lips, and dark skin must be considered ugly. And so it was for Edward Gibbon, who wrote:

> The hand of nature has flattened the noses of the negroes, covered their heads with shaggy wool, and tinged their skin with inherent and indelible blackness. But the olive complexion of the Abyssinians, their hair, shape, and features, distinctly mark them as a colony of Arabs . . . (1977, vol. 2, p. 624).[14]

For Gerald Portal "Abyssinians" are an "extraordinarily handsome, active, and chivalrous race of mountaineers" (1892, p. 240). As in other realms, what was said of the "national character" of "Abyssinians," was a common stock-in-trade of Orientalism (Said 1979, pp. 38-9).

Attempting to understand a people by referring to its so-called national character leads to a blind alley. How can one study about Italians by taking the Mafia as the national character of Italians? Is committing crime second nature to Italians?[15]

Western Ethiopianist discourse identified Ethiopia as the unknown, isolated, remote, inaccessible, hostile, xenophobic

"Other." Ethiopia was the living land of the Bible, of majestic ruin and barbarous splendor, lost in mountain fastness, lost in the recurrence of the same. Ethiopia unknown to the West became *the* unknown Ethiopia. Ethiopia isolated from the West became *the* isolated Ethiopia. *A* deceptive Amhara became *the* deceptive Amhara. The Ethiopian suspicion of European motives in Ethiopia inspired the label "the suspicious Abyssinian": backward, closed, xenophobic. In this Orientalist Semiticist construction of Ethiopian identity, it was the West that was the defining subject, and Ethiopia the defined object.[16] Ethiopians did not define their identity as one of isolation from the West; nor did they call the West the isolated West, the forgotten West.

V

This work deals with the social history of modern Ethiopia from the Battle of Adwa, on March 1, 1896 — which for Akpan was "the greatest victory of an African over a European army since the time of Hannibal" (in Boahen ed. 1985, p. 272), and for Mockler "the greatest single disaster in European colonial history" (1984, p. xxxxi) — to the 1974 overthrow of Emperor Haile Selassie. It is a contribution to the study of the social roots of the Ethiopian misery: famine, war, disease, utter poverty. It deals with the problem of a nation that counts its history in thousands of years, and yet, or perhaps because of it, finds itself unable to feed its people.

I have followed the historical-methodological perspectives of Fernand Braudel, especially his magnum opus, *The Mediterranean* (1972, in two volumes.) I deal with "structural history," with "social time," although "geographical time" and "individual time" (*Ibid*, vol. 1, p. 21) are not ignored. I followed Braudel in situating Ethiopian history through a study of its "economic systems, states, societies, civilizations, and . . . warfare" (*Ibid*). Moreover, I took the *longue duree*-approach to the study of modern Ethiopian history, for in old civilizations like Ethiopia, one simply can not start with an absolute date, ignoring the historical continuum bubbling underneath the surface.

This work discusses Ethiopia's integration into the global network of the modern capitalist system and the concomitant development of bureaucratic institutions, capitalist economic enterprises, and secular education. It elaborates the historical transition from the old order of state/church/peasant trinity into one of a centralized monarchy, wrongly called Absolutism (Bahru Zewde, *JES*, 17, 1984).[17] It closes with 1974, when time ran out on the oldest Christian theocratic monarchy in the world.

Modern Ethiopian history starts with the reign of Emperor Menelik II, 1889-1913 (Tubiana 1980; Rosenfeld 1976). By "modern Ethiopia" we mean not that Ethiopia is modern by the definition of Western Enlightenment (for up until the end of our period, 1974, Ethiopia had been a Christian theocratic state, with no rights of citizens) but that it became part of what Immanuel Wallerstein calls the "Modern World System" (1974; 1980; 1989).

Modernity in Ethiopia meant three things: politically, the recognition of Ethiopia's sovereignty in the global interstate system, on the one hand, and the formation of the modern state with its monopoly of legitimate violence, on the other; economically, peripheralization in the world economy, which began with the export of essential commodities like coffee to the world market; and culturally, the immersion into the universalist project of the modern West, consummated in the secular religion of the Enlightenment: the idea of progress. This was elaborated through the development of modern educational institutions.

The world-system perspective that puts Ethiopia in the periphery of the capitalist world economy, alongside others, is of critical importance for locating the *framework* of the historical processes that transformed Ethiopia from a world empire of long "civilizational project" (Abdel-Malek 1981a) into a peripheral region of the capitalist world economy. And yet, we should be careful not to read too much into the periphery model. Yes, Ethiopia is on a periphery, alongside Burkina Faso and Malawi. But it is also more than that. Peripherality is fragile. It needs to be handled with care.

In order to study the making of modern Ethiopia, cultural analysis is indispensable. After all, what is history if not *cultural* history? Wallerstein wrote: "Our cultures are our lives, our most inner selves, but also our most outer selves, our personal and collective individualities" (1980, p. 65).

Due to my own cultural, linguistic, and religious limitations — I speak no Ethiopian language save Amharic — my cultural explanations are taken from the Christian Amhara cultural universe in general, and its Gojjam details, in particular. I was raised in Dabra Marqos, in a clergy-ridden extended family, drinking from the fountain of Gojjam's Amhara genius, *qene*. What I know in the cultural realm is *tabot* Christian and Amharic. Thus I have not written much about the Oromo, Afar, Kambata, etc., or about Muslim Ethiopians. To write about people whose language one does not speak or whose culture one does not comprehend well does more harm than good to their history.

What has so far been presented as Ethiopian culture is the culture of the Ge'ez civilization, especially in its Amharic form of expression. This emanates from the hegemonic status of the culture of the Ge'ez civilization over other cultures than its being representative of all of Ethiopians' cultures.

If using Amharic culture for social analysis creates problems in the cultural field, it is otherwise with the main body of the text — the social, political, and economic structure of modern Ethiopia. Here the discussion is all-encompassing, covering the social history of modern Ethiopia. The social, political, and economic structures are the skeleton; the Amharic cultural interventions are the flesh. If one is at loggerheads with the other, we cannot help it. There is no singular Ethiopian culture.

VI

Due to the hegemonic weight of the Aksumite and Orientalist Semiticist paradigms in Ethiopian studies, the history of peoples defined as outlandish to the Ge'ez civilization has been referred to in passing footnotes. (The most conspicuous silence is on the history of women.) As a result, the cultural hegemony of "historic Ethiopians" articulated in the two hegemonic paradigms still remains with us. This should change. It is time that the study of Ethiopian history be "liberated" from being a story of a succession of rulers and dynasties, *taameres* (miracles), *gadles* (struggles of saints), and *wudasies* (praises of the powers that be, heavenly or otherwise), wars and expansions, etc., and become a social history of ruler and ruled, noble and base, rich and poor, believer and "infidel," man and woman, victor and vanquished, slave and master, Amhara and "Galla," etc.

By and large, Ethiopian history is written as the narrative of the ruling elites of the Ge'ez civilization, as chronicles of the royalty (Pankhurst ed. 1967). The overwhelming majority of the people, and with them "the ineradicable civilization of the Abyssinian tillers" (Braudel 1981, p. 57), among others, are left out in the night of historical oblivion. John Iliffe reminds us: "In the long term it should be possible to write a true history of the Ethiopian poor . . . but this will need a knowledge of Ethiopian languages not available here" (1989, p. 9). Those of us who know Ethiopian languages need to take the responsibility and the challenge of writing such a history.

The social history of Ethiopia can be written from two aspects: (1) history of women, peasants, nomads, pastoralists, and occupational minorities ("castes"); (2) history of peoples outside or on the margins of the Ge'ez civilization, such as Muslims, Oromos, etc.

As history is "an unending series of efforts" (Braudel 1985, p. 56), so is historical writing. It is time to move beyond what Walter Benjamin called "empathy with the victors," and tell the story of the vanquished, the poor, those who can't "write," those who have no "Book" in their name. The court historians of the Ge'ez civilization were professional flatterers of the powers that be.

Ethiopian history needs to be studied afresh, and should be no longer based on racial, geographical, or dynastic grounds. The "Hamites," condemned by Western Africanists to carry the burden of civilization into Africa (Seligman 1959), are dead.

VII

The book is organized into three parts comprising six chapters, plus Introduction and Epilogue.

Part One, Chapter 1 deals with concepts used in this work for the study of Ethiopian social history.

Part Two (Chapters 2-4) deals with the "old order," what Karl Polanyi called the "archaic" order.[18] It covers the period from 1896 to 1935, from Adwa to the Italian occupation under Mussolini.

Chapter 2 deals with the origins of modern statehood in Ethiopia. It starts with the period around 1855, when the so-called *Zamana Masafent* (Era of Princes, or the Biblical Era of Judges) was coming to an end, and a process of centralization of state power was initiated by Emperor Tewodros II. These were times of increased involvement of Europeans in Ethiopia and Africa at large. The process of formation of modern statehood in Ethiopia is analyzed from a comparative perspective — Western European state formation, African state formation, and Ethiopian state formation.

In the Ethiopian state formation, there were three phases of relations between parcellized and centralized sovereignties. Phase one was when parcellized sovereignty was dominant, centralized sovereignty subordinate. This was the case with the *Zamana*

Masafent (1769-1855). Phase two (1855-1935) runs from Emperor Tewodros II's accession to the throne to the Fascist Italian invasion. It was a long process of conflict and stand-off between parcellized versus centralized sovereignty in which neither was able to assert a sustainable command over the other. Although Ethiopia in the early 1930s was much more centralized than during Tewodros's reign, the private armies of the regional notables were still running at large up until the Italian invasion. Phase three (1941-1974) runs from liberation from Italian rule to the overthrow of Haile Selassie. It was a period of triumph of centralized sovereignty. The 1936-41 Italian occupation was an interregnum. It laid down the preconditions for the transition from phase two to phase three. Although a short period, the five-year Italian occupation inflicted a fatal blow to the power of the regional nobility (Sbacchi 1985, p. 129).

In order to form a sovereign state in the global interstate system, the chief protagonists of modern state formation in Ethiopia had to settle accounts with their local rivals first. For centralized sovereignty in the larger national arena to be established, the lordly power at the regional level must be given decent burial. The private armies of the regional lords had to be dissolved and replaced by a national armed force organized along modern bureaucratic lines.

A detailed comparative study of state formation in nineteenth-century Africa is made, to locate the Ethiopian terrain in the larger African universe. This is in part to help critique the Eurocentric argument made by many Western Ethiopianists (and nationalists from the Horn of Africa) that Emperor Menelik II actively participated in the European Scramble for Africa.[19] Emperor Menelik's 1891 circular to European powers that "If Powers at a distance come forward to partition Africa between them, I do not intend to remain an indifferent spectator" is read as a testimony for his desire to join the Scramble. Instead, by discussing how Africans throughout the continent were forming states so as to face head-on the gathering cloud of the "White Man's Burden," I attempt to show that Menelikan Ethiopia was a cog in the wheel of nineteenth-century African state formation. If one is looking for analogy, then one should turn to this process, not to the European Scramble for Africa. The question, "How did Ethiopia become the only African legal subject in the drawing of her international boundaries with other European colonial powers?" should be addressed from this vantage point. There are many answers to this question, but analogy with the European Scramble for Africa is not one of them.

Chapter 3 deals with slaves and occupational minorities ("castes"). Despite its massive presence well into the twentieth century, slavery in Ethiopia has not yet been studied in detail. It is this paucity of material on slavery in Ethiopia that made this chapter very sketchy. (The study of occupational minorities fares no better than that of slavery.) A distinction is made between slavery inside Ethiopia and the slave trade outside of Ethiopia as the basis for the study of slavery.

Chapter 4 deals with the *geber* system. It is the main chapter of the work in that the *geber* system is the skeleton of Ethiopian society, the pillar of its socioeconomic, political, and cultural foundations. (The concept of the "*geber* system" is discussed in Chapter 1.)

The 1936-41 Italian occupation period was an interregnum, a transition period from the "archaic" to the "modern." The occupation dealt a mortal blow to the archaic order, as it was the harbinger of the new. The Italians were military occupiers rather than effective colonial rulers. Five years was too short for effective colonial rule. And yet, in those five years, they left behind two legacies that are still with us today: a good network of roads, and prostitution. The rest was frenzy of killings gone mad. The ever-ambitious attempt of Italian imperialism to create in Ethiopia what would have been the largest settler-colonial entity in Africa foundered repeatedly (Marcus in Hess ed. *PFICES,* 1979; Villari 1956; Baladacci, *United Empire*, 2, 1911; Pankhurst, *Ethiopia Observer*, 13, 2, 1970).

The Ethiopian resistance against the Fascist occupation helped galvanize anticolonial movements in Africa. One cannot rule out the lessons of the continued armed struggle of Ethiopians against Italian forces to the French and Yugoslav resistance against Nazi occupation. It was not accidental that Emperor Haile Selassie remained the best of friends with both De Gaulle and Tito. Both in the struggle to head off European colonialism and in the persistent campaign to make Ethiopia ungovernable for the Fascist occupiers, Ethiopia became a symbol of unflinching defiance. Africans all over the world took immense pride in this. And this for a land called "the last stronghold of slavery" (Bravelli 1935).

Mussolini's invasion of Ethiopia brought about two significant turning points in the history of relations between the West and the peoples of the "Third World": first, it was the last European colonial conquest; and second, it was carried out by one of the largest modern armies of European colonial invasion ever undertaken since Columbus to occupy a land of "people of color." The Italian invasion heralded the beginning of the end of European colonialism. "Italians" began European capitalism with Venice, and they began the end of European colonial rule with Mussolini's invasion of Ethiopia.

Part Three (Chapters 5-6) deals with the period from 1941 to 1974, the transition to and development of creeping modernity in Ethiopia.

Chapter 5 deals with the gradual demise of the *geber* system and its replacement by a modern bureaucratic state organization. This took place through two related processes: first, politically, through the expropriation of the means of administration from the direct rulers, wherein the parcellized sovereignties of the regional warlords were eaten up by the centralizing forces of Addis Ababa; and second, economically, through the expropriation of the means of production from the direct producers.

Chapter 6 deals with the processes of the destruction of old class relations and the simultaneous development of new ones. It deals with economic expropriation, the separation of the means of production from the direct producers. This process is discussed according to the now conventional distinction between the North-Central regions and that of the South. The existence of *rist* arrangements in the former and their absence in the latter resulted in different outcomes in the expropriation process.

In the Epilogue, we close with a reflection on the "Unmaking of Modern Ethiopia," the nationalist rebellions that are rocking the foundations of the Ethiopian state structure, the various movements "back" to parcellized sovereignties, the metaphorical second coming of the *Zamana Masafent*.

PART I

CONCEPTUAL CATEGORIES

CHAPTER 1

CONCEPTS FOR THE STUDY OF ETHIOPIAN HISTORY

this chapter, I introduce four new concepts, not used previously in Ethiopian studies, for the study of modern (and premodern) Ethiopian history. They are: *geber* system, *tabot* Christianity,[1] Aksumite paradigm, and Ge'ez civilization. Amharic terms (like *geber*) are used as analytic and descriptive categories (with their English translations), rather than the other way around. Many of the mistakes in the historical discipline, as in others, have much to do with mistranslations from one language to another.

The *geber* system is the socioeconomic foundation of the Ge'ez civilization. (The political history of the Ge'ez civilization is by and large the history of war-making among the notables.) The cultural history of the Ge'ez civilization is that of *tabot* Christianity. Aksumite paradigm defines the ideological self consciousness of the Ge'ez civilization. Ge'ez civilization is the larger envelope that defines the overall Ethiopian "civilizational project." Ge'ez civilization is also defined by the Ge'ez script.

The distinctions we made among socioeconomic, political, cultural, and ideological realms are analytic categories that all intertwine in the thread of Ge'ez civilization.

Although the territorial domain of the Ge'ez civilization at times included Yemen across the Red Sea and what was once Enarya in the southwest, its core is concentrated in the region from Dabra Bizan in Eritrea to Dabra Libanos in Shawa. This forms one compact cultural zone of *tabot* Christianity. The chief protagonists of this cultural drama compose the Agaw-Amhara-Tigrayan trinity, with the Amhara-Tigrayan couplet dominant and the Agaw long forgotten. Let us now discuss each concept in detail.

Geber System

The concept "*geber* system" is my own "invention." In the Amharic language, the term *geber* has three different but interrelated meanings. First, *geber* means work, derived from the word *gaber*, with extensions like *gabare* (farm worker, peasant) and *gebrena* (agriculture.) The name *Gabre* is given to servants and slaves. Hence the first meaning of the term *geber* refers to the labor (production) process. Second, *geber* means tax/tribute or labor service paid to the Emperor and the various ranks of the imperial ladder below him. The second meaning of *geber* hence refers to the appropriation of tribute by the ruling class — the *Beta Mangest* (House of State, House of Kingdom is a better term to show the looseness of the state structure), and the *Beta Kehnat* (House of Clergy) — from the *gabbars* (tribute providers.) Interestingly enough, unlike the other two, the *gabbar* has no House. Thirdly, *geber* means banquet. This refers to the redistribution relations of the appropriated tribute among the various segments of the ruling class in the form, among others, of provision of consumables like free food and drinks. If we tie together these three different meanings of the term *geber* and call Ethiopian society a *geber* system, we have the social history of Ethiopia at our fingertips.[2]

The *geber* system consists of three classes, or three orders, based on the tripartite functional division of Ethiopian society: those who fight, organized as the *beta mangest*; those who pray, organized as the *beta kehnat;* and those who provide for daily subsistence, disorganized as *gabbars*. Fighting, praying, and tilling land — these were the social foundations of the *geber* system.

In the *geber* system, the production process, the appropriation process, and the redistribution process formed a systemic whole with the giving and taking of tribute knitting together the entire system.

There were two sets of tributary relations: (1) relations between *gabbars*, on the one hand, and tribute appropriators, on the other; and, (2) relations among the different ranks (orders) of the tribute-appropriating class. The former was the fundamental social relationship of tribute provision and appropriation between producers and appropriators; the latter was the mechanism of tribute distribution and redistribution within the appropriating class itself.

The *geber* system was an inverted pyramid, with the *beta mangest* and *beta kehnat* as parallel power centers extracting tribute from the *gabbar*. Ethiopian history is essentially the history of the *geber* system.

The three orders of the *beta mangest*, the *beta kehnat*, and the *gabbar* were similar to the tripartite division of medieval Europe — those who fight, those who pray, and those who till the land. The great French scholar Gerorg Dumezil wrote that the tripartite division of labor among those who fight, pray, and till the soil was a unique Indo-European phenomenon. But we had it in Ethiopia, as if Ethiopia were Indo-European. In social relations of production, religious culture, and distribution of power relations, *geber*-system Ethiopia of the Ge'ez civilization, with its church/state/peasant trinity, was remarkably similar to medieval Europe, and yet had no peers in Africa.[3] It was also fundamentally different from the social relations of the lowland pastoral-nomadic Afars and Somalis within Ethiopia itself.

The *geber* system was not only a mode of production and appropriation of material life, but it was also a *mode of production of social and moral etiquette.* The three classes of the *geber* system were also classes of manners, values, and moral expectations. They were the subjects of what Gramsci called hegemonic presence, the elaboration and maintenance of social norms. These norms of how each group was to behave defined the cultural contours of the Ge'ez civilization.

Central to the social construction of etiquette of the *geber* system was the concept of honor. Honor meant name, status, prestige, social standing, recognition, and above all, respect. Honor was a class phenomenon; it was above all what defined a person. The producing classes were defined as honorless. Their "honor" was in recognizing the honor of their masters or superiors. There is no better way to see this than look at how the Amharic language defines words of social class and status, for the Amharic words for the three producing classes of nomadic pastoralists (*zalan*), herders (*eragnya*), and peasants (*balagar*) are also terms of social location in the honor hierarchy.

The word *zalan*[4] refers to a mode of production of subsistence, as well as to a mode of ascribed moral conduct. It has a double meaning: nomadic pastoralist, on the one hand, and rude, uncultured, uncultivated, on the other.[5]

The sedentary agrarian counterparts of *zalan* are *eragnya* and *balagar*. Like *zalan, eragnya* and *balagar* have double meanings. *Eragnya* means herder. It also means rude. *Zalan* and *eragnya* are both nouns, nomadic pastoralist and herder, respectively, and adjectives, meaning rude. In the case of *balagar*, however, the word is a noun whose adjective form is *balage*. As in *zalan* and *eragnya*, the word *balagar* has a double meaning. On the one hand, *balagar* means one with the country, man of the soil, tiller of the land, peasant, country person. On the other hand, *balagar* is related to *balage*, which means rude. In all this, there is a symbiotic relationship between class and etiquette, the lower the class, the ruder it becomes, and vice versa. The *zalan, eragnya*, and *balagar* are all defined as rude and lacking in manners.

The contempt for the *zalan* was not simply a superiority complex of an agricultural mode of production over a nomadic-pastoralist mode of production; it was also an extension of the aristocratic contempt for the *balagar*. Unlike in the early Arab, Ottoman, Mongolian, Tutsi, Fulani, etc., cases, in Ethiopia it was not the pastoralists that imposed their dominance over the sedentary agriculturalists, but the other way around.[6]

On the ruling side of the class divide, the opposite of the *zalan-eragnya-balagar* triplet of the "rude" classes — all of whom belong to the macro class of *gabbars* — is the word *chawa*. *Chawa* has four meanings: (1) soldier, as opposed to peasant, on the one hand, and clergy, on the other; (2) free, as opposed to slave (slaves were the most honorless of the entire *geber* system); (3) layman, as opposed to the learned ecclesiastical order; and, (4) cultivated and civilized in manners, as opposed to the "rude" classes.[7] The *beta mangest-beta kehnat* couplet represented the "free," civilized, cultured, cultivated, and well-mannered class; the peasant-herder-nomad triplet that of the uncivilized, uncultured, uncultivated, rude class.[8]

It is quite revealing to see that the Amharic word for soldier is *watadar*, made up of two words, *watito adar*, which means one who spends the night outside the house, as soldiers did during war. Moreover, the word *watata*, the root for *watito*, refers to wandering from place to place, as soldiers went everywhere to fight and loot. It was in opposition to the ever-wandering warrior, the *watadar*, that the *balagar* was defined as one with a country, with a household, with a place of residence and, most importantly, with a place of burial. The *watadar* died anywhere and everywhere, his dead body did not get a decent burial and religious service. Not so with the *balagar.*

To sum up: The *geber* system was made up of three main classes — prayers, fighters, and producers. (Slaves and occupational minorities "castes" cut across class lines). Each class was ascribed a social etiquette, a moral-ethical obligation, and a cultural name. The moral calling of the praying class was to be pious while the warrior class was meant to be gentlemanly. As to the producing class, it was condemned to be rude.

The "rude class" was a negative creation of the "civilized class." After all, what does a Christian Amhara peasant have in common with a Muslim Somali nomadic pastoralist save that both are under the rule of the *beta mangest-beta kehnat* power bloc?

Tabot Christianity

The cultural uniqueness of the Ge'ez civilization resides in its *tabot* Christianity, a Christianity to be found nowhere in the world of Christendom save Ethiopia. From the monasteries of Alexandria and Ireland to the liberal polygamy of the Mormons, one finds no culture resembling Ethiopia's *tabot* Christianity.

By *tabot* Christianity is meant not only a Christianity whose emblem is the *tabot,* but also all the other Judaic practices found only in Ethiopian Christianity. It is different from the Christian West's self-definition as Judaeo-Christian culture (Mazrui 1986, p. 86). The cultural universe of Ethiopia's *tabot* Christianity is one of indissoluble linkage between Judaism and Christianity in which a church is identified more by the *tabot* inside it than by the Cross sign on the roof top of its building. In Ethiopia, the distinction between Judaism and Christianity is so obliterated that when people say Christianity they might as well have Judaism in mind, or vice versa. It was in this sense that Walter Plowden made the remark about "The strong odour of Judaism still clinging to the nation [Ethiopia] and its customs" (1972, p. 53). Judaism is not just an "odor" that could be washed away from the body of Ethiopian *tabot* Christianity. It forms an inseparable part of it (see Hammerschmidt, *JES,* 3, 2, 1965). For anyone in search of religious syncretism, here is a marvelous example.

To discuss *tabot* Christianity in detail, one needs to look at the Judaic infrastructure upon which the Christian superstructure was built. We can identify three most significant presences of Judaism in Ethiopian *tabot* Christianity: The *tabot*; the observation of Saturday as Sabbath; and the distinction between clean and unclean foods.

Tabot

Tabot physically is a portable wooden box like the original Ark of the Covenant. The *tabot* is the most important manifestation of the fusion of Judaism and Christianity in Ethiopia. Every church has at least one *tabot* by whose heavenly name not only the church but also the *daber* (parish) is identified. A church without *tabot* might as well be a brothel. Of all the churches in Ethiopia, Aksum Tseyon (Aksum Zion) church is the most holy and the most revered for Ethiopians claim that the original Ark of the Covenant is kept in this church. From Harrison Ford's Indiana Jones adventure, *The Raiders of the Lost Ark,* to Graham Hancock's desperate search for the original Ark of the Covenant, Ethiopia is the only country in the world of Christendom which has the Judaic Ark of the Covenant as the quintessential representation of the Church. Not even Coptic Egypt, which sent the first Patriarch to Christian Ethiopia as far back as the fourth century A.D. and continued to do so right up to 1959, had anything resembling Ethiopia's reverence for the *tabot*. In a comparative aphorism between the sacred and the profane, the ecclesiastical and the secular power divisions in Ethiopia, is the famous Amharic saying: *kainchat marto latabot kasaw marto lashumet* (the chosen wood for the *tabot*, the chosen man for appointment). Cedar tree is reserved for the making of the *tabot*, just as the best men of the land are called for official appointments. Woe unto him that cuts down that tree that is set aside for the making of the *tabot*. Alas, had the trees in Ethiopia been reserved for the making of the *tabot*, there would have been no deforestation!

Sabbath

In Ethiopic, as in Hebrew, *sabbath* means seven. It is the seventh day of Creation, the day God rested after his six-day work of creating the universe *ex nihilo*. It is Saturday, a religious holiday, the Sabbath of Judaism, the *sanbath* of Ethiopian *tabot* Christianity. Christians are not supposed to work on Saturday, do things like grinding flour, gathering or splitting wood, washing clothes, plowing the soil, etc. But people by custom have made Saturday the most important market day of the week. Ethiopian Christians have two *sanbaths*, Saturday, the Judaic Sabbath, the day of God's rest; and, Sunday, the Christian "Sabbath," the day of resurrection of Jesus from the dead.

Dietary Laws

Christian Ethiopia is the only polity in the world of Christendom that strictly follows the dietary laws of the Old Testament (*Bluy Kidan*), as opposed to the New Testament (*Haddis Kidan*).[9] Christian Ethiopians follow the dietary laws laid down to the Children of Israel in Leviticus 11:3-4, 7. In Deuteronomy 14:21 it says: "Ye shall not eat of anything that dieth of itself." Genesis 32:32 says: "Therefore the children of Israel eat not of the sinew with shrank, which is upon the hollow of the thigh." "Unclean birds" are not to be eaten, while pork is the most abhorred."Ethiopia alone among the Christian nations", Ephraim Isaac notes, "has rejected the traditional doctrine of Christianity according to St. Paul that Biblical law lost its binding force at the Coming of Christ" (1967, p. 46).

Besides these three major Judaic presences in the very heart of Ethiopian Christianity are other Judaic practices including strict observation of the Pentateuchal laws of cleanliness and purity (Hancock 1992, 253). Furthermore, with respect to the Scriptural canon, Ephraim Isaac observes,

> The Ethiopian Orthodox Church follows the teachings of 81 books of Judeo-Christian literature. These are the 39 books of the Hebrew Bible, the 27 Canonical books of the Christian New Testament, and numerous Apocryphal and pseudoepigraphic works. The latter two groups include some of the best known Jewish and Christian apocryphal and apocalyptic literature. Among the apocalyptic books that are most popular in the Ethiopian Church, the Book of Enoch has received worldwide scholarly attention. This book, originally a Jewish work, has been preserved in toto only in the Ge'ez (Ethiopic) version [1967, p. 34].[10]

Of all the religious books of Ethiopia's *tabot* Christianity, the most popular is the *Psalms of David*, referred to as *Dawit* (David) (Tekle Tsadik Mekouria in Mokhtar ed. 1981, p, 418). The religious dance and music (Kebede Ashenafi 1971) — the movement and chanting of the *dabtara* (the non-ordained clergy, similar to the Levites of Judaism), the use of *kabaro* (drum) whose beautiful sound was labelled "barbaric" by Graham Hancock (1992, p. 255), and *tsanatsel* (sistrum), etc. — are similar to that of the Levites dancing in front of the Ark of the Covenant. The dances of the *dabtara* in front of the *tabot* at *Temqat* (Epiphany), held on January 18 (the most celebrated holiday in the Christian calendar), recall the dance of David in front of the Ark of the Covenant.

The inner structure of churches is also profoundly Judaic (Ullendorff, *JSS*, 1, 3, pp. 235-36). The holiest part of the church is the *qedusa qedusan* (holy of holies), where the *tabot* is located. This part of the church is revered more than any other, including that where Holy Communion is administered to the public. Lay males and females can be in the first two chambers, but never in the third where the *tabot* is located. This zone is the exclusive domain of priests and deacons only.

The *qedusa qedusan* is not only the place where the *tabot* is kept, but also where Holy Communion is prepared. With the *tabot* witnessing, the miracle of transubstantiation takes place in the *qedusa qedusan*. The actual mechanism of how this process works is not to be discussed by a layperson like me. It is a secret to be known by priests and deacons only!

In the special, glittering garment worn by priests during religious ceremonies, one can see a profound Judaic presence: the *maqanat* (belt), "corresponding to the High Priest's girdle;" the *qobe* (skull-cap), "corresponding to the mitre;" and the *askama* (scapular), "with its twelve crosses in four rows of three, corresponding to the priestly breast-plate which, as Chapter 28 of the Book of Exodus makes clear, was adorned with twelve precious stones also arranged in four rows of three" (Hancock 1992, pp. 253-4).

In New Year celebration, the Ethiopian New Year festival (*enqutatash*) corresponds to the Jewish New Year (*rosh ha-shanah.*) Both are held in September and they are followed a few weeks later by "a second festival (known as *maskal*, the founding of the True Cross, in Ethiopia and Yom Kippur in Israel). In both cultures . . . this second festival was connected to the New Year by a period of expiation and atonement" (*Ibid,* p. 253).

When we come to circumcision (*gerzat*), Ethiopians are the only Christians that follow to the letter the Old Testament law laid down in Leviticus 12:3: "And in the eighth day the flesh of his foreskin shall be circumcised." So male Christian babies are circumcised accordingly, eight days after birth. Ullendorff comments:

> The date of circumcision on the eighth day is shared . . . by Jews and [*tabot*-Christian] Ethiopians only. This is the

> more remarkable because members of the Coptic Church in Egypt are circumcised at an age between six and eight years, and Gallas [Oromos], Muslims and other influences in Ethiopia, with widely varying dates, would all combine to shake the Ethiopian confidence in the eighth day. Yet this date has been steadfastly maintained, no doubt under the influence of the Pentateuchal injunction . . . I have no doubt that the maintenance of circumcision among Abyssinians is part of those elements of Hebraic-Jewish lore which have been so tenaciously preserved in that part of Africa [*JSS*, 1, 3, 1965, pp. 249-50].

While male babies are circumcised on their eighth day after birth, they are baptized on the fortieth day. Female babies are baptized on the eightieth day. Male Christian babies pass through the initiation rite of Judaic circumcision before they are baptized as Christians.

What can we make of all this? Of this weird-sounding religion to which Christian Ethiopians have shown dog-like fidelity? The answer seems to be that there was Judaism in Ethiopia before Christianity, and that the latter adapted itself to the prevailing Judaic faith, for "it would be inconceivable that a people recently converted from paganism to Christianity . . . should thereafter have begun to boast of Jewish descent and to insist on Israelite connections, customs and institutions" (*Ibid,* p. 227). The Judaic faith was the pillar, the skeleton, the inner soul upon which the Christian faith was built.[11] Getachew Haile concludes that:

> Only a Christianity of a nation or community which first practiced Judaism would incorporate Jewish religious practices and make the effort to convince its faithful to observe Sunday like Saturday. In short, the Jewish influence in Ethiopian Christianity seems to originate from those who received Christianity and not from those who introduced it. The Hebraic-Jewish elements were part of the indigenous Aksumite culture adopted into Ethiopian Christianity [*JSS*, 33, 2, Autumn 1988, p. 246].[12]

What makes the Beta Israel (House of Israel, known otherwise as "Falasha") different from the Christians is not that they follow Judaism *per se,* but rather that their Judaism does not contain Christian elements.[13] For Christian Ethiopia, the temporal primacy of the Old Testament over the New Testament has a very different meaning altogether.

Finally, fasting. Wednesday and Friday, except for forty days beginning from Easter (*fasika*), are fasting days. There is also Lent and other fasting periods. During fasting, no meat or dairy products are to be consumed. In all, there are 165 fasting days in a year for the ordinary Christian, with up to 250 for the pious to the letter. Ethiopian Christianity, which has more fasting days than any other branch of Christianity, can rightly be called part-time-vegetarian Christianity. The billions of dollars Americans spend annually on dieting would be incomprehensible to Ethiopian *tabot* Christianity.

Aksumite Paradigm

The Aksumite paradigm is the paradigm of the ruling class of the Ge'ez civilization. It articulates three fundamental ideas that are central to its discourse:

Origin

Once upon a time there was an Ethiopian queen known by the various names of Saba, Makada, and Azeb. She heard of the wisdom and glory of King Solomon of Jerusalem. She decided to pay him a visit. During her stay at King Solomon's court, she conceived a child by him known as Ebna-Hakim, Bayna-Lehkem or Ibn Al-Hakim in Arabic, and Walda-Tabib (son of the wise man, ie., King Solomon) in Ge'ez. He was also known as Menelik I. When he came of age, he went to Jerusalem to visit his father. Upon his return back to Ethiopia, twelve thousand of King Solomon's people followed him. Some of Solomon's men removed the original Ark of the Covenant from the Temple of Jerusalem and brought it with them to Ethiopia. They replaced the original with a replica. Queen Saba abdicated the throne in favor of her son Menelik I. That became the foundation of a long line of civilizational genealogy known as the Solomonic dynasty. Thus begins Ethiopian history, with Aksum at its center.[14]

The Solomon-Saba story is the centerpiece of the *Kebra Nagast* (Honor of Kings, otherwise translated as Glory of Kings) (Budge 1932). It is Donald Levine's "national epic" of Ethiopia (in Marcus ed. 1969, p. 12), Eike Haberland's "*magna carta* of the Ethiopian empire" (in Ogot ed. 1992, p. 705). The *Fetha Nagast* (Law of Kings) (Paulos Tzadua 1968)[15] is the legal code of the Ge'ez civilization. Of the two, the *Kebra Nagast* is, to use the now fashionable language of postmodernism, the "master text," the canon, of the Aksumite paradigm.[16]

Historical Essentialism

Ethiopian history has been written as the story of dynastic narratives. Like his Byzantine and Chinese counterparts, the Ethiopian court historian was a professional flatterer of the reigning monarch, elevating him to the sky, while diminishing the stature of the previous rulers. In the hands of some modern Ethiopian historians, the narrative of Ethiopian history became one of essentialist reproduction of the same (Taddesse Tamrat 1972, p. 302; Sergew Hable Selassie 1972, p. 292). Although the historical succession of Aksumite, Zagwe, and Shawan dynasties, each expanding the territorial domain of the Ge'ez civilization in a southerly direction, was recognized, Ethiopian history from Aksum to Haile Selassie was seen as being basically the same.[17] Ethiopian *tabot*-Christian *denominationalism* has found its utmost expression in this essentialist reading of Ethiopian history.

Woe Unto Unbaptized Heathens!

The third component of the Aksumite paradigm is one of self- consciousness of the religious and cultural supremacy of the Ge'ez civilization over the "Others" — Muslims, Beta Israel,[18] and "pagans" (*aramane*) — all known by the collective negative identity of *yaltatamaqu ahzab* (unbaptized heathens.)

As Aksumites and their heirs moved further south into the domain of the "infidels," it was seen as a positive expansion of the Ge'ez civilization, of its Christianity, of its "high culture."[19] When the expansion took the opposite direction, like the Oromo expansion of the sixteenth and seventeenth centuries, it was perceived as the invasion of "barbarian hordes" (Merid Wolde Aregay 1971). The cultural borrowing of the Ge'ez civilization from "Others" was acknowledged much less than the other way around. The divine calling of the Ge'ez civilization was to assimilate "Others" (through Christian proselytization), not to be assimilated by them. Like Senghor's colonialism, the Ge'ez civilization was to be a nonassimilating assimilator. Zewde Gebre Selassie wrote thus: "The central theme of Ethiopian history . . . has been the maintenance of a cultural core which has adapted itself to the exigencies of time and place, assimilating diverse peoples" (1975, p. 1). The "cultural core" Zewde is referring to is, of course, the Ge'ez civilization.[20]

The Christian God of the Ge'ez civilization was *yaesrael amlak* (God of Israel), the ruling Solomonic dynasty *esraelawi* (Israelite), its emblem *moa anbasa zaemnagada yehuda* (Conquering Lion of the Tribe of Judah) (Rubenson, *JES*, 3, 2, 1965), and its State *mangest egziabherawit* (God's State, Holy Empire). Solomon and Saba, the transfer (or stealing?) of the original Ark of the Covenant from Jerusalem to Ethiopia, and with it the privileged title of "Chosen People" from Jews to Ethiopians, the claim of Aksum as the Second Jerusalem, the divine calling to proselytize the "heathen" in the name of the Lord Jesus Christ, etc., were all woven to form the quilt that was Ethiopian identity. This makes "Christian Ethiopians the chosen people of both the Old and New Testaments for, unlike the Jews, they have accepted the Gospel" (Haberland in Ogot ed. 1992, p. 706).[21] Therein lies the heart of the Aksumite paradigm.

It is astonishing how a paradigm based on a myth of sex (between Solomon and Saba) and theft (of the Ark of Covenant) has had such a powerful hold on so many people who were to follow the divine mandate, "Thou Shall Not Steal!" Shouldn't we call the Aksumite paradigm the "sex and theft paradigm"? The paradigm of fornicators and thieves? Sarcasm aside, myth plays a profound role in peoples' consciousness about themselves.

The cultural-cum-religious discourse of the Aksumite paradigm elaborated a geographical terrain of expansion in space, a maturation over time of the Ge'ez civilization "moving" in a north-south direction: hence the Aksumite-Zagwe-Shawa dynastic sequence. Each of the latter perfected upon the former, building on the original model that was Aksum. After all, what was the Zagwe dynasty but one of Christianized Agaws, and the Shawa dynasty but of Christianized Amharas? Is it so surprising that the Aksumite paradigm does not include the Walasma dynasty or the Kingdom of Damot as one of its own?

To sum up: the Aksumite paradigm is one that claims a triple supremacy for the Ge'ez civilization over those outside its cultural embrace: superiority of its civilization over "Others'" barbarism; superiority of its *tabot* Christianity over "Others'" heathenism; and superiority of its Ge'ez script over "people without writing." Armed thus, the Aksumite paradigm articulated a consciousness of having a History, which "Others" lack. In the words of Marc Bloch, "Christianity is a religion of historians" (1953, p. 4), for it has a Book, as well as a script.

The fundamental building blocks of the Aksumite paradigm are articulated not only by the literate class of the Ge'ez civilization, but also by Western Ethiopianists. The *Kebra Nagast*, referred to by both paradigms, became the source for substantiating the claim of the triple supremacy of the Ge'ez civilization. The *Kebra Nagast* became not only a "national epic" and a "*magna carta*," but also the most authoritative canon of the Ge'ez civilization.[22]

Ge'ez Civilization

Every civilization has its "barbarians."[23] The Ge'ez civilization is no exception. The "barbarians" of the Ge'ez civilization are known as *yaltatamaqu ahzab* (unbaptized heathens.) *Tabot* Christianity is the boundary that sets apart the world of believers from that of "infidels." Accordingly, the barbarians of the Ge'ez civilization were: (1) "pagans" proper, (2) the Beta Israel, and (3) Muslims. Strictly speaking, while all were seen as unbelievers, the former was perceived as the "real pagans", while the latter two were "impostors."

The downfall of Aksum was attributed in part to the attack of the Bejas, the Ethiopian "pagan" counterparts of the Germanic "barbarians" that overran the Roman Empire. There was also the tenth-century revolt of a woman variously referred to as Yodit or Gudit (Judith), Esato (fire), and Aster (Esther), who brought utter destruction to the tottering power of Aksum. She ruled for forty years. Her identity is controversial. For some she was an Agaw *ayhud*,[24] for others a "pagan" queen from the kingdom of Damot that was located just south of the Abbay (Blue Nile) river (Sergew Hable Selassie, *JES*, 10, 1, 1972).[25] She drove the last nail into the coffin of Aksumite power.

The war unleashed by Imam Ahmed ibn Ibrahim al Ghazi (1527-43), nicknamed in the Christian literature as "Gragn Muhammad" (Muhammad the left-handed), has left by far the most enduring negative memory in the collective consciousness of Christian Ethiopia. Based in the Harar region, his *jihad* almost destroyed Christianity in Ethiopia. The might of Portugal and the tenacity of the Ethiopian Christian establishment saved Christian Ethiopia from the fate that befell Christian Nubia.

Islam is a child of Ethiopia, and a Christian Ethiopia at that. Christian Ethiopia has a unique privileged place in the annals of Islam; it is the "Land of the First Migration." It was the Christian king of Aksum who gave protection to the persecuted followers of Prophet Muhammad, thereby saving Islam from possible infantile extinction. But then Christian Ethiopia was later engaged in a life-

and-death struggle against the very faith that it helped survive. Other than religion, the Christian-Muslim rivalry was over the control of trade routes (Abir 1980).

It was the fear of Islam that brought Christian Europe into the consciousness of Christian Ethiopia. The *faranj* — the Arabic *Al-Faranj*, a corruption of the word "Frank," a general Ethiopian reference to people of European descent — is pictured with a Janus-faced identity. On the one hand, he is a Christian, a cobeliever. To this extent, he is an ally in the struggle against the Muslim menace that encircles Ethiopia. Christian Europe is hence closer to Ethiopia than the Afars living in the lowlands of Ethiopia itself. The image of a Christian island encircled by a Muslim sea that informs the Christian Ethiopian identity has looked beyond the Muslim desert onto the lavish green of Christian Europe for a common religious stand against the followers of Prophet Muhammad. Despite this Christian fraternity, however, Ethiopian Christianity is suspicious of the authenticity of its European counterpart (Mathew 1974; Caraman 1985; Crummey 1972). The *faranj* is seen as following a corrupted and debased form of Christianity, one that is not true to the teachings of Christ. He is a *botalik* (Catholic), hence an imposter, a heretic, a blasphemer.

The most important group since the sixteenth century singled out as "pagan barbarian" *par excellence* is the "Galla," as the Oromo are called by the non-Oromo. The massive Oromo expansion into the heart of Christian Ethiopia in the sixteenth and seventeenth centuries[26] was understood as the invasion of "barbarian hordes" into the midst of Christian civilization. The Oromo were perceived as the Mongolian "hordes" of Ethiopia, as the destroyers of Christianity and civilization. They were seen as the killers of the Amhara,[27] the dread of the Ge'ez civilization that had just emerged from its fifteen-year dread of Gragn's *jihad*. For Christian Ethiopia, the "Galla" presented a doubly negative image of fear and contempt: fear in that the Oromo were formidable fighters until the large-scale introduction of firearms in the nineteenth century tilted the balance of power against them; contempt in that they were identified as "pagan barbarians." Hence the "Galla" were seen as a rough, sharp-edged bone in the throat of the Ge'ez civilization, tempted to choke it, but preferring instead to bleed it.

The depiction of the Oromo as "barbarian hordes" was not only a prejudice of the Ge'ez civilization, but also of some very well-known European travellers to Ethiopia and prominent names in Ethiopianist scholarship. The Portuguese Jesuit Manoel de Almeida, who was in Ethiopia during the seventeenth century, called the Oromo the "crueller scourge" than "Gragn," sent to punish Christian Ethiopia for its refusal to convert to the Roman Catholic faith, resulting in "almost the total ruin of that contumacious empire" (in Bahrey, Almeida, Huntingford and Beckingham 1993, p. 58). The British Major W. C. Harris, who came to Shawa in 1841 seeking a "treaty of amity and commerce" with *Negus* Sahle Selassie of Shawa, pictured the Oromo as "barbarian hordes who brought darkness and ignorance in their train" (1844, vol. 3, pp. 72-3). Edward Ullendorff saw them as having "nothing to contribute to the civilization of Ethiopia" (1960, p. 76).[28]

In the collective memory of post-sixteenth-century Ge'ez civilization, the "barbarian infidel" is pictured as a two-headed hydra: one "Galla," and another Muslim. Anyone who studies post-sixteen-century Ethiopian history and fails to recognize this or ignores it does immense damage to the history of the region. The history of Ethiopia of the last 400 years is essentially the history of the relationship — at times of bloody conflict, at other times of conciliation and assimilation — between the protagonists of the Ge'ez civilization, mainly the Amhara and the Oromo.

Once an "infidel" was baptized and took a Christian name, he was eligible to join the Christian Ge'ez civilization. In some cases, baptism went along with the granting of high official status in the imperial power hierarchy. In this way, "infidels" were assimilated into the high culture of Christian civilization, replacing their "primitive barbaric" culture by a "civilized" Christian culture. For the "barbarian infidels," the road to civilization passed through *tabot*-Christian assimilation.

The civilized/uncivilized distinction of the Ge'ez civilization had been primarily one of social class rather than of ethnic or regional origin. The Christian *balagar* was the pedestal of the uncivilized in the very midst of the Ge'ez civilization itself.[29] Being Christian was not sufficient to be considered civilized, although one could not be civilized without being Christian. The civilized group was one, Christians in authority, while the uncivilized were classified into two groups: uncivilized Christians (the *balagar*) and the "barbarians" proper. If the *balagar* felt superior to the barbarian, it was a cultural simulator illusion on his part. Of course, if an opportunity arose for individual social mobility, the uncivilized Christian was in a better position than the barbarian "*afun yalfata Galla*" (a "Galla with untied tongue", i.e., an Oromo who can't speak Amharic). One of the most telling expressions of cultural chauvinism against the Oromo is the Amharic saying: *yagalla chawa yagomen choma yalawim* (There is no Galla gentleman any more than there is fat in greens). *Gallana sagara eyadar yegamal* (Galla and human feces stink more every passing day), and *galla sesalaten bacharaqa jantela yeyezal* (When a Galla thinks he is civilized, he stretches his umbrella in moon light) are some of the others. The most notorious came in the form of a query: *saw naw galla?* (Is it human or Galla?).[30]

The *geber* system as the social foundation, *tabot* Christianity as the cultural formation, and the Aksumite paradigm as the ideological expression define the specificity and unity of the Ge'ez civilization.

PART TWO

THE OLD ORDER, 1896-1935

CHAPTER 2

THE ORIGINS OF MODERN STATEHOOD

henever human societies have attempted to achieve an integrated existence as a national unit around a power centre which is itself the instrument of hegemony of one or several dominant classes, the army has been at the heart of the process as a whole. The army as spearhead has cleared the way, guarded the national power, patrolled the frontiers and whenever circumstances raised the question of unity, unified the various components of the national entity around a hegemonic centre. Certainly this has often been executed by fire and sword: yet always on the basis of a national political project, and often in the context of a whole world view. [Anouar Abdel-Malek, *Social Dialectics, vol. 2: Nation & Revolution,* 1981b, pp. 49-50].

The processes of modern state formation in Ethiopia can be studied through a comparative analysis of analogous processes elsewhere.[1] We isolate three realms of modern state formation during the nineteenth century: Western Europe, "renascent" old states, and Africa. The Ethiopian process of modern state formation is discussed in relation to and within the framework of these three realms.

The Western European Realm

State formation in Western Europe coincided with the rise of capitalist relations. The process was one that Max Weber called "expropriation of the immediate bearers of political power" (1974, pp. 82-83). In Perry Anderson's apt statement, the formation of European absolutist states was one of replacement of "parcellized sovereignty" by "centralized sovereignty" (1979, p. 19). The formation of absolutist states, the rise of capitalist relations, and the constitution of state-framed nations took place simultaneously. This is the formation of state-nations, as contrasted with that of nation-states (Pflanze, *Review of Politics,* 28, 2, 1966). The most important cases included England and France.

In the excellent collection of articles edited by Charles Tilly under the title, *The Formation of National States in Western Europe* (1975), Tilly wrote, "War made the state, and the state made war" (in *Ibid,* p. 42). The process of modern state formation meant "Building differentiated, autonomous, centralized organizations with effective control of territories [which] entailed eliminating or subordinating thousands of semiautonomous authorities" (*Ibid,* p. 71). Comparing the medieval "state" with the modern, Samuel Finer observes:

> . . . *territorially,* the medieval state was *differentiated.* By contrast the public and the private *functions were consolidated* in one and the same office or individual.
>
> In contrast, the contemporary state consists of formerly differentiated territories which have been brought together and whose populations have become *consolidated* under the same common organ of rule — be it prince, or dictator, or Parliament [in *Ibid,* p. 87; emphasis in the original].

Essentially, "the twin process — from consolidated service to differentiated service and from differentiated territory to consolidated territory — is what constitutes *the development of the modern state"* (*Ibid;* emphasis in the original).

Within the Western European realm of modern state formation, but without a long process of centralized sovereignty asserting itself over parcellized sovereignty, were the Italian and German instances, in the latter case the so-called conservative revolution (Moore, 1966). In the 1850s there was no Italy. "Italy was not a country, then, but an idea: the idea, precisely, of persons who longed for Italian unity and independence" (Davidson 1992, p. 121). In 1870, Italy was finally made a state, a result of the Risorgimento (Holt 1970). In 1896 Italy had its Adwa. In 1848 there was no Germany.

There were dozens of Germanic-speaking principalities, with Prussia as the most powerful. The 1848 revolution failed to create a democratic, united Germany. In the 1870s, there was Germany, a powerful state unified under the hegemony of Prussian junker-bourgeois alliance, with Bismarck's iron-and-blood policy. In 1885, Berlin was to host the conference for the so-called Scramble for Africa. By the time Italy and Germany became colonial adventurers in Africa, they were barely three decades young. But then, they had a long European tradition to draw from.

The Italian and German cases were examples of centralized sovereignty being formed in a hothouse fashion, as they were also processes of nation-state formation. In the English and French cases, modern state formation was evolutionary; in the Italian and German cases, it was revolutionary. In the former, states created nations; in the latter, nations became states.

Renascent Old States

The second realm refers to old civilizations. Within the framework of the capitalist world system, they became old-states-turned-new, either of their own volition, in their eagerness to "modernize" by "catching up" with the West (e.g., Japan, Thailand, Persia, Ethiopia) or as they were forced to be modern through colonial occupation (e.g., Egypt, India, Iraq) or somewhere in between the two (e.g., China). These were polities with a long "civilizational project."

Samir Amin argues that the synchronization of state and nation formation with that of capitalism was a Western European experience which, due to Europe's global hegemony, was taken as a universal law of development. There were state-nations prior to capitalism. The best example is Egypt, the "eternal nation" (1980, p. 20), with seventy centuries of centralization.

The third realm refers to states formed in precapitalist settings, within the framework of the capitalist world system but with no centuries-old tradition of statehood as in Egypt, China, Iran, etc. They were political frameworks within which their incorporation and peripheralization into the global network of the capitalist world economy took place (Cooper, *ASR*, 24 June/Sept. 1981, pp. 1-86).[2]

It is to this third category of states formed in and through the processes of incorporation and peripheralization that the various trajectories of state formation in nineteenth-century Africa belong, and to this realm we now turn.

The African Realm

In West Africa, the ending of the transatlantic slave trade and the beginning of so-called legitimate commerce unleashed processes of state formation that would have legitimate control over people and territory and be conducive to incorporation into the capitalist world economy (Ajayi in Flint ed. 1976, pp. 200-221; Wallerstein in Gutkind and Wallerstein ed. 1985, pp. 35-63; Wallerstein in Ajayi ed. 1989, pp. 23-39; Boahen in Ajayi ed. 1989, pp. 40-63). A powerful movement of state formation took place, sanctified by the ideology of Islamic reformism. Slavery for local use flourished to produce the commodities of "legitimate commerce" (Freund 1984, p. 63) whose need for political control added more weight to the process of state formation.

Islam was a great agent of state formation in nineteenth-century West Africa (Webster and Boahen 1990, Part One). Also a great agent of trade and slavery, Islam filled the vacuum left by the end of the transatlantic slave trade by forming vast and powerful centers of political authority. In 1804, the Muslim Fulani scholar, Uthman dan Fodio, led a successful revolt against the Hausa ruler of Gobir. In 1804-10, he conquered Hausaland which became part of the Fulani Empire of the Sokoto Caliphate. It was the largest political entity in nineteenth-century Africa. Influenced by Sokoto, Ahmad Lobbo, also a Fulani, formed a state at Macina on the upper Niger. Al-Kanemi reformed Islam along Sokoto lines in his state of Kanem-Borno. Al Hajj Umar, a Tokolor, also influenced by Sokoto, formed the large Tokolor Empire that stretched from Futa Jalon to Timbuktu (Kwamena-Poh et. al. 1991, p. 32; Hiskett in Flint ed. 1976, pp. 125-69).

One of the most ambitious efforts at state formation in West Africa in an intense conflict with European imperialism was Samori Toure's (Legassick, *JAH*, 7, 1, 1966). For more than three decades, he formed the loosely connected Mandinka Empire, while simultaneously engaging in a series of battles with the French. In 1898, he was he finally silenced.

The Islamic-revivalist states of West Africa, especially the Sokoto Caliphate, were formed by and large through *jihad* and were the locus of the Islam-slavery-state-formation symbiosis (Hiskett 1984; Last 1967; Johnston 1967; Lovejoy, *JAH*, 19, 3; Willis ed. 1985, vols. 1 & 2; Trimingham 1962; Hopkins 1973; Willis, *JAH*, 8, 3, 1967; Fisher and Fisher 1970; Lapidus 1990, Chap. 20; Batran in Ajayi ed.

1989, pp. 537-54). Islam may have provided the apparent religious justification for slavery and state formation (Last in Ajayi and Crowder eds. 1974, vol. 2, pp. 1-47). Beneath the religious veil, however, was a secular sediment. The historical conditions of nineteenth-century West Africa were such that for "legitimate commerce" to work, a corresponding political "superstructure" was necessary. It is this political "superstructure" that keeps "law and order" for the smooth flow of commodities that we call the modern state. It was in West Africa that state formation was more widespread during the nineteenth century than elsewhere on the continent, which can be explained in part by the fact that West Africa was incorporated into the capitalist world economy earlier than the rest of the continent, save the South African region.

In non-Muslim West Africa — in the southern savannah, forest, and the Guinea coast — states like Asante (Wilks 1989), Dahomey (Herskovits 1938), and the Yoruba states of Ibadan and the Egba Confederacy were enlarged and strengthened in the context of "legitimate commerce" (Boahen 1986, Section II). The wars in Dahomey and Yorubaland were fought to control the new palm oil trade to the world economy "which came to dominate the economies of Benin, the Niger Delta city states from Ebrohimi to Opobo, Calabar, and the Igbo communities" (Kwamena-Poh, et al. 1991, p. 32).

In North-East Africa, from Muhammad Ali of Egypt to the Somali coast, processes of state formation in the nineteenth century were essentially similar to that of West Africa. Muhammad Ali's objective in the early part of the nineteenth century was "to give Egypt the military, political, economic and cultural institutions that would make it the driving force behind the reconstitution of a new Islamic empire to replace senescent Turkey" (Abdel-Malek in Ajayi ed. 1989, p. 327).

Muhammad Ali's intent was to avoid Egypt's peripheralization in the world economy (Marsot 1984). His was a Herculean project of making Egypt a major industrial power through what later came to be known as import-substitution industrialization. "In fact, Egypt in the 1830s was exporting a significant quantity of manufactured goods, especially textiles, to neighboring countries" (Stavrianos 1981, p. 215). As Abdel-Malek saw it: "Muhammad Ali was alone among contemporary Eastern Islamic rulers in considering economics as underpinning politics, and this is what made this canny Albanian officer a statesman" (in Ajayi ed. 1989, p. 337). Mohammad Ali began a state-led modernization of Egypt that invited comparison "only with those of Peter the Great in Russia and the Meiji Emperor in Japan . . . . By the 1830s Egypt was second only to England in its modern industrial capacity" (Bernal 1989, pp. 246-7).

Despite this fascinating beginning, Egypt was unable to be, like nineteenth-century Russia or Japan, a semiperipheral power. Egypt's "failure" was not accidental, though. Peripheries are never given; they are always made. So was Egypt. What could have been a major industrial power at the northern tip of North-East Africa was forced to pull back to peripheral status. In the words of Bowring: "A manufacturing country Egypt never can become." Instead, it was to Egypt's "comparative advantage" that it follow, in Bowring's words, "the peaceful development of her agricultural aptitude" (cited in Stavrianos 1981, p. 220). Egypt's quest for industrial status had to be blocked "by any means necessary". And it surely was.

The 1838 Anglo-Turkish treaty made Egypt a supplier of raw cotton to Manchester. Western commercial houses in Alexandria sent their agents to Egyptian villages to buy cotton directly from peasants. Egypt's army was crushed by the British navy, reduced from 130,000 to 18,000. The forced peripheralization of Egypt was now complete. Egypt could no more dare to process its raw cotton into finished textiles. Nor could she become a manufacturing nation creating a periphery of her own in the Sudan, Ethiopia, and the Horn of Africa at large. Both during Muhammad Ali's time and later under the rule of Ismail and Tawfik, Egypt's repeated attempts to create a periphery out of Ethiopia foundered repeatedly. By the time the Suez Canal was built in 1869, the fate of Egypt as a cotton-growing periphery of Manchester had reached a point of no return.

Egypt could not have become an industrial power without creating a peripheral zone of its own somewhere. That somewhere was the Horn of Africa. Once again, Christian Ethiopia stood in the way. The might of the British Empire from the North, and a nervous Christian Ethiopia from the South, choked Egypt's ambition for semiperipheral, and eventual core, status. So ended the story of Muhammad Ali, the most ambitious and most successful quest for industrial power ever attempted by a non-Western leader in the nineteenth century, save Japan. To historical capitalism that produced only one non-Western core power in its 500-year history (i.e., Japan), this comes as no surprise.[3]

Muhammad Ali's attempt was "an example of non-Europeans

beating Europeans in their own games . . . . Where the racial stereotype of natural European superiority failed, artificial intervention was necessary to preserve it" (Bernal 1989, p. 249). The stopping of Muhammad Ali was just such an artificial intervention to preserve "natural European superiority." In the race-intoxicated terrain of the nineteenth-century West, who was this Albanian "adventurer," trying to block the natural progress of the European mind and skill? In the words of Lord Palmerston, the then British Foreign Minister: "I hate Muhammad Ali whom I consider as nothing but an ignorant barbarian, who by cunning and boldness and mother-wit, has been successful in rebellion" (cited in Temperly 1936, p. 89).

The repercussions of Egypt's failure were felt elsewhere in Africa. As Abdel-Malek remarked: "Sudan, Ethiopia, the Horn of Africa and the region of the Great Lakes in Central Africa, were to learn from the experience of a renascent Egypt at grips with the forces of imperialism" (in Ajayi ed. 1989, p. 354). He forgot to add: When Egypt was crushed by Britain, Christian Ethiopia thanked God and took a sound nap. After all, what was Egypt's heroic attempt at industrialization but Muslim imperialist conquest for Christian Ethiopia? (Dye 1969). For Islamic Africa, especially the Horn of Africa, nineteenth-century Egypt may have symbolized the Crescent standing up to the modern Crusaders of the West. Not so for Christian Ethiopia. As usual, Ethiopia spoils what would have been the clean slate of an Islamic North-East Africa.

In the Sudan, Islamic reformism, similar to that of West Africa, was unleashed by a vigorous Mahdist movement, led by Muhammad Ahmed ibn Abdallah, a man of Dunqulawi origin who in 1881 despatched letters from the island of Aba in the White Nile, declaring himself the Mahdi. The Mahdist movement in the Sudan was also directed against Turco-Egyptian rule and British control of the Sudan (Ibrahim in Ajayi ed. 1989, pp. 356-75). The Mahdist Ansars scored victory over General Gordon at Khartoum and became masters of the country. The Ansars fought a *jihad* and made the *bay'a* (oath of allegiance) which made their war of liberation holy (Ibrahim in Boahen ed. 1985, p. 74).

From Egypt's Muhammad Ali to Sudanese Mahdism, the forces of Islamic expansion and state formation dashed their head repeatedly against the hard wall of Christian Ethiopia. A late comer, Islam in North-East Africa found in Christian Ethiopia an insurmountable barrier against proselytizing the entire region. Christian Egypt had succumbed to the forces of Arab-Islamic expansion of the seventh century A. D. What was left was a pocket of Coptic Christian believers. Thanks to Saladin, Christian Nubia was written off the map of the Nile Valley, for it dared to come to the aid of European Crusaders. Christian Ethiopia was the remaining impediment. "Gragn" Muhammad almost succeeded in saying farewell to Christian Ethiopia, but that was reversed. The Mahdist Ansars attacked Christian Ethiopia and killed Emperor Yohannes IV in 1889, but overrunning the country was not their aim; nor would they have succeeded had they attempted. It is one of those aspects of history that we cannot help pondering how different African history would have been had Christian Ethiopia not been at the critical intersection of Islam's nerve center, keeping off everything that smelled of Islam, confining it to the periphery like a loose belt around her waist, watching nervously that it not come up close to her neck and choke her. Located in the "wrong place," Christian Ethiopia "spoils" everything in the region. Trimingham's point that Christian Ethiopia has been the main obstacle to Islam's bid for overall hegemony in the rest of Africa is well made. He wrote:

> Abyssinia, by its purely individualistic resistance . . . has helped to change the course of African history. Its highland fastness have been a rock against which the waves of expansion of the Islamic civilization from the Arabian Peninsula and East African coast on the one hand, and from the Nile valley on the other, have dashed themselves in vain endeavour, so that Islam could not establish that stable rule on the east coast which would have led to interior expansion and possibly the religious unification of Africa under Islam [1965, p. xv].

In Eastern Africa, the process of state formation and consolidation was not directly run by Islam as its agency. Nevertheless, Arabic-Islamic presence was considerable. The "sub-imperialism of Buganda" (Roberts, *JAH,* 3, 1962) under Kabaka Mutesa I garbled the Islamic pressure that made him Muslim neophyte, only to be a Christian later, and at other times to revert back to Islam or to his African "traditional" religion (Oded 1974). The primary concern of the Arab presence in Eastern Africa during the nineteenth century was the procurement of slaves to the various regions of the decaying Ottoman Empire and the eastern flanks of the capitalist world economy. The greatest slave dealer of nineteenth-century Eastern

Africa, Tippu Tip, was not engaged in state formation (Farrant 1975; Wills 1990, pp. 73-82). The Zanzibar Sultanate, with slave plantations as its economic foundation, was the only instance in which Islam, slavery, and state formation coexisted in triple symbiosis in this part of Africa (Cooper 1977; Sheriff 1987).

Nineteenth-century European abolitionists of all kinds pictured the slave dealer in Africa in the image of the Arab. The Arab became the "master slaver" (Bennett 1986). Other attempts at state formation in East Africa have been studied recently in Salim ed. (1985).

In Southern Africa also, states were being formed, the most famous and most ambitious of which was the *Mfecane* (Ngcongco in Ajayi ed. 1989, pp. 90-123; Parsons 1986, Chaps. 4 & 5). Shaka succeeded in creating the most well-disciplined army in nineteenth-century Africa. His *impis* sent shock waves throughout Southern Africa. E. A. Ritter observed, "The very name of Shaka made every tribe tremble from the Great Kei River in the Cape to the Zambezi, and from the Indian Ocean to the farthest confines of Bechuanaland" (1935, p. 338). Alas, how else could states have been made? Commenting on Shaka's accomplishments, Ritter wrote, "From a rabble of 500 men he had increased his army to 50,000 warriors whose discipline exceeded that of the Roman legions at their best" (*Ibid,* p. 345). From a mere 100 square miles, Shaka's new empire grew to 200,000 square miles, "whilst the fragments broken off from his empire were rapidly expanding till they would ultimately extend far over a million square miles."

In the meantime, in 1821, one of Shaka's allies, Mzilikazi, rebelled against Shaka and headed north with a small coterie of warriors. They came to be known as Ndebele or Matabele. Using Zulu military methods, they carved out a state between the Vaal and the Limpopo rivers, "conquering several Sotho and Tswana chiefdoms, and incorporating many of their people as subordinates, exacting tribute from others, and, like the Zulu, sending impis out to terrorize distant communities" (Thompson 1990, p. 86). And then there was the formation of the kingdoms of Gaza and Swaziland (*Ibid*).

The other significant process of state formation in Southern Africa was that of Lesotho. Reacting partly to the *Mfecane,* and partly to the ever-relentless drive of white settlers in all directions, Moshoeshoe of Lesotho used diplomacy and war to create a state structure in the domain of his rule. As Kuper observed, "Throughout

Southern Africa in the late eighteen century [and well into the nineteenth] nations were rising rapidly to power under ambitious rulers" (1947, p. 13). Moshoeshoe was one such ambitious ruler.

The Ngwenyama of Swaziland, the Mwamis of Rwanda and Burundi, the Morena of Lesotho, etc., formed and re-formed states in the context of the distant sounds of the trumpet of the "White Man's Burden."

What was taking place in nineteenth-century Africa was not just an "adaptation" of Africans to the lure of incipient modernization. Nor was it a case of Africans "responding" positively to the West, or as the jargon of Weberian rationality would have it, Africans responding "rationally to the market" by forming states as political frameworks for economic rationality to work. The *Mfecane,* and its larger Southern and Central-African impacts, were caused by fundamental *internal* factors, one of which was population growth (*Ibid*).

The Ethiopian Realm of State Formation

In the global survey of modern state formations made earlier, where does the Ethiopian variety fit in?

State formation in modern Ethiopia shares some of the fundamental aspects of the three realms discussed earlier. Like the first, state formation in Ethiopia proceeded by the triumph of centralized sovereignty over the parcellized sovereignties of the *Zamana Masafent* — the four quasi-independent regional polities of Tigray in the North, Amhara in the Center, Gojjam in the South-West, and Shawa in the South. The process was a long and protracted one. Through the initial protagonist, Kassa-Tewodros, the principle (at least, lesson) of hegemony of centralized over parcellized sovereignty was established. That but cracked the tip of the iceberg. Under Yohannes IV, there was more centralization; but parcellized sovereignty still remained at large. But under Yohannes IV, Ethiopia was "imagined" as a political entity, with well-defined territorial boundaries. In a letter written to the Kaiser, Wilhelm I, King of Prussia, dated February 17, 1881, Emperor Yohannes IV said:

> To the east and the south [east] the boundary is the sea. To the west and north, where there are not seas, it is bounded by Nuba, Suakin, Khartoum, Berber, Sennar, Ennaria, Sudan, and then Dongola, Haren Dawa, Gash, Massawa, Bedun, Shoho, and Tiltal. Further, the regions inhabited by Galla, Shankilla, and Adal is [*sic*] all mine, and yet

> recently in the middle of Shoa, a place known by the name Harar, was taken [from us]. All the same I listed these places so that my country's boundaries be known [cited in Zewde Gebre Selassie 1975, p. 258].

Compared to Yohannes's imagined boundaries of Ethiopia, Menelik's accomplishment was rather limited. Yohannes IV was a key architect in the making of modern Ethiopia. Emperors Tewodros II *initiated,* Yohannes IV *elaborated,* Menelik II *consolidated,* and Haile Selassie I *completed* the process of transformation from parcellized sovereignties to centralized sovereignty.

Going back to our varieties of states, the Ethiopian case also shares a basic similarity with the second. Ethiopia is not like Chad or Burkina Faso, Central African Republic or Malawi — a piece of territory carved out by a European power and given a name.[4] Ethiopia is like Egypt, China, Iran; very old, but also very young. True, Ethiopia did not have the same degree of centralization as "seventy-centuries-old" Egypt. It was more akin to China, where parcellized and centralized sovereignties changed place intermittently, as dynasties rose and fell within its cultural universe.

Still, state formation in nineteenth-century Ethiopia resembles the third variety — the various attempts at state formation in Africa during the nineteenth century. Situated within a comparative framework of state formation in Africa, the Ethiopian case was similar to the formation of states elsewhere in Africa. Two essential processes were at work: (1) Expansion of territorial claim and possession; the bringing of various previously autonomous and semi-autonomous groups and polities under centralized rule; the predominance of the use of force (Tilly's "war creates states"); and the imposition of tribute on the newly incorporated. The means of destruction, the instruments of warmaking, were local (spears) or imported (guns) or both. As the Zulus were "washing their spears," the Ethiopians were waxing their guns. The historical protagonists of African state formation knew well the role of the army as the paramount agent of state formation. Emperors Tewodros II and Menelik II, as well as Samori Toure, Shaka, Mutesa, Muhammad Ali, etc., recognized the critical importance of the army in the formation and consolidation of states (Pankhurst, *BUPA,* 2, 1966; *JES,* 5, 1, 1967; Merid Wolde Aregay, *JES,* 14, 1980). (2) State formation in Africa, including Ethiopia, took place in a process of collision with European expansion. For this, the acquisition of firearms was simply indispensable.

The role of firearms in the making of modern Ethiopia can be seen from two angles, internal and external. From within, superior firepower, and the locale that commanded this superior firepower, asserted its dominance over the rest. Shawa was that locale. Geographically speaking, the Center, Shawa, was dominant over both the North (the hitherto dominant locale of arms superiority) and the South. The uneven distribution of firearms in Ethiopia meant the uneven distribution of military power. The hierarchy was Center-North-South, in descending order (Pankhurst, *JES*, 9, 1, 1971; *Ethiopia Observer*, 11, 2, 1967; 12, 2, 1968; 15, 1, 1972; Abir 1970, p. xxiv; Caulk, *JAH*, 12, 4, 1972).

Externally, the combined strength of Ethiopian firearms enabled the Adwa victory. Overall, the political sovereignty of Ethiopia was established through the dominance of Addis Ababa — the political, cultural, administrative, geographical, and economic hub of the country.

The critical role of firearms in state formation was well understood by Europeans, for they saw superior firearms as the invincible impediment to the initiative of Africans to form their own states. As Hilaire Belloc had it:

> "Whatever happens we have got
> The maxim-gun and they have not."

State formation in Ethiopia involved three main processes. First, in the domain of the Ge'ez civilization (Northern and Central Ethiopia), where parcellized sovereignty reigned supreme, the process was one of a series of campaigns to replace parcellized sovereignty by centralized sovereignty.

The state of the Ge'ez civilization was by and large a *predatory, plunderer state* that lived by looting the *gabbars*. There being hardly any towns, or the towns being no more than temporary military camps of the royal entourage (Pankhurst 1982; 1985), the life force of the predatory state was one of *institutional plunder*; its "income" was derived from mobile predatory appropriation. By and large, the Ge'ez civilization was an agrarian civilization (Gamst, *CSSH*, 12, 1970). It was a loose aggregate of semi-independent polities tied together by a shared culture of *tabot* Christianity (Zewde Gebre Selassie 1975, p. 2]. We now turn to this predatory plunderer state.

The Predatory State

The predatory state thrived in part on plunder and predatory appropriation of *gabbars'* belongings, as well as the belongings of other plunderers. Predatory appropriation was the taking away of whatever belonged to the *gabbar* by force, making the concept of "surplus appropriation" meaningless. In predatory appropriation, "necessary" and "surplus" become one. Predatory appropriation is one of "compulsory transfer of wealth", as opposed to "voluntary transfer of wealth."[5] Concepts like "surplus" and "necessary" may help explain the capitalist mode of production where a minimum of subsistence must be left for the workers so that the extended reproduction of accumulation can take place without interruption.

With predatory appropriation, the case was otherwise. Its motive was plunder of consumable resources. Unlike his bourgeois counterpart, the predator had no interest in leaving a certain amount of the produce with the peasant. The predator was not a businessperson looking for market; he was a warrior in search of plunder. And in the profoundly war-ridden Ethiopia, virtually a pervasive *war culture,* to the victors went the spoils.

The predator took whatever he could and destroyed the rest. The outcome was intermittent destruction of productive forces. Unlike his bourgeois counterpart, who constantly revolutionized the conditions of production, the predatory warrior was a professional destroyer of productive forces.[6] After consuming whatever he could, like the Biblical locusts of Egypt, the predator burnt houses, slaughtered or drove away cattle, set fire to crops. His destructive fury was worse than his voracious consuming appetite. And then there was the rape of women, which was simply second nature to the warrior class. Pankhurst observed:

> The fact that the soldiers of former times [prior to the mid-twentieth century] were unpaid meant that they were obliged to requisition or loot whatever they required from the countries through which they passed, irrespective of whether the inhabitants were friends or foes [1968, p. 563. See also Pankhurst, *Ethiopia Observer,* 7, 2, 1963].

The nomadic warriors, wandering from place to place, were the basis of the predatory nature of the warrior class. The imperial warriors camped at different places following strict protocol according to their rank, with the Emperor's tent in the middle, and the higher echelons of the imperial hierarchy surrounding the Emperor

(Pankhurst 1968, pp. 545-48; *Azania*, 18, 1983, pp. 181-95). It was this constantly mobile force of tens, sometimes hundreds of thousands of armed men and their retainers — slaves, wives, concubines, etc. — that was so devastating to the peasantry upon which it preyed for its subsistence.[7] By and large, the state of the Ge'ez civilization was always on the move, the "wandering capitals of Ethiopia" (Horvath, *JAH*, 10, 2, 1969), led by the king of kings, in search of loot. In times of war, looting and booty were the source of livelihood of the warrior class, for there was no payment of salaries (Pankhurst 1968, p. 551). For the warrior, war spelled plunder. For the tiller of the soil, war was a dreaded scourge that put him at the mercy of that human locust, the warrior class. Since the manner of exaction was predatory, there was no customarily recognized uniformity in the demands of the warriors.[8]

The most destructive aspect of the predatory relation was the massive death of people due to epidemic diseases, the germs of which were carried on the backs of the warriors. Given the unsanitary conditions of the warrior class, the costs of the epidemic diseases like typhoid and amoebic dysentery were appallingly high. The decimation of entire villages in the aftermath of war was not uncommon. Besides epidemics, famine quite normally followed war. Famine and epidemics were the two most devastating results of the predatory relation (Pankhurst, 1991; for the medieval European parallel, see Cipolla 1976, p. 151).

In the *longue duree* of the *geber* system, the *gabbar's* burden of providing whatever the warrior needed has been described by many contemporary observers. The chronicle of Emperor Eskender (1478-1494) wrote that "his [the Emperor's] soldiers ruined all the people," while the Chronicler of Sartse Dengel (1563-1597) noted that the Emperor once said, "If I prolong my stay in Tigre, the country will be ruined because our soldiers are numerous, indeed innumerable" (cited in Pankhurst 1966, p. 53). Almeida, who witnessed the plunder of peasants' resources in the seventeenth century, wrote:

> Big companies of men, soldiers and lords bringing many servants come daily to quarter themselves in small villages. Each one goes to the house he likes best and turns the owner into the street, or occupies it with him. Sometimes it is a widow or a married woman whose husband is away, and then by force he gets at not only food and her property, but her honour [in Beckingham and Huntingford eds. 1967, p. 80].

What Almeida witnessed was still going strong up until the Italian occupation. Pearce wrote:

> In Abyssinia, it is a custom even when the King, Ras or governor are at home, for their soldiers to form themselves into small parties and put one, whom they consider worthy, at their head, and go into the country from farmer to farmer living at free quarters, no one daring to deny them, unless they are too exorbitant and unreasonable in their demands. On these occasions the villagers will give a general alarm, and raise the neighbouring villages to their assistance, and many lives are lost on both sides [1831, vol. 1, p. 91].

The saying *yaabateh bet sizaraf abrah zeraf* (when your father's property is looted, join the looting) is a recognition of how plundering was a means of livelihood not only of the warriors, but also of some peasants who, unable to stop the looting, would join the looters. "Indeed part-time soldiering was almost the only way a farmer could escape for a time from being prey to others by participating in the plunder" (Caulk, *IJAHS*, 11, 3, p. 466). The common practice of peasants hiding their grain in deep pits outside their homes so as to save it from looting by the warriors was a typical form of class struggle in the conditions of predatory appropriation.[9] Peasants also rose up occasionally in rebellion against the warriors to protect their belongings (Caulk, *IJAHS,* 11, 3, p. 491).[10]

Basing himself on Plowden's eyewitness account, Pankhurst estimated that the size of the predatory warrior class in the second half of the nineteenth century was at least 200,000 men, half a million with the camp followers (1966, p. 92).

Predatory extraction of tribute was the normal means of livelihood of the warriors in times of war. In both internal wars among the various ranks of the notables, and aggression from outside, the warriors consumed the produce of those peasants that happened to be on their way to the battlefield and back. Between 1868 and 1896, there were major battles fought against the British (1868), Egyptians (1875, 1876), Sudanese Ansars (1885, 1887, 1888, 1889), and Italians (1887, two major wars in January 1895, two in December 1895, one in January 1896, and one on March 1st, 1896 (Adwa) [Pankhurst 1968, p. 572]. As Pankhurst noted:

> These wars impoverished many hitherto prosperous areas of the north and west, damaging most of the principal

> towns of the north, including Adowa, Gondar, Asmara, Sokota, Maqale, Chelicut and Antalo, as well as rendering unsafe the two main trade routes to Massawa and the Sudan [*Ibid*. See also Pankhurst, *JES*, 4, 2, 1966].

Predatory appropriation continued well into the Italian occupation of 1936. During the 1935 Fascist invasion of Ethiopia, despite Haile Selassie's warning to the fighters that "All who ravage the country or steal from the peasants will be shot," the predatory character of the warriors continued unabated. George Steer, in his account of the war, wrote that the Ethiopian Army of 1935-36 was like a "trail of brown ants . . . eating up everything" (1936, p. 137). Even in times of peace, the peasants were not safe from plunder by the warriors (Wylde 1970, pp. 262-3; Caulk, *IJAHS*, 17, 2, 1984, p. 221).

Although predatory appropriation was based on the extraction of tribute from peasants by force, this does not mean that tribute payment was necessarily predatory. The tributary relations among the various ranks of the appropriating class were not predatory, although the potential threat of the use of force by the higher ranks to levy tribute from the lower ranks was always there, acting as the "invisible hand" of the *geber* system.

The predatory relationship between producers and the appropriators had two distinct regional and systemic forms. The first was that of the warriors and peasants discussed previously. The second was between nomads and pastoralists, mostly in the lowlands, on the one hand, and appropriators on the other. In the Ogaden, for example, the *naftagna* carried out "intermittent expeditions, not far removed from raids" of Somali livestock (Perham 1969, p. 338).

Predators were also active along the long Sudanese border. Periodic campaigns for plunder in these areas were additional means of revenue for the warrior-administrators. These campaigns lasted for a short time. They were expeditions which, in the early decades of the twentieth century, included hunting for slaves (Lange 1982, p. 78; Pankhurst 1976, p. 43; Bahru Zewde 1976; Triulzi 1981; Johnson in Donham and James eds. 1986; Shack 1974, p. 25).[11] Moreover, nomadic people were assigned as *gabbars* to the *naftagna*, although they were more difficult to collect tribute from than the agricultural *gabbars*. Hence pillaging (McClellan, *IJAHS*, 17, 4, 1984, p. 666).

Another dimension of predatory extraction was *sheftenat* (banditry). It was widespread in Ethiopia. It took three forms: fleeing from injustice and the Robin Hood-type *shefta* (outlaw, bandit);

rebellion against a ruler by making a claim to a certain imperial title; and as a mere means of livelihood. The Robin Hood-type *shefta* protected peasants against abuse by notables, reminiscent of Haddis Alemayehu's Abeje Belew in his *Feqer Eska Maqaber*, although he himself was a plunderer too since he could not live otherwise. The imperial aspirant became *shefta* for he claimed that power belonged to him instead of the one ruling. When he rebelled and became *shefta*, he was putting pressure on the high-ranking notables to enable him rise up the power ladder. That was his means of social mobility (Caulk, *IJAHS*, 17, 2, 1984, p. 203). Many emperors in Ethiopia, like Tewodros II and Yohannes IV, started their careers as *shefta*, reminding us that banditry in Ethiopia was more than just being a bandit (see the pieces by Crummey, Fernyhough, and Caulk in Crummey ed. 1986). Some of the *shefta* used to hide in and around the international boundaries of Ethiopia, Italian Eritrea, and the Sudan (Garretson, *IJAHS*, 15, 2, 1982).

State Centralization

The formation of the modern state in Ethiopia involved three processes: First, centralization of power in the domain of the Ge'ez civilization; second, territorial expansion of the Ge'ez civilization beyond Shawa; and, third, collusion and collision of interest between Ethiopian rulers and European powers engaged in the Scramble for Africa.

The process of state centralization in the domain of the Ge'ez civilization was initiated by Kassa Hailu, later *Atse* (Emperor) Tewodros II, who put an end to the *Zamana Masafent* (Abir 1970; Rubenson 1966). After defeating the Tigrayan notable *Dajjach* Wube at the Battle of Darasge on February 8, 1855, *Dajjach* Kassa Hailu was coronated *Atse* Tewodros II, supposedly on a prophecy that a man with that name will reign over Ethiopia and return her to her former glory. Bahru Zawde wrote: "Soon after the Battle of Darasge, he [Tewodros II] turned his attention to the south — to Wallo and Shawa. With that action, he brought to an end the northern focus of the *Zamana Masafent*" (1991, p. 30).

When we discuss how Kassa Hailu-Tewodros brought about the end of the *Zamana Masafent*, it is seldom noted that the struggle against the *Zamana Masafent* was not just one of creating a centralized power, but also that it was a struggle against the Oromo dominance at Dabra Tabor, which was the epicenter of an Oromo arc of rule running through North-Western Wallo, Southern

Gondar, Damot, and Gojjam. In a letter sent to Queen Victoria in 1862, Emperor Tewodros declared:

> My fathers the Emperors having forgotten our Creator, He handed over their Kingdom to the Gallas and Turks. But God created me, lifted me out of the dust, and restored this Empire to my rule . . . . By His power I drove away the Gallas. But for the Turks, I have told them to leave the land of my ancestors. They refused. I am going to wrestle with them [cited in Pankhurst, in Ajayi ed. 1989, p. 397].

Even less noted is how deep the Oromo expansion of the sixteenth and seventeenth centuries had resulted in the Oromization of the ruling house of Gojjam. Since *Atse* Susenyos's coronation, where he billeted Oromo *chawa* known as Illmana Densa (still a name of a region in Gojjam), on the *balagar*, Gojjam was ruled by Christianized, Amharic-speaking, assimilated Oromos. From *Dajjach* Yosedek — the eighteenth century Gudru Oromo ruler of Gojjam — to *Ras* Hailu the Great, *Negus* Tekle Haimanot, and *Ras* Hailu Tekle Haimanot, the rulers of Gojjam were Oromos who assimilated with the Amhara, converted to Christianity, and spoke Amharic (Tekle Tsadik Mekouria, in Amharic, 1981 Eth. calendar, pp. 250-1).

Hence, Kassa Hailu-Tewodros's military engagements in Gojjam were against the assimilated Oromo chieftains of that region. Gojjam elders often say: *Gojjam galla naw* (Gojjam is Galla.) As for the Battle of Embabo, we should not forget that the generals of both armies were Oromo — *Ras* Gobana of *Negus* Menelik, and *Ras* Darasso of *Negus* Tekle Haimanot.

Thus, the process of incipient centralization of state power in the domain of the Ge'ez civilization unleashed by Kassa-Tewodros was also a process of the first-round defeat of Oromo power located in the very heart of Amharaland. For the Ge'ez civilization to emerge from the night of the *Zamana Masafent*, the light of the 85-year "intruder" (the Yajju Oromo ruling house at Debre Tabor) had to be extinguished. That was accomplished by Kassa-Tewodros.

The second aspect of state formation relates to the southward expansion of the territorial domain of the Ge'ez civilization beyond Shawa. Emperors Tewodros and Yohannes unified the classical domain of the Ge'ez civilization from Tigray to Shawa (Rubenson 1966; Zewde Gebre Selassie 1975). Their forces were spent when they reached Shawa. It was now Menelik's turn to push it further south (Darkwah 1966; 1972; 1975; Marcus 1975; Bulatovitch 1971; Beauregard, *TAJH*, 5, 2, 1976). Menelik's drive south unleashed the second-round defeat of the Oromo. This time, it was Menelik's turn to be the intruder in Oromoland. The Oromo, soon to be conquered in a massive campaign of terror and intimidation, were located outside the domain of the Ge'ez civilization. In a period of half a century, from the rise of Kassa-Tewodros to the creation of modern Ethiopia in 1900, the history of modern state formation in Ethiopia was by and large a history of the double victory of the Ge'ez civilization, led by the Tewodros-Yohannes-Menelik triumvirate, over the Oromo, and the equally double defeat of the Oromo from *Ras* Ali the Great of Dabra Tabor/Gondar to Abba Jiffar of Jimma. The rise of modern Ethiopia heralded the demise of Oromo power.

But before Menelik could carry out his task, one last contender had to be neutralized, Gojjam. That was decided at the Battle of Embabo (in North-Eastern Wallaga) on June 6, 1882. The defeat of the Gojjames opened the South for Menelik's war horse to gallop with ever relentless speed. As Bahru noted, "The Embabo victory was Menelik's passport to the southwest" (1991, p. 62). And we might add, a passport with no need of visa. With the Gojjames cleared off the path, "the Battle of Embabao made Menelik the only serious candidate for the succession to Emperor Yohannes IV" (*Ibid*. See also Caulk, *JES*, 13, 1, 1975).

Once victorious over the Gojjames, the Menelikan octopus spread its tentacles in all directions south, sucking in the soft and crushing and "pacifying" the rebellious (Donham and James eds. 1986). In the Menelikan campaign of territorial conquest of the last two decades of the nineteenth century, Christian Ethiopian power was revived with indomitable vigor that made the Ethiopia of 1900 larger in size and more heterogeneous in ethnic composition than what it had been just a quarter of a century earlier.

The only analogy to the magnitude of the Menelikan expansion was the Oromo expansion of the sixteenth and seventeenth centuries. But the Oromo had occupied *land*, for they were in search of grazing and settlement space; the Amhara "occupied" *people*, for their aim was tribute exaction, to enhance the life of the leisure class. While the "Oromo genius for assimilation quickly claimed any non-Oromo, defeated or otherwise" (Mohammed Hassen 1990, p. 21), the Amhara conquerors imposed a rigid class system of ruler and ruled. The relative egalitarianism of the former and the hierarchical order of the latter led to the different results of their territorial conquests.

Two key concepts epitomize the Menelikan Christian-Amharic conquest: *Agar maqnat*, and *dar agar. Agar maqnat* refers to colonization, cultivation, (and christianization) of land defined as "empty," waiting to be made use of.[12] *Dar agar* (frontiers) pertains to the end horizon of the expansion, the boundary of colonization. Accordingly, the term "Galla *agar*" (Galla country) came to be identified with a fictitious empty land. With that came the idea of the "idle, lazy Gallas," not working on the land they possess, a land wasted for lack of hard-working people, a land occupied by "infidels."

One may think this analogous with the European concept of *terra nullius* (empty land), a concept used to justify the European Scramble for Africa (Fisch in Forster et al. eds., 1988). But despite the temptation to draw this analogy, we should beware of reading Menelik's expansion to the South as being similar to the European Scramble for Africa. True, colonialism, both old and new, does not have to be racial. There can be black- on-black colonialism, just as there was white-on-white colonialism (England-Ireland), or yellow-on-yellow colonialism (Japan-Korea). Black colonialism can't be ruled out a priori on racial grounds, as if blacks can't colonize other blacks. Colonialism is based on an unequal *relationship* of power between the colonizer and the colonized. And it is no divine mandate that the two sides of the power divide be of different races. Colonial relationships *create* racial distinctions *ex nihilo*. After all, the Irish were depicted as belonging to a *race* apart from and inferior to the English, as were Koreans by the Japanese. It is not the prior existence of races that gives rise to racism; it is racism that has manufactured groups called "races" (Balibar and Wallerstein 1991). And this is a historical phenomenon; racial groups are defined and redefined periodically. Hence, the Japanese are treated as "honorary white" in apartheid South Africa, but not the Chinese.

The concept of empty land was not meant to be understood literally. It was a metaphor for land to be occupied by force, if necessary, and rights on it transferred to the new occupying authorities. If the land was to be occupied by force and the "natives" dispossessed of their previous rights, then the land became "empty"; it became ownerless *ex post facto*.

The concepts *agar maqnat* and *dar agar* were not invented during Menelik's expansion. They were part of the vocabulary of the Ge'ez civilization that was ever expanding.

Menelik's conquest was carried out by a force of *predominant-*

ly Amhara extraction, for there were non-Amharas also. (*Ras* Gobana was a key architect in Menelik's relentless drive to the lavish green of the South.) Nevertheless, although non-Amharas played a role in that historic drama, the chief protagonists and beneficiaries of the drama of Pax Menelika were predominantly Amhara.[13]

Menelik's territorial expansion was legitimized as being the "reunification" of Ethiopia through the reconquest of the former tributaries of the Christian kingdom,[14] cut off from the main Christian entity in the aftermath of the Oromo expansion.[15] As Emperor Menelik himself said in his now infamous 1891 circular letter to the European powers: "While tracing today the actual boundaries of my Empire, I shall endeavour, if God gives me the strength, to reestablish the ancient frontiers of Ethiopia up to Khartoum, and as far as Lake Nyanza with all the Gallas," and the "Arussi country up to the limits of the Somalis, including also the Province of Ogaden" (cited in Sheik-'Abdi 1993, p. 110). Like Tewodros before him, Menelik zeroed in on the Oromos. But unlike Tewodros who swore to throw the "Galla intruders" out of Ethiopia, Menelik wanted to incorporate them and their resources in the South within Ethiopia. The Ethiopian reconquista was understood and justified in the name of *tabot* Christianity.[16] Few argued the reunification thesis as strongly as Tekle Tsadik Mekuoria:

> That the southern regions of Ethiopia — Hararge, Sidamo, and the areas settled by the Oromo — had been part of Ethiopia from the time of Aksum, Zagwe, and Shawan dynasty, 13th-16th centuries, during the reign of *Atse* Amda-Tseyon, Zara-Yaqob until the rise of *Gragn* Ahmad, is clearly proven by documentary evidence [1981 Eth. calendar, p. 211; my translation from the Amharic original].

Other than justifying the Menelikan expansion, it is ludicrous on Tekle Tsadik's part to say that Aksumite civilization, whose territorial extent at its largest was confined to what is now Eritrea, Tigray, Northern Wallo, and at times parts of Arabia, could have in any way included Sidamo and Hararge, far south of Zagwe territory. In the post-"Solomonic-restoration" period, regions like Northern Hararge, Arsi, Sidamo, Inarya, and Kaffa were paying intermittent tribute to the Christian kingdom. But to push this back to the Zagwe period, not to mention Aksumite, is fictitious. (In our schooldays, we were told that in antiquity, Ethiopia's borders extended from Egypt to Madagascar! This was obviously a confusion of the Ethiopia of the Greeks, which referred to people of "burnt faces," with Aksumite Ethiopia).

The Menelikan conquest took two distinct forms, with two different outcomes, depending upon the degree of resistance from the local population. In areas like Wallaga and Jimma, where military resistance against Menelik's forces was mute, the incorporated regions were left with their previous sociopolitical arrangements, and a tributary relationship was established between them and the central administration. Direct armed occupation and the dismantling of the indigenous status-quo was found unnecessary. In the immediate aftermath of the Battle of Embabao, Menelik's forces obtained the "peaceful" submission of South-Western regions. Bahru Zawde wrote:

> With little or no resistance, the Oromo states [of the southwest] submitted to Menelik one after another. In the years between 1882 and 1886, Menelik was able to obtain the submission of Kumsa Moroda (later *dajjazmach*, and baptized Gabra-Egziabher) of Leqa Naqamte, Jote Tollu (also made *dajjazmach*) of Leqa Qellam, Abba Jiffar II of Jimma, and the rulers of the other Gibe river states, as well as of Illubabor, further to the west [1991, p. 62].

In these regions, intermediary rule was established, with the former notables linking Addis Ababa with the local population. They were the *balabbats*, the transmission belts, the human bridge connecting "their" people with the *matie* (newcomers). Some converted to Christianity, and their baptismal name became their secular name. Gebre-Egziabher (servant of God,) Gebre-Maryam (servant of Mary,) etc., were typical. The servants of the new conquerors converted to a new religion that made them servants of the Christian God. By being Christian, they joined the ranks of Christian Amharic speakers. They mixed their blood with that of the royal court at Addis Ababa. In this way, the Oromo rulers of Wallaga became extensions of the imperial royal house radiating from Addis Ababa.

In other regions where the people fought back, the military factor played a key role. In Western Gurage, Arsi, Walayta, Kaffa, and Harar, stiff resistance was put up by the population against Menelik's forces. The Gurage split into two, the Kesante (northern Gurage) submitting "peacefully," while the western Gurage fought back. The Kesante, with "their relative geographical proximity, and their religious affinity with Christian Shawa, together with the threat of the Oromo that surrounded them, rendered resistance impolitic" (*Ibid*, p. 61). The Western Gurage, on the other hand, were subdued after fierce engagement. Subsequently, a Muslim revivalist movement led by Hassan Injamo of Qabena spread in the area which was finally crushed by *Ras* Gobana in 1888 (*Ibid*).

The most fierce resistance of all was put up by the Arsi Oromo. Facing guns with spears and arrows, the Arsi stood up against Menelik for four years, 1882-86. In December 1883, Menelik himself barely managed to escape alive. The final assault on the Arsi Oromo was led by *Ras* Darge Sahle Selassie, Menelik's paternal uncle. At the Battle of Azule, on September 1886, the Arsi Oromo were finally silenced (*Ibid*, pp. 62-63). No wonder then that the Arsi Oromo came to be the most hated, the most feared, and the most despised in the whole country, while the Wallaga Oromo were not only respected, but became part of the ruling elite through intermarriage with the royal family.

With Arsi now "pacified," it became a "a stepping-stone to Harrar, the commercial centre of eastern Ethiopia" (*Ibid*, p. 63). On January 6, 1887, the Harari were defeated at the Battle of Chalanko, and Menelik entered Harrar triumphant.

Harrar was a city-state *par excellence* (Burton 1987; Waldron in Hess ed. *PFICES*, 1979). Just free of Egyptian suzerainty in 1885, Harar was an urban civilization in the midst of agrarian and nomadic life, a city-state that was a center of Islamic learning, well-organized trade, and an elaborate fiscal system. Compared with any place in Ethiopia during the nineteenth century, it had no equal. Only Jimma came close. After the Battle of Chalanqo, the Hararis gave in to Menelik, "outgunned, outnumbered and outmanoeuvred" (Bahru Zewde 1991, pp. 63-4. See also Caulk, *JES*, 9, 2, 1971). Abdullahi, the Emir of Harrar, was deposed. In his place, *Dajjach* (later *Ras*) Makonnan Wolde Michael, Emperor Haile Selassie's father, was appointed to rule over the region.

West of Harrar, the same fate as the Arsi befell Walayta, which resulted in one of the most horrendous campaigns of Menelik's expansion. *Kawa* (King) Tona of Walayta's forces succumbed to the Menelikan war machine in 1894 (Bahru Zewde 1991, pp. 64-5). In 1897, Kaffa went through the same horror as the Walayta. *Tato* (King) Gaki Sherocho of Kaffa was in chains and taken prisoner to Addis Ababa, as had been King Tona before him. *Ras* Wolde Giorgis took over the governorship of Kaffa (*Ibid*, pp. 65-6). The resources of Kaffa, once a well-organized monarchy of legendary wealth (Huntingford 1955; Orent, *AHS*, 3, 2, 1970), were now at the disposal of the new rulers.

In the southwest was Jimma, a city-state of tremendous wealth based on trade, mainly slaves and ivory (H. S. Lewis 1965; Wilkinson, *JRGS*, 25 1855)). In both Kaffa and Jimma, trade in slaves and ivory was a monopoly of the imperial court, from whom the *jabartis* carried it over to the Christian areas and beyond.

The regions conquered after military engagements paid dearly, for they dared to resist Menelik's might. Hence was imposed that infamous order, the *naftagnya* system (McClellan, *Africa* [Roma], 33, 3, 1978).

The word *naftagna* is derived from the word *naft,* (Arabic for gun). *Naftagna* means "one with gun." The degree of the *naftagna* presence in the newly-conquered territories depended upon the degree of resistance put up by the local population. In regions of local military resistance, the *naftagna* system was imposed once the resistance was "pacified." *Naftagna* and *gabbar* faced each other without mediation, directly and fiercely. The language of the gun was the means of communication. So was formed the dual society: conqueror and conquered, victor and vanquished, civilized and barbarian, believer and infidel, clean and dirty, Amhara and "Galla." Gebru Tareke wrote:

> Paternalistic and arrogant, Abyssinians looked upon and treated the indigenous people as backward, heathen, filthy, deceitful, lazy, and even stupid — stereotypes that European colonialists commonly ascribed to their African subjects. Both literally and symbolically, southerners became the object of scorn and ridicule [1990, p. 71].

Yes "Abyssinians" were all that. But it is a mistake to draw analogy with European colonialism, even at the level of stereotype. Yet this analogy has been so pervasive in critical Ethiopian studies that it evades even such a careful and shrewd observer as Gebru. But even Gebru, on the very next page, retracts his positive analogy with European colonialism thus:

> There were no culturally defined areas of settlement [in southern Ethiopia], and the northerners were far less demarcated from the indigenous population than the European colonialists elsewhere in Africa. Moreover, set-

> tler society [in southern Ethiopia] was open, and anyone could become thoroughly Abyssinianized by adopting Amharic and Orthodox Christianity. The French or Portuguese were far less successful with their policies of assimilation for, in the final analysis, no *assimile* or *assimilado* could ever cross the racial barrier. In Ethiopia, the "superior-inferior" complex had a cultural connotation only [Ibid, p. 72].

European colonialism came to Africa with racism, partly left Africa with racism, and partly remained in Africa with racism. This was not the case with "Abyssinians"'s relations with southern peoples.

It is racism, more than any other characteristic, that sets apart the most vicious *naftagna* from his most benevolent European colonial counterpart. The former was not racist, the latter was. *Negus* Mikael of Wallo, Empress Mannan, Haile Selassie's wife, Haile Selassie's grandfather, Walda Mikael Gudissa, *Ledj* Eyasu, the Wallaga notables who joined the royal family through marriage, etc., were all Oromos. And yet, even for them, the word "Galla" carried the stereotypical connotation that Gebru refers to above. As Gebru correctly noted earlier, the dominant\subordinate divide in the South was cultural, as much as it was class; it was one of *culture-class*. It could be crossed over, but through a one-way assimilation process into the Ge'ez civilization. Marriage into the dominant group was one way of doing so. Imagine a Zulu "paramount chief" joining Buckingham Palace in holy matrimony!

It is of critical importance to comprehend that "Amhara" and "Galla" were not ethnic terms. *Amhara was a metaphor for power, and Galla for the relative lack of it*. For the conquerors, the word "Galla" was a shorthand for the conquered "Others," be they Gurage, Kafficho, Gudela, Oromo, Walayta, etc. For the conquered peoples of the South, Amhara meant "one with power," and the person identified as such could as well be an Oromo from Shawa, a Gurage, a Tigrayan, or an Amhara. For Muslims and followers of "traditional" African religion, Amhara meant a Christian with a gun.

The *naftagna/gabbar* system was based on the establishment of settler "colonies" during the processes of "pacification" and after the establishment of the Pax Menelika. These settler "colonies," called *katamma* (from the root word *maktam*, which means to camp), were initially garrison posts that included warriors, administrators, and clergy. They were the locale for "maintaining law and order" and the smooth flow of tribute to the imperial treasury at Addis Ababa. The location of the *katammas* was with defense purposes in mind. A good many of what are today towns in Ethiopia had their origin in the military consideration of their founders.

Once "pacified," the people living on the land were "distributed" as *gabbars* to the *naftagna* (see McClellan, *Africa*, 33, 3, 1978, p. 434). People from Northern and Central Ethiopia, mostly the poor, moved to the South, to the Galla *agar* (Galla country,) in search of a better life. This had significant impact on the balance of the people-land ratio in the *rist* regions. McClellan wrote:

> For the individual northerner, emigrations provided an opportunity to relieve pressures on the northern household unit, insuring more land for those left behind as well as to gain power, status and wealth in the south. Attraction was strongest for the young who had the last opportunity in the north. Life would be hard, but the chances for both economic and social mobility were better [*IJAHS*, 17, 4, 1984, p. 660].

The hegemony established by the *naftagna* over the *gabbar* was based on the claim of superiority of the former over the latter.[17] The mutual fear and respect that existed between the Amhara and the Oromo since the latter's massive expansion in the sixteenth century,[18] a relationship understood by the former as a conflict between Christian civilization and pagan barbarism, a relationship wherein intermittent series of military victories and defeats were experienced by both sides, a relationship where the Oromo had been active participants in the power struggles of the post-Susenyos period until they became dominant during the *Zamana Masafent* — these relationships of equity were transformed into a lopsided relationship of dominance and subordination by the beginning of the twentieth century. In Mohammed Hassen's words:

> Never since the first half of the sixteenth century had such a radical change in the balance of power occurred in the Horn of Africa and with such speed as it did during the second half of the nineteenth century. The new weapons [of war] not only made victories easier for the Amhara, but also enabled their leaders to set up administrative and military colonies in Oromo territory at a long distance from their home base [1990, pp. 197-8].

Thus was ushered in a new era, one in which the Oromo were beaten, or threatened with being beaten into submission by a terrifyingly superior military force. The very mention of the word *naftagna* struck terror. Hence the saying: *and amara mato galla yenadal* (one Amhara can chase away a hundred Gallas). The historical process that transformed the mutual fear and respect between the Amhara and the Oromo into one of dominance and hegemony of the former over the latter is one of the most important aspects in the making of modern Ethiopia.

The third aspect of modern state formation in Ethiopia refers to the collusion and collision of interests among the various warlords in Ethiopia and European powers — primarily Italy, France, and Britain — that shaped the process and outcome of state formation. In their zealous passion to outcompete each other, European powers supplied arms to the various warlords of Ethiopia to instigate rebellions against the *negusa nagast*. The Italian supply of arms to *Negus* Menelik in order to incite him against *Negusa Nagast* Yohannes IV is a case in point. By the end of the nineteenth century, *Negusa Nagast* Menelik II was the biggest gunlord in Africa, commanding tens of thousands of rifle-carrying warriors. Different warlords received and bought guns from different European powers to out-compete each other. To this extent, there was a common interest between Ethiopian warlords and European powers. And yet, it was the combined military strength of Ethiopia against Egypt, Sudanese Ansars, and Italians that preserved the country's sovereignty. Here we see conflicting interests between Ethiopia and outside powers.

The process that began as the gradual supremacy of centralized sovereignty over parcellized sovereignty in the domain of the Ge'ez civilization ended up in a larger project of state formation through territorial expansion which, by the beginning of the twentieth century, resulted in the formation of the geopolitical entity coterminous with the present international boundaries of Ethiopia, excluding Eritrea (see Hamilton 1974).

Commenting on the historical significance of the newly-formed Menelikan state, Bahru Zewde wrote:

> It was to be Menelik's main claim to historical distinction that he presided over the realization of an idea that had first been kindled in the fiery mind of Tewodros. Yet the final result bore little resemblance to the initial dream. Tewodros's vision of Ethiopia was limited to the central

> provinces, with Shawa marking the southern limit. Yohannes's conception, while extending further in the north, was broader in the south only by proxy, through the agency of his vassal Takla-Haymanot, who was made *negus* of Gojjam *and* Kaffa. Menelik, on the other hand, pushed the frontier of the Ethiopian state to areas beyond the reach even of such renowned medieval empire-builders as *Negusa Nagast* Amda-Tseyon (r. 1314-1344.) In the process, the Ethiopia of today was born, its shape consecrated by the boundary agreements made after the Battle of Adwa in 1896 with the adjoining colonial powers [1991, p. 60].[19]

By using diplomacy and/or war, and by exploiting the inter-European rivalry, Menelik presided over the formation of the modern Ethiopian state (Rendell Rodd 1923, pp. 162-91; Greenfield 1965, pp. 115-28; Marcus 1975, pp. 135-213; Caulk 1966; Sanderson, *JAH*, 5, 1, 1964; Marcus, *JAH*, 7, 1, 1966).

In summary, the process of formation of modern statehood in Ethiopia was one in which an old polity was struggling to become a born-again modern state, to find a place under the sun of the interstate system.[20] This involved four processes: (1) the simultaneous processes of *creative destruction* [21] of the *Zamana Masafent* and the *innovative introduction* of state consolidation and centralization in the domain of the Ge'ez civilization; (2) the destructive annihilation of states and proto-states in the southern regions;[22] (3) the heroic resistance in Northern Ethiopia against Egyptian and European imperialism by *Ras* Allula and Emperors Yohannes and Menelik; and (4) the southern push of Menelik that brought him on a collision course with nearby European colonial powers, mainly Britain. Bahru wrote:

> The race for territory [between Menelik and European powers] became even more acute after the victory of Adwa in 1896, as Menelik's troops pushed further outwards with reinvigorated *elan*, and the colonial powers, particularly Britain, rushed to check them [1991, p. 61].[23]

So was born modern Ethiopia, with the defeat of the Oromo, Walyata, Kaffa, Gurage, etc., in the South, and Egypt and Italy from beyond the Sea. As elsewhere in state formations, the unity of modern Ethiopia was formed through "the means of brutality" (Renan in Bhabha ed., 1990, p. 11). With the triple victory over Muslim

Egypt, Catholic Italy, and the "pagan" and Muslim South in the last quarter of the nineteenth century, a new era began in Ethiopian history, that of modern Ethiopia. The "Conquering Lion of the Tribe of Judah" had triumphed! In these aspects, Ethiopia is without peers in modern African history.

The fundamental aspect of state formation in nineteenth-century Africa, including Ethiopia, was one of expansion-assimilation-centralization. Polities expanded their domain of territorial jurisdiction. This was followed by the formation of centralized sites of power, which in turn necessitated the political and cultural assimilation of some of the new subjects, at first the notables, thereby incorporating them within the domain of the expanded relations of rule. All this took place through an elaborate system of the giving, receiving, and redistributing of tribute. Tribute payment, whatever the form, including slaves as in West Africa (Polanyi 1966; Fisher and Fisher 1970, p. 150), was the social cement that forged the fragile unity of the newly-formed states. In all these, the fundamentals of state formation in Ethiopia found themselves quite at home with the rest of Africa.

So Ethiopia was sitting on three stools — the modern Western, the historic old states, and the new fragile states of nineteenth-century Africa. The domain of its Ge'ez civilization was one of showdown of parcellized versus centralized sovereignties. Relations of rule were moving away from autonomous and semi-autonomous polities to relatively centralized states. As the new centers of power were growing larger in size and population, they were getting smaller in number. Like its other African counterparts, Menelikan Ethiopia was expanding its size, centralizing its power, and assimilating the notables of its new subjects. With these two at hand, modern Ethiopia baptized its cultural mosaic with the holy waters of its old civilizational vocation — its *tabot* Christianity, on the one hand, and the Amharic language, on the other. It declared both to be the sole official seals of its identity. Its throne was the exclusive possession of the Christian descendants of the House of Solomon and Saba, and its emblem the "Conquering Lion of the Tribe of Judah." All those outlandish to its religious-cultural universe that happen to live inside Ethiopia were declared unfit to rule. Ethiopia was a Christian island surrounded by a heathen sea. Thus Ethiopian Muslims were referred to as "Muslims living in Ethiopia"!

Despite the three distinct realms of statehood in the modern world, there were some essential similarities that are observable in all of them. These included: territorial expansion and integration; formation of centralized authority (the degree of centralization varying with the degree of economic and cultural cohesion); predominance of the role of the army in the initial process of state formation; a more or less defined boundary; an elaborate system of taxation; and membership in the interstate system.

If these were some of the similarities, what were the differences?

State formation in Western Europe proceeded simultaneously with that of nation formation. From Absolutism to the twentieth century, the West ushered in nations that developed through a highly elaborate system of mass communication. Roads created nations. The "sack of potatoes" that was once Western Europe was transformed into modern, nationally-integrated political units (E. Weber 1976; Skocopol 1979, Chap. 5). Subjects became citizens endowed with "natural rights" (Schama 1989, Chap. 4). Even then, Northern Ireland, the Basque, and Southern Italy, to mention but few, defied the general trend. West European states became the core of the capitalist world economy. On the other hand, a good many of the old states like Hindustan and Egypt ended up being colonies of the West, while the new states of nineteenth-century Africa succumbed to the overwhelming power of the European war machine. No nations were formed in Africa, while those like Somalia are now breaking down into their atomistic, clannish components.

Superiority of European firepower brought to a halt the various attempts at state formation in Africa.[24] From Zululand to Sokoto, from Mahdist Sudan to the Tokolor Empire, the various political entities in Africa succumbed to the dictatorship of European military technology. The victories of Isandhlwana and Khartoum were to be epic memories in the annals of African resistance. Shaka was deified as hero, embellished in Mofolo's *Chaka*, and Kunene's *Emperor Shaka the Great: A Zulu Epic.* The heroes of Isandhlwana were glorified, for "like lions they fought" (Edgerton 1988). And yet, on the historical scene, Kitchener avenged Gordon. Isandhlwana was not allowed a second coming, for Zulu power was crushed (Guy 1979). Lugard raised the Union Jack on the knees of the once mighty Sokoto. Cecil Rhodes's childhood fantasy of painting Africa red came partly true, but was goldish in color (Rotberg 1988). From slavery to "legitimate commerce," from "legitimate commerce" to colonialism, the half-millennium relationship between the West and

Africa continued along the same line of dominance\subjection, with only the form changing. It is from this perspective that the significance of Ethiopia's success in becoming a sovereign state in the midst of colonized Africa should be assessed.

How did Ethiopia achieve sovereignty in contrast to the rest of Africa (save Liberia)? There were three main reasons. First, more than any other place in Africa, there were more firearms imported from Europe into Ethiopia.[25] Second, the history of centuries of statehood — the existence of an armed body separate from the rest of the population, the warrior class (*chawa, watadar*), specializing in the art of warmaking as a vocation — proved effective in preventing Ethiopia from succumbing to the European onslaught. Third, the cultural unity established by the Ethiopian Orthodox Church cemented a sense of identity beyond the parish and region onto the higher plane of Ethiopia as a Christian island surrounded by a hostile heathen sea. That Europeans were Christians did not matter for Ethiopians. The Emperor's nagarit (war drum) sounded the war cry: *ristehen yamiqema haimanotehn yamiarekes mistehen yamidafer telat keruq metobehalena tanasa! Gulbet yaleh bakendeh yalelah batsaloteh takatalegn.* (An enemy has come from a distant land to take away your land, to destroy your religion, to defy the honor of your wife. Rise up! If you are strong, follow me and render me your arm. If you are weak, follow me with your prayer for my victory.) Such was Ethiopian emperors' call for war mobilization. Land, Religion, Wife — these were the sacred trinity of Ethiopian war "nationalism," *tabot-Christian denominationalism*, a "nationalism" as ephemeral as the length of the battle itself, after which it broke down into its parish and shire components. For the hundreds of thousands of volunteer fighters, the three principles worth dying for had been the rallying ground for saving Christian Ethiopia from "Gragn Muhammad" in the sixteenth century all the way up to Mussolini in the mid twentieth.

In contrast to the Ethiopian story, state formation in the rest of nineteenth-century Africa failed due to two main reasons.[26] First, the states formed were new and fragile, based on "shaky social and cultural foundations . . . and ruled over peoples who had been subjected for less than a century, some for only one or two generations" (Coquery-Vidrovitch 1988, p. 67). The exception was Egypt. But Egypt was too important for the West to be left to the Egyptians. Second, there was an immense gap in military power between Europeans and Africans. Europe's was one of maxim-gun colonization; Africa's was not. True, Africans had guns too. But they were no match for Europeans. Besides, Africans hardly united among themselves against Europeans. How could they? They were not Africans in consciousness yet. The Asantehene's responsibility was for the well-being of the Asante nation, not for the land mass called Africa. African nationalism came onto the scene in the twentieth century. The common colonial experience had then created a common African identity (Mudimbe 1988; Appiah 1992).

CHAPTER 3

SLAVES AND OCCUPATIONAL MINORITIES ("CASTES")

lavery is the permanent, violent domination of natally alienated and generally dishonored persons (Orlando Patterson, *Slavery and Social Death*, 1982, p. 13; emphasis in the original.)

Slavery

The relation of enslavement as instituted practice, no matter under what name designated — household, plantation, harem, temple, military, etc. — has existed across historical formations of the most diverse kind. From the Mamlukes of Egypt to the Victorian gentleman of the Carolinas, from the Circassian women in the galaxy of Ottoman Porte to the *Zanj* eunuchs who looked after them, from the monks and nuns of Christian Russia to that of *Dar al-Islam* with *jihad* both as a means and justification of war against the *Dar al-Harb*, "whether on the throne or in chains" (Hegel 1977, p. 121), slavery existed across historical time and cultural distinctions such that, "There is no region on earth that has not at some time harbored the institution [of slavery]" (Patterson 1982, p. vii).

The universality of slavery across geocultural space and historical time presents a formidable challenge to rigorous conceptualization. In his celebrated piece "Slavery," included in the *International Encyclopedia of the Social Sciences* (14, 1968), Moses I. Finley classified slavery into two kinds:

> *genuine* slave societies — classical Greece (except Sparta) and Rome, the American South and the Caribbean — on the one hand, and *slave owning* societies as found in the ancient Near East (including Egypt), India, or China, on the other hand [*Ibid*, p. 308].

He wrote that "slavery attained its greatest functional significance, and usually its greatest numerical strength, in societies in which other less total varieties of bondage had either disappeared or had never existed" (*Ibid*). Since slavery is "a species of dependent labor and not the genus," and since in most cases non-slave dependent labor was largely available, it was only in genuine slave societies that slavery became the most important form of dependent labor. Finley wrote:

> In classical Roman law, slavery was defined as an institution "whereby someone is subject to the *domination* of another contrary to nature" . . . . *Dominium* can be translated as "power," but the idea of property is also implied. This definition may be accepted as universally applicable without the controversial phrase, "contrary to the nature" [*Ibid*, p. 307. See also Buckland 1969].

Freedom

The concept of "freedom" is as complicated as that of slavery (Patterson 1991). Just as there is no abstract slavery, so also there is no abstract freedom. Freedom is no metahistorical essence, but a historical relation of rights, "positive" and "negative" (Berlin 1960). And since "Right can never be higher than the economic structure of society and its cultural development conditioned thereby" (Marx 1968, p. 324), freedom understood as individual personal right did not exist under all forms of slavery.

Two conceptions of freedom can be identified: freedom as *resid-*

ual right (whatever is not authoritatively appropriated by someone else), and freedom as a legal-philosophical principle concerned with positive *rights of persons* in relation to constituted authorities.[1] In slave societies, the abstract individual as a person endowed with natural rights, including freedom, was an exception, not the rule (Patterson 1991, p. x). It was the modern liberal state that combined the abstract notion of personal freedom with that of slavery. Thomas Jefferson and slavery were contained within the same systemic envelope. Orlando Patterson wrote:

> In the Western world the paradox [of slavery] is compounded by another historical enigma. Slavery is associated not only with the development of advanced economies, but also with the emergence of several of the most profoundly cherished ideals and beliefs in the Western tradition. The idea of freedom and the concept of property were both intimately bound up with the rise of slavery, their very antithesis. The great innovators not only took slavery for granted, they insisted on its necessity as a way of life [1982, p. viii].

The simultaneous existence of slavery and the concept of personal freedom should not be seen as a paradox. At the heart of bourgeois theory of freedom is the concept of property. Since slaves are property, to own them does not contradict freedom; it rather complements it. The right of the free persons includes the right to make others unfree; the right to own them as slaves.

When we come to the non-Western world, "freedom" has a different connotation, for slavery is different too (Watson ed. 1980). Here to be free may mean to be ostracized from the community. In Africa, for example, an individual attains humanity by "belonging *in*" the community as an active participant in civic affairs (Kopytoff and Miers in Kopytoff and Miers eds. 1977, p. 10). The very word "freedom" as understood in the West does not exist in many languages (Patterson 1991, p. x). In Africa, including Ethiopia, the concept of freedom, and its relation with slavery, is quite different from that of the West. In Ethiopia, the word for freedom is *natsanet*, which means political independence, not personal freedom as understood in Western liberalism. Kopytoff and Miers wrote:

> In the Western conception, the antithesis of "slavery" is "freedom," and 'freedom' means autonomy and a lack of social bonds . . . . In most African societies, 'freedom' lay

> not in a withdrawal into meaningless and dangerous autonomy but in attachment to a kin group, to a patron, to power — an attachment that occurred within a well-defined hierarchical framework [in Kopytoff and Meirs eds. 1977, p. 17].

The residual notion of freedom in relation to slavery is a negative conception that denotes that one is not a slave. Put otherwise, as the Arab proverb from Mecca had it, "The slave is he who has no slave" (Sersen in Willis ed. 1985, vol. 1, p. 101). Strictly speaking, this was not the case everywhere, as there were "slave aristocrats," to use Max Weber's expression (1976), ie., slave-owning slaves, as there were serf-owning serfs in Russia (Hellie 1982, p. 74).

To conclude our discussion of slavery and freedom, both conceptions should be understood *historically*. The general features of slavery across historical and cultural formations should be sorted out of the historical details, rather than taking one aspect, like slavery in the Americas, and impose it as an ideal type upon the rest. Having discussed some theoretical aspects of slavery and freedom, albeit in a nutshell, let us now turn to the Ethiopian scene.

Slavery in Ethiopia

> All men share liberty on the basis of natural law . . . . War and the strength of horses bring some to the service of others, because the law of war and victory, makes the vanquished the slaves of the victors [*Fetha Nagast*].

The discussion on slavery in Ethiopia can be seen from two angles: slavery in Ethiopia; and the slave trade out of Ethiopia, mostly to the Arab and Ottoman empires. Slavery in Ethiopia belonged to Finley's category of slave-owning society; there was no genuine slavery. Slavery took mostly the form of household slavery. Pankhurst wrote:

> Slaves were generally relegated to inferior types of work. Male slaves were engaged in porterage, and in time of war often accompanied their master, carrying not only his supplies, but his spear, shield and rifle. Women slaves had to grind corn and carry firewood and water. They also prepared the spices, did the cooking, cleaned the house, collected manure for burning, poured mead, chased away flies and held the candle. In many cases, especially where the

> master's wife bore no child, they might also serve as concubines. Numerous slaves were employed at Menelik's palace. The most handsome men, particularly among the Shanquellas, were enrolled as a special guard, while others acted as subordinate servants and porters. Female slaves and children were engaged in all types of domestic work and accompanied the army on expeditions [1968, p. 74].

Yes, slaves in Christian Ethiopia carried their master's rifle. Trotting behind their master's decorated mule, slaves had the gun, the very instrument that made their enslavement possible in the first place, in their hand. And the master trusted them! Baum saw the scene in early twentieth-century Addis Ababa where the "slave boy, [was] trotting at the right side of his master's mule, gun in bright satin case over his shoulder" (1927, p. 30). Alas, in modern, democratic, rational America, slaves were not allowed to use drums! It was feared that they might use it for communicating among themselves.

Although the principal owners of slaves were from the higher echelons of the noble hierarchy, even very low-ranking officials did own slaves. A good many of the slaves in Northern and Central Ethiopia came from Oromo, Sidama, Kaffa, and Beni Shangul ("Shanqella") regions.

The primary means of getting slaves was through raids and warfare. Organized slave raids were dispatched periodically by slave merchants. Occasionally, prisoners of war were sold into slavery. Such were the cases of Oromos selling Gurages into slavery, and vice-versa (Shack 1966, p. 137).

The idea that Christians were linked to slavery only as buyers, not as sellers, did not square with the fact that during Menelik's campaigns in the South, prisoners of war were enslaved by the thousands. Pankhurst cites the eyewitness account of Vanderheym, who joined Menelik during the Walayta expedition of 1894, and who himself took eleven slaves:

> Menelik's army captured 18,000 slaves, one-tenth of which were considered as the Emperor's booty, the rest as the property of his soldiers. Slaves, he adds, were at this period given as presents from one chief to another almost like visiting cards. A British diplomatic report for 1895 stated that 15,000 slaves were captured in Welamo and that persons obtaining them were subjected to a tax of a dollar per slave [1968, p. 105].

And Harold Marcus called Emperor Menelik "Ethiopia's greatest slave entrepreneur" who "received the bulk of the proceeds, along with a tax for each slave brought into Shoa and one for every slave sold there. It was not until his resources had grown considerably that Menelik could attempt to eradicate the trade" (1975, p. 73).

In Amharic and Tegregna languages, the word for slave is *barya*. The term *barya* has three main connotations: slave; a name of an ethnic group in Northwest Eritrea; and a phenotypical designation (very dark skin, kinky hair, flat nose, thick lips.)

In his Amharic article, "*Yabarya Sem Baamaraw Bahel*" ("Slave Name in Amhara Culture", *JES*, 10, 2, 1972), Seifu Metaferia discussed the sociocultural significance of the word *barya*. The public perception of the barya was expressed in images and metaphors referring to disease, sexuality, skin color, hair, virginity, behavior, manners, etc. Accordingly, epilepsy was known as *yabarya beshita* (slave disease). The implication was that epilepsy makes one fall anywhere; it is a disease as low and degrading as a slave. *Barya yezotal* (he is possessed by a slave), was a reference to madness and insanity. The mad person did many unconventional things, as the slave was thought of doing the same. *Barya dengay* (slave stone), was to mean black stone, since slaves were "black." *Yabarya tsegur* (slave hair) meant kinky, wooly hair. To say *barya dengel* (slave virgin) was to make a sarcastic remark about something that is hardly possible, ie., finding virgins among slave women (*Ibid*, p. 159).

In the case of "slave character," the most well-known expression is *yabarya tebay* (slave behavior.) *Yabarya tebay* refers to a number of things: untrustworthiness, prone to lying, stealing, constant fornication, cheerfulness, uncaring for tomorrow, laziness, etc. One of the most important identifications of slave behavior is the attribute that slaves do not know how to behave when respected. The question: *Barnet alebeh*? (Do you have slave lineage?) refers to "free" people who don't know what to do when respected or considered as one's equal. This emanates from slavery being based on lack of honor and respect for the slave.

In the realms of sexuality — perhaps the most pervasive aspect of the culture of slave/non-slave dialectic — the term *barya* strikes a cord of immense sexual prowess. Like its Middle Eastern counterpart, the non-slave population in Ethiopia projected a formidable sexual appetite upon its slaves, both male and female. Since the *barya* woman was seen as being sexually overwhelming, even some of the *teleq sawach* (big men) could not resist the temptation of their female slaves. Of course, the master of the female slave had every right over her, including the right of free access to her sexual service. If the slave woman had a baby from her master, the identity of the real father would be covered up, and some male slave or non-slave retainer would be designated as a fictitious father. It was an opprobrium for the *teleq saw* (big man) to have sexual relations with his slaves, although it was one of those open secrets. Even the Biblical story of Abraham and Hagar could not wash away the stain of public shame that came with the embrace of a slave woman.

The *emabet* (lady) had the same fantastic image of the sexual prowess of the male slave, as that of the *getoch* (gentleman) had of the female slave. In the *tabot*-Christian morality, "perversion" and "deviance" found their utmost expression in sexual union across the slave/non-slave divide.

In the sexual union between noble and slave, a momentary phase of equality was established. All the altars of order and status crumbled to the ground upon which the two extremes of the social divide embraced. In their "animal" needs, noble and slave became one; in their social positions, they were the extreme ends of the societal divide. Noble-slave sexual relations established sudden and spasmodic moments of "social mobility" up and down, the result of which was absolute levelling of status distinctions. The seemingly universal attribute, at least in the Middle East and the Western world at large, about the sexual prowess of slaves was a popular prejudice in Ethiopia. Deep down the surface contempt for the slave was a jealousy of the freedom of slaves from conventional morality in sexual norms. Haddis Alamayahu's moving description of the prison-like life of Sable Wengel, a character of a noble family, contrasted with the freedom enjoyed by her slaves in his historical-sociological novel, *Feqer Eska Meqaber,* is a classic representation of everyday life in Ethiopia. In sexual matters, things were topsy-turvy: the slave was free; the free was slave to *tabot* Christian morality.[2]

Marriage or non-marital sexual relations between the slave and non-slave population were not uncommon. This led to a mixed population of part "free," part slave descendants. Accordingly, $^1/_2$ slave was called *wullaj,* $^1/_4$th slave *qennaj,* $^1/_8$th slave *fennaj,* $^1/_{64}$th slave *manbete,* and $^1/_{128}$th slave *darababete. Manbete* and *darababete* refer to "houses." The former is an abbreviation of the question: *yaman bet naw?* (whose house is it?). In the case of the latter, *darababete* means "My house is a hut" (Pankhurst 1992, pp. 112-13). In

Christian Amharic Ethiopia, slaves were referred to as *yabet ledjoch* (children of the house). This emanated in part from slavery being household slavery, and in part from slaves reproducing within the master's household itself rather than being bought new.

The slave/non-slave divide took the form of "color" designation. The distinction between *tsalim* (dark, night, black) and *qayh* (red), or *tequr* ("black") and *qay* "red", was the "color" signifier of the non-slave population to set itself apart from that of the slave. The chronicler of Emperor Susneyos referred to the "Shanqella" as *tsalim*, and the *saba* ("free") as *qayh* (Pankhurst in *CEF*, 1976, pp. 41-2). Saba literally meant man or human, implying, as in all forms of slavery, that non-slave is human while the slave is not fully human; the slave is socially dead (Patterson 1982). The distinction between the *saba qayh* (red men) and the *tsalim barya* (dark slave) was also made during the Aksumite period (*Ibid*, p. 2). Color differences and military weakness of the peoples along the Sudanese border made them easy prey for slave hunters. "Shanqella" and *barya* became common terms for slaves (*Ibid*, p. 1).

The non-slave population's depiction of the *barya* was expressed by ridiculing their phenotypical features. In this case, it was not Oromo or Gurage slaves that were the object of scorn, since they "look" the same as the non-slave population, but the peoples along the long Sudanese border — the "Shanqella." (We should not forget that owning slaves was widespread throughout Ethiopia up until the early 1940s. It was not an Amhara-Tigrayan monopoly.) To counter the phenotypical similarities between slaves and non-slaves, most Oromo and Gurage slaves, and some Amharas and Tigrayans, were exported out of Ethiopia, while for internal use most of the slaves were from the Sudanese region whose phenotypical features were distinct from the non-slave population of Northern, Central and Southern Ethiopia. With characteristic nineteenth-century Victorian racism, W. C. Harris described a "Shanqella" slave that he saw at Dabra Berhan in the middle of the nineteenth century as follows:

> The huge black Shankela, with blubber lip and bloodshot eye, is resting for a moment against the broken wall, and stretching a brawny limb which might have supported the bully Hercules himself. Grinning from ear to ear as his burly neighbour sports some savage joke in license unrestrained, he seized with a three-horsepower his bundle of split wood, which two Amhara could with difficulty raise, and poising

> it like a feature upon his wooly head, walks away in all the vigour of a young giant [1844, vol. 2, p. 56].[3]

The contempt of the non-slave population for *barya* phenotype — thick lips, flat nose, very dark skin, kinky hair, etc. — may not be seen different from W. C. Harris's description of the "Shanqella" he saw at Dabra Berhan. But the similarity ends there. To see racism in the contempt for the *barya* phenotype in Ethiopia is to completely misunderstand the social structure of racism altogether. The phenotypical arrogance and aquiline prejudice of most peoples of the Horn of Africa has no *historical structural* resemblance to that of Western racism. A detailed discussion of the issue is beyond our concern here.[4]

In Ethiopia, as elsewhere in other slave relations, slaves did not have full names, for they were deprived of their fathers' names. In Ethiopia, a name is a name only when a father's name is added to it, the addition of the grandfather's name too being common. Hence the expression *yatabatu, yatabatua* (Where is his father?, Where is her father?, respectively), meaning that one is without a father, i.e., a slave. Patterson noted:

> A man's [and woman's] name is, of course, more than simply a way of calling him [her]. It is the verbal signal of his [her] whole identity, his [her] being-in-the-world as a distinct person. It also establishes and advertises his [her] relations with kinsmen [1982, pp. 54-55].

Since slaves did not have a father's name, let alone a grandfather's, their name was not called name. It was called *materia* (appellation). Name versus appellation — that was the nominal side of the substantial divide between *chawa* (free) and *barya* (slave). The former was also known as *yasaw ledj* (child of man), as opposed to the latter, referred to as *yabet ledj* (child of house). *Yasaw ledj* means that one belongs *in* the community, while *yabet ledj* means one belongs *to* the household, i.e., to household slavery. *Yasaw ledj* is *chawa*.[5]

Since slaves were expropriated of their names, their acquisition was accompanied by giving them new names, appellations, to be more precise. The change of name is "almost universally a symbolic act of stripping a person of his former identity . . . . The slave's former name died with his former [pre-slave] self" (*Ibid*, p. 55).

The typical name for a male slave was *Gabre* (derived from the word *gabre* which means to work or to serve), and that of a female slave was *Amate*, the female version of *Gabre*. *Gabra* and *Amata* are common Amhara-Tigrayan adjective prefixes with nouns to qualify. Hence names like Gabra-Egziabher (servant of God) and Amata-Mariam (servant of Mary) are names of non-slave men and women, respectively. They are Christian names of submission to divine authority. (Every Christian had two names — one "secular" name given by his parents, mostly fathers, and another Christian, baptismal name given by the Church at christening of babies. Baptismal names are hyphenated, as in Gabra-Egziabher.)

On the slave side of the social divide, *Gabre* and *Amate* were names of servants of the earthly master, the slave owners. Unlike the non-slave population, slaves had only one "appellation," with no adjective to qualify a noun. It was coupled neither with an earthly fatherly name, nor with a divine one. The former defined their status as slave, the latter their status as "infidel." Their "infidelity" justified their enslavement. So there were two masters — one divine, to be served by the non-slave Christian, and another human, to be served by the slave. Hence there were also two "slaves" — the non-slave "slaves" of God; and slaves of the non-slaves. Since "one can not serve two masters at the same time," different names were applied to the status distinctions.

Slaves were known not through their "names," but rather through the name of their master. "Whose slave are you?" was the conventional way of asking the identity of the slave. As the master was known, so was the slave's identified thereby.

It was common for the average person to own slaves. The number of slaves owned increased with one's status in the social hierarchy, from one or two for the average person up to thousands for the king of kings. Slavery was widespread not only in the Christian Amhara-Tigrayan region, but also in the South. Pankhurst quotes Giaccardi who said that the slave population of Kaffa in 1897 was no less than 80,000. In 1921, Jimma was "a country of slaves" with Abba Jiffar owning thousands (Pankhurst 1968, p. 75; Tekalign Wolde Mariam in Taddese Beyene ed. *PEICES*, vol. 2, 1989, pp. 309-318).

The number of slaves in Ethiopia was quite large. Pankhurst gathered a set of guesses for the 1910s and 1920s:

> In 1914 Merab believed that at least a quarter, perhaps a third of the population were slaves, and that there were some 20,000 in Addis Ababa and 3 or 4 million in the country as a whole. A decade or so later Civinini put the capi-

> tal's slave population at 30,000, while Noel-Buxton later stated that slaves comprised about one-fifth of the whole population of the empire, Emperor Haile Selassie shortly afterwards saying that they numbered about two million [1968, p. 76].

The question of slavery in Ethiopia was a sensitive international issue (Matthew, *The Church Overseas*, 6, 1933). Because of it, Ethiopia was prevented from joining the League of Nations at its founding in 1919. Like the Ottoman Empire in the nineteenth century, Ethiopia was under tremendous pressure from Western powers, especially Britain, to put an end to slavery (Miers in Taddese Beyene ed. *PEICEs*, vol. 2, 1989, pp. 253-266). On March 31, 1924, the then Regent, *Ras* Tafari Makonnan (later Emperor Haile Selassie), issued a decree for the emancipation of slaves. A decade passed between this decree and the actual end of slavery. The call to an end of slavery in the 1920s was "nothing short of a social revolution" (Pankhurst 1968, p. 108). The end of slavery had economic and social consequences for the slave-owning population. It was tantamount to a declaration of war on them. The ending of slavery brought about an economic reorganization of Ethiopia (Edwards, *AEH*, 2, 1982).

Symbolic Slavery of the Notables

In a qualitatively different setting was the association of the word *barya* with self-reference in the power rank of command and obedience. It was common practice for a low-ranking official or an ordinary person to refer to himself as the *barya* of the Emperor. War boasts (*fukara*) repeated words like *yanta barya*, *yanta ashker* (your slave, your servant, respectively), to show one's cliental status to a superior. To sign a letter with the words *baryawe* (your slave), was standard procedure. The person who signed *baryawe* was not a slave at all. He *considered* himself to be one. In this context, the entire population was treated as the "slave" of the *negusa nagast*. This is quite akin to Marx's discussion of "generalized slavery of the Orient," where, according to Hegel's *Philosophy of History*, only one man, the "despot," was free.

A good many of the people who called themselves "slaves" of the Emperor were members of the high-ranking nobility. What we have here is *symbolic slavery* of the nobility, as opposed to the *real* slavery of the real slaves. In the former, we are in the realm of patron-client relationship; in the latter, that of master-slave relations. As Patterson noted of the Islamic Middle East: "It was inevitable that the master-slave and patron-client relationships should influence each other, a fact that largely accounts for the semantic confusion" (1982, p. 309). The "semantic confusion" Patterson refers to above is applicable to Ethiopia where the word *barya* referred to both the patron-client and the master-slave relationships. Reminick wrote thus:

> To be 'slave' to someone doesn't necessarily mean that the person was bought as a slave and kept as one . . . . To be one's slave also shows one's unfailing, unwavering loyalty to one's superior; to be always at the beck and call of his master. This is given in exchange for the supervisor's protection and keeping of his servant, a patron-client relationship. To be 'slave' to Menelik himself was only in value proper for the nobility of high rank. There was too great a social status distance between the peasantry and the emperor to claim direct association [1973, p. 91].

Not only did the non-slave population consider itself to be the "slave" of the king of kings, but the latter thought so.[6] The Emperor of Ethiopia spoke of himself as *We*, to mean the plural in the singular, to show the universality in the singularity, to emphasize his singular ultimate power over his "slave" subjects — "the dotting of the i," as Hegel called it. Symbolic slavery was such that the Emperor could take away official titles he bestowed upon his appointees at any time, for any reason, with no questions asked. After all, "Kings change their minds" (Maitland 1987, p. 298). It was in this sense that the power of the Emperor over anyone under him resembled the power of the master over his slave. Symbolic slavery defined the claimed status distinction between the Emperor and the nobility, and between the nobility and lower-ranking officials.

Slave Trade Out of Ethiopia

Ever since the rise of Islam and before, the region we now know as the Middle East had been an octopus that sucked in countless Ethiopian slaves, mostly female.

It is difficult to calculate the magnitude of the slave trade out of Ethiopia during the nineteenth century. The only attempt made to study quantitatively the scale of the trans-Red Sea Islamic slave trade is in Ralph A. Austen's article, "The Islamic Red Sea Slave Trade: An Effort at Quantification" (in Hess ed. *PFICES*, 1979). In this article, Austen estimated that between 450,000 and 500,000 slaves were exported through the ports of Zeila, Tajura, and Berbera during the nineteenth century (*Ibid*, p. 451). Pankhurst came with an estimated figure of 1,250,000 slaves in the period 1800-1850 (*TAJH*, 5, 1, 1976, pp. 98-99. See also Pankhurst, *JSS*, 9, 1, 1964). The principal routes of the slave trade passed through Massowa, Metemma, Tajura, Zeila, and Berbera (Abir 1970, p. 69).

The Gurage, Oromo, and Sidama constituted the majority of the slaves for export.[7] The slave trade in Ethiopia, both domestic and for export, was run by the *jabartis* (Abir 1970, p. 71; Darkwah 1975, p. 167). Slaves and ivory were the main export items from Ethiopia during the nineteenth century (Darley 1969). In the 1880s, in addition to slaves, the Kaffa region exported coffee, cardamon, civet, and ivory (Huntingford 1955, p. 111).

In the nineteenth century, the most important destination of Ethiopian slaves was the Ottoman Empire (see Inalcik 1985, p. 34). Ottoman slavery then had a triple hierarchy of slaves — "white" slaves, mostly women from the Black sea regions of Georgia and Circassia at the top; "black" slaves (*Zanj*) from Eastern Africa at the bottom; and "brown" slaves (*Habashi*) from Ethiopia at the intermediate rung (Toledano 1982; Baer *JAH*, 8, 3, 1967; Beachey ed., 1976; Elbashir 1983; Fisher and Fisher 1970; Walz 1978; Udovitch ed. 1981).

There were differences among the slave dealers too. In Egypt, dealers in black slaves were called *jallaba*, and dealers in white slaves *yasiriyya*. "While dealers in black slaves were included in a group of 'cursed and impious' guilds of low social status, dealers in white slaves were grouped with the highly respected guilds of the Khan al-Khalili merchants" (Baer, *JAH*, 8, 3, 1967, p. 428). The status of the slave dealers was hence determined by the status of the slaves they dealt with.

The hierarchical arrangement of slaves also had direct relation to their owners. In Egypt, the most prestigious slaves were white slaves owned by the Turkish upper classes. The Egyptian upper and middle classes that came next in the social hierarchy owned Ethiopian slaves. Black slaves were owned and used for household labor by the average Egyptian (*Ibid*, p. 441). This does not mean that the Ottoman Turks did not own *Zanj* or Ethiopian slaves. Actually, the most expensive slaves were black eunuchs who were the caretakers of the imperial harem and the treasury. Owning them was of the highest status.

Ethiopia was one of the sources of eunuchs for the Arab and Ottoman Empires. (Eunuchs were also found at the imperial court in Ethiopia). According to Patterson, "Ethiopia has an unenviable reputation as a major source of eunuchs throughout the world from ancient times" (1982, p. 316).

That Ethiopia was one of the sources for the procurement of eunuchs has left a profound impression in the minds of many an Arab and Ottoman about the *Habashi*. The *Habashi* became identical with slave (*abd*), and the most despised slave at that, the eunuch. And yet, the beauty of Ethiopian women slaves washed away the "dirt" that was the eunuch.

Popular consciousness in Ethiopia pictures the Arab as a sex-crazed being who will do anything to get Ethiopian women. The stereotype is a reflection of the Arab slave trade that sucked out countless women from Ethiopia for centuries.

The slave "trade" was a demographic curse that bled Ethiopia dry. Ethiopian blood runs through the veins of many an Arab, Indian, Iranian, Turk, etc. Ethiopia was the favorite hunting ground of slaves to provide the insatiable need of the Arab and Ottoman worlds for their harems, bureaucracy, army, and menial jobs. And then was Bilal, the first *muzeen* in the Islamic religion, who was born of an Ethiopian slave mother.

Although slavery was widespread in Ethiopia up until the early 1940s, and although the surplus extracted from slaves fattened the bellies of slave owners, it was the *gabbar* that was the main object of exploitation. Hence, when slavery was legally reabolished for the last time in 1942 (it was abolished repeatedly earlier, including by the Italians during the occupation), the social structure of the *geber* system did not collapse.

As to what happened to ex-slaves after the end of slavery, we can hardly say anything substantial. They melted away in the larger society. Carlo Conti Rossini's Ethiopia as "museum of peoples" does not just mean that different ethnic and religious groups live in Ethiopia side by side, like objects arranged in a museum. Ethiopia has been a melting pot *par excellence*. That included slaves and ex-slaves. That is partly why it is difficult to find out what happened to ex-slaves. Research on this issue would be invaluable. One thing we are certain about is that in many cases, household slavery was replaced by household servitude such that ex-household slaves became household servants.[8] This was the case with freed ex-slaves who "preferred" to stay with their ex-masters rather than venture into an unknown world. Freed ex-slaves who left the households of their former masters became "coolies," guards, servants, maids, wood choppers, tree climbers, thieves, soldiers, prostitutes, etc.

Interestingly enough, while slaves and ex-slaves could "integrate" into the larger society with relative ease, this was virtually impossible for the occupational minorities ("castes") up until very recently, in a good many cases to this day. To this theme of the occupational minorities, we now turn.

Occupational Minorities ("Castes")

Occupational minorities, wrongly referred to as castes, were found throughout Ethiopia, cutting across ethnic, class, and religious distinctions. These were segregated groups despised for the types of labor they were engaged in: hunting, tanning, smithing, fishing, pottery-making, and weaving. Reviewing the overall position of craftspeople in Ethiopia, Hallpike wrote:

> . . . the artisans most commonly despised are weavers, smiths, potters, and tanners, and we sometimes hear of hunters, such as the hippopotamus hunters of Lake Tana, and the woodworkers among the Gurage, who are considered inferior. Weavers tend to be the least and tanners the most frequently despised. In many cases such groups are said to have a different, more negroid appearance than their superiors. There are some instances where these groups have a religious basis, as with the Moslems and Falashas in Amhara areas. We frequently find that despised classes are forbidden to own land, or have anything to do with agricultural activities, or with cattle. Commensality and marriage with their superiors seem also to be generally forbidden them [*Africa*, 38, 3, July 1968, p. 258].

The occupational minorities were called by various names like Wayto, Watta, *tebib* (wise), *buda* (one with evil eye), etc., by the Amhara and the Oromo, Manjo by the Kaffans, and Manni by the Konso (Levine 1974, p. 57; Simoons 1960, pp. 23-50; Pankhurst 1968, Chap. VII; Cerulli 1956, pp. 61-62; Hallpike 1972). Among the Konso, there was a distinction between the *hauda* (craftspeople) and *edanda* (cultivators) (Hallpike 1968, p. 258). In some cases like Christian Amhara-Tigrayans, the segregative division of labor was rationalized on religious grounds. The Wayto and the Beta Israel belong to this category.

Among the Sidama people too, there were occupational minorities:

> The Hadichos are a client people of the Yemericho, of a different order than the other tribes. The Hadicho are conceptualized as potters, one of the despised castes in parts of East Africa. Together with the blacksmiths, Tontichos, and the tanners, Hawachos, they are regarded as unclean (*dekerancho*) and may neither marry nor eat together with Yemerichos and Wollabichos, who regard themselves as clean (*kerancho*) [Brogger 1986, p. 34].

William Shack, in his study of the Fuga among the Gurage — whom the latter classify into *fuga* (woodworkers), *nafura* (blacksmiths), and *gezha* (tanners) — observed that weaving and pottery-making, which are despised professions among other groups in Ethiopia, are "'respectable' semi-professions undertaken by some Gurage men and women to supplement their farming income. But smiths, tanners, and woodworkers are members of a low-status occupational caste, regardless of specialization" (*Man*, LXIV, March-April, 1964, p. 50). Shack noted the "essential characteristics" of the Gurage-Fuga relations as being: "endogamy; restrictions on commensality; status hierarchy; notions of pollution concerning food, sex and ritual; association with traditional occupations; ascribed caste status . . . more or less in that order" (*Ibid*). Marriage between Fuga and Gurage is forbidden, the rationale being:

> Because Gurage fear contamination from direct contact with Fuga, they are forbidden to enter Gurage homesteads without permission, which in fact means until the occupants are at a safe distance, after which the homestead must be ritually cleansed. Rank and status among the Gurage are based on ownership of land and the relative size of one's *asat* holding. Contrariwise, Fuga own no land and are prohibited from cultivating *asat (Ensete edulus)* . . . the staple subsistence food crop of the Gurage . . . . Similar restrictions entail crossing an asat field and herding cattle. These prohibitions are ritual safeguards for the Gurage, who believe that Fuga will destroy the fertility of the soil, injure the breeding capabilities of cattle, and change the milk of a cow into blood or urine. Occupations which Fuga perform are to the Gurage despicable (and yet indispensable) and to hunt or eat large game is ignoble. Reinforcing

> these attitudes is the belief that Fuga take the form of hyenas at night and consume all the domestic animals that have died in the village [*Ibid*].

There were occupational minorities among the Muslims too. The Wayto, despite their acceptance of the main tenets of Islam, were segregated by their coreligionists. The Wayto's consumption of "unclean" food, like hippopotamus, was enough to shut them off completely (Trimingham 1965, p. 224.)[9] The Somalis also had their own occupational minorities.[10]

Among the Amhara, craftspeople are occupational minorities. Weavers and smiths are thought of as possessing the "evil eye." Legend has it that these despised groups were the ones that made the cross upon which Jesus was crucified!

Another case of occupational minority is the Beta Israel. The Beta Israel, like other craftspeople, did not have access to land ownership. They were tenants. What is interesting about the Beta Israel is that they were the only group that practiced their own occupational minority-like segregation against all those who were not one of them (Quirin 1977, p. 231; see also *IJAHS*, 12, 2, 1979).[11] Theirs was more of a religious than an occupational segregation.

In pre-Menelikan southwestern kingships, the occupational minorities were attached to the royal court. Haberland wrote:

> In Kafa they guarded the frontiers and their gates. In Wolayta one king even tried to muster a mounted bodyguard, exclusively from members of the special castes [sic]. Everywhere that the ritual of the sacral killing of the king can be found, members of these groups are the executioners [in Hess ed. *PFICES*, 1979, p. 132].

The occupational minorities were social constructs of those who discriminated against them. In the case of the Wayto's hunting of hippopotamus for food, it is quite possible that they might have been hunters of other games, or not hunters at all, before they were pushed out and squeezed by the southward expansion of the Ge'ez civilization from the north. Since the land of the Wayto was occupied by the Christians, the ideology and practice of discriminating against them and the whole nonsense of their being sorcerers, possessors of evil eye, etc., might have been a rationalization for the discriminatory practices.

Interestingly enough, the Gojjames have the reputation of being *buda*, as well as the morate in Shawa, and the people of Aksum in

Tigray. All these people are Christians, not engaged in the profession of the occupational minorities. How they came to be identified as *budas* needs another study.

The Amhara aristocrat and the Konso *gabbar*, the most fundamentalist Christian and his Muslim counterpart, shared, despite their class, ethnic, and religious differences, the same segregationist practice against the occupational minorities. This despite the fact that these minorities speak the same language as the community around them. From the standpoint of division and integration of labor, the occupational minorities were part of the larger society. The entire agricultural life of the discriminators would have come to a virtual halt without their labor. Who but they made the plows, the knives, the clothes? Economically, they were internal to the community; culturally, they were externalized, marginalized, and ostracized.

Despite the segregation of the occupational minorities, it is a mistake to talk of a caste *system* either in Ethiopia or elsewhere in Africa.[12] A caste system exists when social groups are organized as castes, i.e., there is no one-caste system. "One caste cannot exist in an otherwise casteless society, for castes are interdependent social phenomena [in which each group is a caste in its relation to the other which is also a caste]" (Cox 1970, p. 3).

Having discussed slavery and occupational minorities, albeit schematically, let now us turn to the fundamental social structure of Ethiopia in the period of our interest, the *geber* system.

CHAPTER 4

THE *GEBER* SYSTEM

he most distinguishing feature of each social formation, each 'mode of production'. . . is not so much how the bulk of the labour of production is done, as how the dominant propertied classes, controlling the conditions of production, *ensure the extraction of the surplus* which makes their own leisured existence possible.

[de Ste. Croix, *Class Struggles in the Ancient Greek World*, 1981, p. 52; emphases in the original].

The Amharic maxim *gabare yamibalaw enjie yamikaflaw ayatam* (the peasant may not have anything to eat, but he always has something to pay) is a telling commentary on the tradition of tribute extraction from the peasant by the powers that be.

Two fundamental divisions existed within the tribute-appropriating class: the lay, and the ecclesiastical (the *beta mangest* and the *beta kehnat*, respectively). In the lay establishment, tribute appropriation took two historic forms: predatory, and customary. In predatory appropriation, tribute extraction was based on the use of force, the demand of appropriators was chaotic, there was constant recurrence of destruction of productive forces by the appropriators, and appropriator/producer conflict was common. The war-making class of the *geber* system was mobile, fragmented, and unsalaried. Predatory appropriation emanated from the recurrent cycles of war caused by the warrior class. This was discussed in detail in Chapter 2.

Customary appropriation was different. Here there was a customarily-recognized "legitimacy" in the extraction of tribute from the producers. Unlike its predatory counterpart, customary appropriation was relatively peaceful, the extraction of tribute did not entail the direct use of armed force, and there was a semblance of "voluntary transfer of wealth," as opposed to the "compulsory transfer of wealth" of predatory appropriation.

Although predatory appropriation is logically distinct from the customary, both took place within the same social relation, the former in war times, the latter during peaceful periods. Predatory appropriation took place after the end of the rainy season, or before its beginning. The ideal months for war were between January and March, immediately after the harvest time. The rainy season spelled peace. Customary extraction of tribute also took place immediately after the harvest time. The rainy season was one of hunger in the peasant households. During war (and many of the wars in Ethiopian history took place in February), it was a double burden on the *gabbar* who had to pay tribute customarily, while whatever was left was consumed by the warriors predatorially. For the *gabbar*, if rain meant peace, it also meant hunger. The harvest time of plenty of food was also the beginning of wars, plunder, and customary appropriation.

Appropriation by the *beta kehnat* belongs to the customary variety since the Church used no sticks to force its power over the *gabbar*. A mere mention of hell was enough to strike terror in the heart of many a *gabbar*. In times of war, the clergy joined their regional notables, carrying the *tabot* of their parish, as did the ancient Israelites. They were not fighters but prayers invoking God's help to render victory for their respective notables. If victory was achieved, it was thanks to the heavenly figure of the parish, if not, it was due to the sin of the people. The Ethiopian victory at the battle of Adwa was attributed to the presence of St. George in the battlefield on the side of Ethiopians!

Since wars did not take place all the time and warriors live on pillage and plunder alone, what provided warriors with subsistence was a complex series of customary rights of tribute appropriation from the producers granted to them by the Emperor. This was based on an intricate system of rights to land possession which gave warriors, clergy, and peasants equal rights of access to land possession in *rist* (*risti* in Tegregna) arrangements, and tribute extraction by warriors and the Church from peasants in *gult* (*gulti* in Tegregna) arrangements.

People's right to land and to other people's produce had four forms: *rist*, *gult*, pastoralism, and "tribal communalism." These were not only systemic variations, but also geographic and religious. The *rist* relations were located in the Christian highlands. The *gult* relations were concentrated on the highlands of both sides of the Rift valley. The pastoralist relations were found in the lowlands of the Rift valley, and east of the Rift valley. The "tribal-communal" relations were located in the long Sudanese borderline (Cerulli 1956). Of these, the *gult* system was the dominant form of social relations of production.

In religion, the people of the *rist* system belong predominantly to the Ethiopian Orthodox Church. In the *gult* system of the South, they are a mixturc of Muslims and "pagans," with few Christians. Muslims predominate. The pastoralists are mostly Muslim, and the tribal-communal areas "pagan."

The *Rist* and *Gult* Systems

In his work, *Yaityopya Maretna Geber Sem*, translated by Mengesha Gessesse as *Ethiopia's Traditional System of Land Tenure and Taxation*, (*Ethiopia Observer*, 5, 4, 1962), Gebre Wold Ingida Work made a comprehensive study of the *rist* and *gult* systems. Gebre Wold wrote the piece in 1944, while he was the Director General of the Land Revenue Department. In a simple statement he said: "It was the custom that a person had to pay tax for the use of his land or *rist*" (*Ibid*, p. 302).

Rist

The word *rist* is derived from the word *wurs*, which means inheritance. (*Mawras* means to inherit, and *warash* inheritor.) *Rist* is land held and transmitted hereditarily.

Rist is based on "descent corporate estates" and individual "claim to descent" (Hoben 1973, pp. 130-1).[1] It is "a form of freehold, with rights and privileges resembling those of a medieval European entail" (Messing 1985, vol. 1, p. 10).

Rist is both *ancestral descent claim* and *effective possession* of land. The ancestral descent claim is much larger than that of the effective possession. The contradiction between descent claim (that is descent-based) and effective possession (that is individual) is the foundation of the people-land and people-people relations in the *rist* system. This contradiction is manifested in the so-called social psychology of Amhara individualism (see Levine 1967, pp. 75-76).

The contradiction between ancestral descent claim and effective possession of *rist* land led to the formation of a suspicious personality type in which every descent claimant was seen as a potential or actual antagonist. This suspiciousness, which was a reflection of the conflict among many descent claimants for effective possession of the same land, was captured in the well-known saying, *saw maman qabro naw* (You can trust a man only after he is buried dead). The custom of *qemesha* (tasting) in which every host, including a wife in relation to her husband, tasted the food and drink before others start eating and drinking was due to the fear of being poisoned. Intra-kin killings were not abnormal, and the basic source of conflict was the contradiction between descent claim and effective possession of *rist* land. As much as every newborn child was an occasion of merry-making, he/she was also seen as the future claimant of land by everybody, from brothers and sisters to the remotest possible kin. Hence the infamous Amhara lack of trust of others (*Ibid*, p. 93).

The typical morning well-wish in Amhara culture, *bachar yemalseh* (May you come back safe), emanated from a cultural universe in which the world outside the household was seen as one of Hobbesian war of all against all. The Amhara leaving his home in the morning prayed *katabagna adenagn* (Save me from the quarrelsome). This popular Hobbesianism was rooted in the *rist* system, which generated enmity and antagonism. The best testimony to the social psychology of Amhara polity is epitomized in the famous adage: *yaltaratara tamanatara* (One who is not suspicious is uprooted). Everybody is on the lookout for everybody else.

The claim to *rist* possession is based on belonging to a descent line of an original father who happened to be the first to occupy the land. He is known as the *aqni abbat* (original father) or *wanna abbat* (main father). And "The names of first settlers are widely known and generally agreed upon" (Hoben 1973, p. 118).

Rist land was transmitted along both parents' line of descent (cognatic descent.) Hence, every person had two lines of inheritance. When a man got married, he added a third line to his *rist* rights, his wife's *rist* land. Hoben observed:

> A man classifies his *rist* land and his potential *rist* rights

> into three types in accordance with the way he traces the validating pedigree. Thus he refers to all the *rist* land rights he validates with pedigrees traced through his father as 'father *rist*'; he refers to all birth pedigrees traced through his mother as 'mother's *rist*'; and he refers to all the *rist* land and *rist* rights he validates with pedigrees traced through his wife as 'wife's *rist*.' It is important to note that this schema classifies *rist* land in accordance with the way the person in question traces his pedigree and not in accordance with his relationship to the person from whom he acquired the land. Thus, a man classifies a field as "mother's *rist*" even though he received it from his father, provided, of course, that the man traces his validating pedigree to the land through his mother (in other words, provided that the man's father held the land as his "wife's *rist*" [*Ibid*, p. 136].

In *rist* right, the mother was considered as the father's wife. (Of course, she was. The point is that she was more than just that). In *rist* rights, men had advantage over women since women could not trace *rist* claim/possession through their husbands, while men did through their wives. In other words, men had three lines of claims — through their father, through their mother, and through their wives — while women had only two, father's and mother's. However, two critical factors mitigated what would have been an outright patriarchal domination. First, the difference between father's *rist* and mother's *rist*. Hoben wrote:

> The most important difference between "father's *rist*" and mother's *rist* . . . is that the former cannot by custom be claimed from the widowed mother so long as she continues to head her deceased husband's household, while the latter can be claimed from the father once the mother is dead. On the other hand, a man can claim "wife's *rist*" *only after his wife has given him a child* and can keep it only so long as he continues to support that child. In other words, a man does not have any rights to *rist* in virtue of his marriage to his wife but only as trustee or custodian for the children he has with her. For this reason, wife's *rist* is also referred to as "children's *rist*" [*Ibid*; emphasis added].

Wife's *rist* was children's *rist*. Accordingly, then, the husband did not have three lines as we thought earlier but two, just like the wife's, since the third line, that of his wife's, was actually their children's. And yet, the husband had three lines of effective possession of *rist* land.

So, for married men, there were three lines of effective possession of *rist* land; for children of both sexes, two lines of *rist* descent rights; and for married women, two lines of *rist* descent rights. The two lines of *rist* rights of the female child became one of the three lines of effective possession of *rist* land of her future husband. What both sexes enjoyed equally at birth, the female lost to the husband when she got married. Being a wife was hence a loss of her ability for effective possession; not of her right to pass her *rist* to her children. But what if the widowed mother remarried?

> If the widow remarries, her grown sons will almost never permit her to remain in her former husband's [the son's father] homestead; for they say the new husband is trying to steal from them their father's *rist*. Subsequent to her remarriage and consequent removal to her new husband's homestead, the widow cannot retain control over any of her deceased husband's *rist* land which he held as his "father's" or "mother's" *rist*; that is, through descent lines traced through his mother or father. It may be claimed in equal shares by all of the dead man's children. Those fields which are her own, fields which her deceased husband held as "wife's" or "children's" *rist*, cannot be taken from her and are cultivated by her new husband. Upon her death these fields can be claimed equally by all her children [of both sexes] by either husband [*Ibid*, pp. 147-8].

Given the patrilocal removal of women (since it was women that were "given away" as wives), they were at a disadvantage vis-a-vis men. It was this "circulation of women" as wives that was the basic hindrance to the real equality of the sexes in relation to *rist* land rights *and* effective possession. Both sexes had equal *right* to claim *rist*; they did not have equal *access* to its effective possession. Donald Crummey wrote of the Gondarine period that "Men and women *may* have equal rights in land in Gondarine Ethiopia, but they did not exercise these rights equally. Men dominated and controlled land; and when the women had it, men tended to get it" (*IJAHS*, 14, 3, 1981, p. 465). And yet, the *rist* arrangement was such that

> Christian Ethiopians lack the patrilineal, narrow descent groups of western Christianity, and have a set of rules for

> transmitting property which tends towards radical fragmentation [Crummey, *JAH*, 24, 2, 1983, p. 207].

The contradiction between gender equality in *rist* rights and effective possession tilting toward men can be partly explained by the gender division of labor wherein men were identified as the food providers, the tillers of the soil, while women's role was perceived as one of rendering help. This despite the fact that the entire household work, fetching water, gathering wood, raising children, etc., was done by women. Nevertheless, the wife was not a housewife, stuck inside the household.[2] Equal access of both sexes to *rist* land was not sufficient for an equal access to the instruments of power, both in the household and outside. There was more than mere property relations for the "world-historic defeat of the female sex" (Engels, in Marx and Engels, 1968).

Rist was barred from commodity circulation. However, it was not uncommon for people to sell their share of *rist* to another person, in which case it became the private property of the buyer (Pausewang in Hess ed. *PFICES*, 1979, p. 705; Crummey in Hess ed. *PFICES*, 1979). If the buyer of the land was a foreigner, prior permission should be obtained from the government. The authority of the central government in *rist* was that, "Transfer of *rist* land either by sale or inheritance, was not valid without a permit from the Government" (Gebre Wold, *Ethiopia Observer*, 5, 4, 1962, p. 305). Hence, "When a *rist*-holder died the heirs paid one mule to the government for the right to register the land under their own names" (*Ibid*, p. 304).

In regions where land measurement was customary, "When a landowner failed to pay the tax for his land [to the government] before a given date, his *rist* was put up for sale" (*Ibid*, p. 314). For land not yet measured, the claimant of the land requested the Emperor for property right recognition. The Ministries of Interior and Pen registered the land in the person's name in the Bahar Mezgeb. "The land was then divided into diverse categories, as follows: 1) Sisso; 2) Desseta; 3) Guber; 4) Guindebel; 5) Semone; 6) Yemengist Metekeya; 7) Meulmeul" (Mahteme Selassie, *Ethiopian Observer*, 1, 9, 1957, p. 284). If anyone of the *rist* kin members wanted to sell their part of *rist* land, their relatives were given the first option to buy the land (Gebre Wold, *Ethiopia Observer*, 5, 4, 1962, p. 304).

Rist was neither communal nor private landed property. It was not communal property in that it was fragmented into individual possessions by kin members. It was not private property in that *rist* could not be bought and sold so that it stayed in the possession of the same kin group. But with the development of commodity production and the "cash nexus," *rist* land became more prone to alienation to non-kin buyers.

Scholars have vacillated on the status of *rist* between communal and private (Lundstrom 1974). Since *rist* was not to be sold, it was seen as communal lineage property.[3] And since *rist* was possessed individually, it was seen as private holding. *Rist* contained both elements. It was a marvelous compromise between collective kin "ownership" and individual claim and effective possessive right.

To claim *rist*, one need not be married and have their own household. Anyone living anywhere at any time could claim *rist* provided they could prove that they belonged to the descent line of the kin group. The saying *rist bashe amatu labalabatu* (*rist* belongs to the possessor after a thousand years) means that there is no statutory limitation for claiming *rist*. People living in urban areas, far removed from agriculture, had the same right to claim *rist*. The innumerable claimants on the limited *rist* land led to continuous fragmentation of land possession and deterioration of soil fertility worsened by the lack of modern agricultural techniques.

Having discussed *rist*, let us now try to define it: *Rist is the right of Christians of both sexes to claim, possess, inherit, and pass on to their children land on the basis of belonging to the same cognatic-descent kin group.*

Since kin descent was the only way one could claim *rist*, the study and memorization of one's kin descent was very important. One of the first duties of parents, especially fathers, was to teach their children the pedigree of their kin-descent all the way back to the original father, as well as the various locations of their *rist* lands. The kin-descent pedigree was cited in Biblical pattern, along the male line, including those married to and begotten. In the pedigree, women were referred to as mothers, wives, sisters, or daughters.

Gult

Literally, *gult* means something immobile or stationary. And yet, the *gult* under discussion here was anything but immobile. *Gult* was tribute appropriation right granted by the Emperor to the lower echelons of the power hierarchy — "local rulers, members of the royal family, the nobility, or priesthood as well as to religious establishments" (Pankhurst 1966, p. 305). It was the Emperor's prerogative to create and transfer *gult* right at will. Pankhurst wrote:

> [T]he Emperor could create *gult* in any part of the country merely by transferring his taxation rights to a third party; no confiscation was involved, nor was there necessarily any change in the property relations of the area [*Ibid*].

Land grants to religious, military, and administrative institutions was an old tradition that goes back to the conversion of the Aksumite King Ezana to Christianity during the fourth century A.D.[4]

Now, let us define *gult*. *Gult is the right of tribute appropriation from peasants granted by the Emperor to the various ranks of the warrior class, the Church, and others in return for military, administrative, and religious services rendered to the Emperor by the gult grantees.*

Gult was an arrangement whereby the Emperor got less tribute from his subjects in return for service from his clientele. "*Gults were a medieval substitute for salaries and provided the King with a ready means of rewarding his loyal servants*" (Taddesse Tamrat 1972, pp. 102-3; emphasis in the original. See also Merid Wolde Aregay 1971, p. 80). What was supposed to be all his, the entire tribute of the land, was shared out among his *gult* grantees. Ultimate power and authority resided with the Emperor, who could determine the degree of power distance between him and that of his clients. Emperors shuffled and reshuffled their clientele according to their disposition, their imperial prerogative, their power of the *shum-shir* (appoint-remove).

Gult grants were of two kinds: grants to lay men and women, and grants to religious institutions. *Gult* grants to the former lasted for life or less (they could be revoked by the Emperor at any time and be given away to others), while that of the latter were given permanently in the form of *rista-gult*, i.e., *gult* held as *rist* (Taddesse Tamrat 1972, p. 12). Let us discuss this distinction between lay and ecclesiastical *gult* grants in detail.

Lay Gult Grants

Lay *gult* grants were first and foremost grants to warriors. As Huntingford observed, this was due to the fact that "Ethiopia south of Tigre was gradually acquired by occupation and conquest, and it is probable that the land here was regarded from the first as belonging to the king" (1965, p. 13). Not only south of Tigre, but the entire Christian territory of the North was originally occupied through conquest (Taddesse Tamrat, 1972, pp. 98-9).

The *bala-gult*, (the *gult* possessor), was not a landlord in that "*he had originally no rights on the land itself, but only on the peasants living and working on it*" (*Ibid*, p. 101; emphasis in the original). In the domain of Ge'ez civilization of Christian Ethiopia, land remained in the hands of the local people in the form of *rist* holdings.[5]

Built in the *gult* system was an "insecurity of tenure" which was "very convenient for the maintenance of effective control by the royal Court over the activities of the provincial officers" (*Ibid*, pp. 102-03).

Church *Gult* Grants

> Let the King give honor to the order of the clergy . . . . Let him give from his wealth to each of them, according to their rank. He shall exempt them from tribute, presents, and the other things to be given to the rulers. . . . And let the King assign to God a part of the presents and of the spoils of war, as King David and other righteous kings did. Let him not raise his hand against priests or God's saints, so that what befell the evil kings of Israel and others may not befall him [*Fetha Nagast*, pp. 272-73].

Why did Emperors grant *gult* to religious institutions? The answer lies partly in what Georges Duby called "obsession with sin and damnation" (1980, p. 322) that was the primary concern of believers. In *tabot* Christian Ethiopia, where the divine right to interfere in the internal affairs of everyone was never doubted for a moment,[6] the concern about sin and damnation was second nature to all. Famine, pestilence, disease, death, demotion from power, etc., were all seen as being due to a single cause, sin. Obsession with sin was so dominant in Ethiopian *tabot* Christianity, and identified with the lust of the flesh (like sex), that the Amharic word for the male semen and sin itself is the same, *hatiaat*. In this culture of sin paranoia, the help of God was constantly invoked through the mediation of the Church. The Church received *gult* grants from the lay notables in return for prayer for the health, well-being, and redemption of the soul of the *gult* grantor. The Church prayed for the soul of the entire pedigree of the *gult* grantor — those who died, those who were alive, and those yet to be born. If the grantor was the Emperor, the Church prayed for the continued reproduction of his rule through his descendants. Although there was no money-back guarantee in *gult* grants to religious institutions, there was an *anticipated salvation of the soul in afterlife*. After all "What gain is there for a man to have everything but lose his soul?"

There was another dimension of *gult* grants to religious institutions: the exercise of hegemony. In the Gramscian division and integration of labor between repression and hegemony, the former was exercised by the State, the latter by the Church. The Church had been the sole institution of the exercise of hegemony for 16 centuries. Church and State had different foundations of power, different forms of land control, different functions in the social structure. The most important difference was that the State commanded the means of destruction, while the Church controlled the means of salvation. The Church was the carrier of the literate-religious culture; the State was its defender. The Church had veto power of excommunication; the State did not. The Church carried out intellectual and cultural hegemony; the State practiced repression. The Church condemned the sinful and urged them to repent; the State punished wrongdoers and reminded others to learn from their mistakes.[7]

In the division and integration of labor between the State and the Church, it is sometimes difficult to say which one of the two was more powerful. In some cases, the Church was more powerful than the State in that, by using its veto power, the prerogative of excommunication and curse, it could undermine and eventually overthrow an established royal power. The success of the Portuguese Jesuits in making Emperor Susneyos a Catholic neophyte could not last long, for the Ethiopian Orthodox Church cursed those who would follow him. Emperor Tewodros II's fall was due in part to his antagonism with the Church. His rule was based on repression, without the buttress of Church hegemony. And then there was Emperor Yohannes IV, who went to the opposite extreme of Tewodros and became obsessed with religion (Caulk, *JES*, 10, 1; *TAJH*, 1, 2, 1971). Yohannes IV, whose official title was "The Elect of God, Yohannes, King of Seyon, King of Kings of Ethiopia" was "a nobleman by birth, a cleric by education, a zealot by faith, moralist by tendency, a monk by practice, a nationalist by policy, and a soldier and emperor by profession" (Bairu Tafla 1977, p. 15). In an Emperor of these characteristics, the State seemed to have devoured the Church.

In terms of material power and control over land, the State was always dominant over the Church. And yet, Church and State needed each other; and, as in European Christianity, they "enjoyed a mutually self-perpetuating relationship" (Wood 1990, p. 352). Overall, like his Byzantine counterpart, the Ethiopian Emperor was the head of the Church.

Gult grants to ecclesiastical institutions were known as *semon*, and the grantees were called *semongnas* (those with *semon*) (Gebre Wold, *Ethiopia Observer*, 5, 4, 1962, p. 308). Pankhurst noted that the popular notion that land in Ethiopia is divided into three domains — *siso laarash, siso laqadash*, and *siso laangash* (one-third for the tiller, one-third for the prayer, one-third for the Crown [*angash* means coronator] respectively) — such that the Church's share was one-third of the wealth derived from land was historically unfounded (1966, p. 28). *Semon* land was given to the head of church or monastery under the title of *maderia*, "a certain area deducted from the lands appertaining to it. Such land he held as long as he remained in office. If he pressed the founder of the Church for it, he often became the permanent owner of this land" (Mahteme Selassie, *Ethiopia Observer*, 1, 9, 1957, p. 285). This may partly explain why Christian Ethiopia had so many churches.[8] Establishing a new church was hence not just an act of laying the groundwork for eternal salvation of the soul, but also for the needs of the flesh here on earth.

While in some cases *semon* lands were cultivated by priests and deacons, in others the clergy lived off the tribute levied from peasants living in their parish. In the case of monasteries and convents, monks and nuns were engaged in the production of their meager needs, as a good part of the year was spent on fasting.

The extremely slim body and twisted long hair identified the men of monastic asceticism. Theirs was a Christianity of egalitarian poverty, one that marked the monastic order off from the parasitic and pompous lifestyles of priests and *dabtara*. "Rejected are all vain glorification of the self and of all other things of the flesh" (Weber 1978, vol. 2, p. 1200). In monastic asceticism, celibacy was the watchword against the "peculiar irrationality of the sexual act" (Weber 1964, p. 238).[9]

Rist and *Gult*: A Comparison

There are two fundamental distinctions between *rist* and *gult*.

First, *rist* pertains to *right to land possession*, while *gult* refers to *right to other people's produce*. Second, *rist* is hereditarily transmittable, while *gult* is not (except in the case of *resta-gult*). In *rist* we are in the realm of equal rights of access to land possession for all Christians. (Muslims, slaves, and craftsworkers were not allowed to have *rist* rights). *Gult* is the basis of the class distinction between the provider and taker of tribute. The *gult* system is the foundation of the class structure of the *geber* system. Accordingly, despite the multiplicity of regional variations, the *gult* system was essentially the same in both "historic Ethiopia" and the South. *Rist* and *gult* "are not different types of land but distinct and complementary types of land rights. Normally, they extended over the same land" (Hoben 1973, p. 5). As the saying had it: *habtam bagultu, daha baristu* (The rich by his *gult*, the poor by his *rist*).

In "historic Ethiopia" (what I called the Ge'ez civilization), the *gultagna* was both a *gultagna*, separating him from the *gabbar*, and a *ristagna* (one with *rist*), making him one with the *gabbar*. He had two rights — right over land (*rist*), and right over *gabbar* 's produce, (*gult*). Conventional wisdom notwithstanding, the fact that the *gultagna* shared the same *rist* right as the *gabbar* in "historic Ethiopia" does not at all mean that the two were comrades-in-arms.

The ideological bases of legitimacy for the dominance of the *gultagna* were different in "historic Ethiopia" and the South. In the former, the *gultagna* could pass as one among the people, a *ristagna*, just like the *gabbar*. He could hide behind the curtain of religious sameness and genealogical kinship with the *gabbar*. In the South, he was naked and exposed. In "historic Ethiopia," the *gultagna* was opaque; in the South he was transparent. In "historic Ethiopia," the *gultagna's* power was mediate; in the South it was immediate.

The degree of exploitation, and the complicated layers of demands from the *gabbar*s, were the thinnest in nomadic areas, which were almost exclusively Muslim. The clergy were concentrated in "historic Ethiopia." They consumed a good part of the peasant's produce in the form of consumption of food and drinks, other than the fact that they received tribute of all sorts in the name of church property. The degree of exploitation of the *gabbar* was higher in regions where Church and State existed in symbiosis than those where they did not.

Taxation and Tribute

There were so many variations in the forms of titles and land rights under the *geber* system that it is demanding to present a systematic and coherent account of them.[10] Hence we focus on the major aspects that can be taken as frameworks within which the minute details can be subsumed as mere variations on substantially similar themes.

Terms like tax, tribute, and tenant are very much confused in usage, especially in the works of Mahtame Sellassie, Gebre Wold, and Richard Pankhurst (Mahteme Selassie, *Ethiopia Observer*, 1, 9, 1957; Gebre Wold, *Ethiopia Observer*, 5, 4, 1962; Pankhurst, *JES*, 5, 2, 1967; 6, 1 & 2, 1968).

Taxation

The structure of taxation was based on an intricate hierarchy that reached from the imperial court (*gebbi*) down to the *chiqa shum* (village official). The three most important local tax officials were the *mislene, malkagna*, and *chiqa shum*, in descending order of rank. The *malkagna*, as it was called in Amhara and Tigrayan regions, was known under a variety of names in the South.[11] So was the *chiqa shum*[12]

The Mislene

Mislene means "like myself." The *mislene's* task was to "supervise the collection of taxes and to punish law-breakers" (Gebre Wold, *Ethiopia Observer*, 5, 4, 1962, p. 313). He had an assistant known as *dug*. "Because a *Mislene* appointed him . . . [the *dug's*] office was not officially recognized by the government. He was given neither salary nor land from the *Mislene*" (*Ibid*). The *mislene* was appointed either directly by the emperor, or by provincial governors.

The Malkagna

Under the *mislene* was the *malkagna*. There were two kinds of *malkagna:*

> [T]he first was either a soldier serving in the national forces or a soldier of a shalekh [head of thousand]; the second was a head of many landowners whose kinsmen called him melkegna. A melkegna enforced orders from the Mislene and supervised tax collection [*Ibid*, p. 319].

The role of the *malkagna* was to see to it that peasants paid their land tax in time. He also acted as a disciplinary officer.

The *Chiqa Shum*

The *chiqa shum* was appointed from among the *gabbars* for one year. Like the *malkagna*, the *chiqa shum's* main task was the "collection of taxes and the enforcing of orders from superior officials"

(*Ibid*, p. 313). The *chiqa shum* also deliberated on judicial matters arising from local disputes. For his service, he took minor receipts for himself.

Above the *mislene* were district and provincial governors through whom the taxes collected at the local level passed to the central administration at Addis Ababa. Almost all of the officials above the *mislene* were appointed by the emperor. Taxes were collected after the end of the harvest season, between *Tahsas* 1 (December 8) and *Megabit* 30 (April 6). Taxes were paid either in cash, kind, or both.

Taxes in Kind

There were seven kinds of taxes in kind: grain tax, crafts tax, livestock tax, spices tax, mining product tax, wood tax, honey tax, and ivory tax.

Grain Tax

Asrat (tithe): The payment of tithe to the central administration on a national scale started in 1901 by order of Emperor Menelik II. The tithe was paid both by warriors and peasants and was then collected and stored in the imperial granary.[13]

Crafts Tax

Payment of tax in craftsworks was derived from *milmil maret*. (*Milmil* means pruning, and *maret* means land.) Under this category was included a tax called *shamma geber* (toga tax), paid in cotton clothes. Ten different kinds of cotton clothes were made by weavers and presented as tax (Gebre Wold, *Ethiopia Observer*, 5, 4, 1962, p. 309). Other than cotton clothes, clothes made of sheep wool (*barnos* or *zetat*), were also offered as tax. There were different qualities of woolen clothes for different ranks of people (*Ibid*, pp. 309-10).

Taxes paid in craftsworks included *koricha geber* (saddles), *qurbat geber* (hides), *mitad geber* (*mitad* is large clay used to bake *enjara*), *tagara geber* (long, cylindrical iron used for making sickles, hoes, axes, ploughs), *kasal geber* (charcoal), *qalam geber* (ink used for writing secular and spiritual books for the royal palace), *doma matrabia geber* (hoe and axe), *machid geber* (sickle), *leguam geber* (bits used to fit into the mouths of horses and mules), *erkab geber* (stirrup), *marasha geber* (plough-share), *tor geber* (spears), and *barud geber* (gunpowder) (*Ibid*, p. 310).

All these taxes were paid by weavers, blacksmiths, potters, and tanners. (On taxes levied on Muslims, Waytos, and Beta Israel, see Pankhurst 1968, p. 515).

Each tax form had the name of the tax and the word *"geber"* (tax) attached to it, like *korcicha geber*, i.e., tax paid in saddles. In the above description of taxes, the word "tax" is avoided in the English brackets. The tax form was also identified together with the land (*meret*), wherein each tax was allocated specific land for its production.

Livestock Tax

Like the grain tithe, there was also a tithe on cattle. Chicken, pheasant, and fish were paid as tax for the use of the imperial kitchen. The fish was used in the long Lent season and other fasting periods, including Wednesdays and Fridays. Taxes were also levied on camels. "In the semi-desert zones where the inhabitants live by stock-raising, the land belonged to the state. The nomadic herdsmen deduced a tenth of their stock for the Government" (Mahteme Sellassie, *Ethiopia Observer*, 1, 9, 1957, p. 293).

A tax called "slaughter tax" (although not as common as it used to be in previous times when peasants did not have the right to slaughter their cattle without the consent of and payment of tribute to the notable) was also practiced in some parts of the country. In Borena, in the 1930s, a tax of one Ethiopian dollar for every cow or ox slaughtered was collected (Pankhurst, *JES*, 5, 2, 1967, p. 49).

Spice Tax

Taxes in pepper, ginger, cloves, and many other kinds of spices were paid to the central administration for use in the imperial kitchen.

Mining-Products Tax

Under this category were found mostly salt and gold. Salt was available from Tigray, and gold from the western and southwestern parts of the country. *Amole chaw* (salt bar) was used as a currency in former times. Salt was also used for cooking, and, mixed with fodder, for cattle, horses, and mules (Gebre Wold, *Ethiopia Observer*, 5, 4, 1962, p. 310).

Wood-Products Tax

Taxes were paid in *indod* (a plant used as soap) and *zabia* (wooden handles). Koso tree was paid as tax which was used as a cure for tapeworm that comes from eating raw meat. An incense called *bergud* was paid as tax "so as to make the smell of food in the dining rooms of the royal palace disappear" (*Ibid*, p. 311). *Kasma* (a wooden peg used to erect government tents), and *chibo* (torch) were also paid as tax. The *chibo* was used for lighting roads at night, and also for lighting torches during *Maskal* (Founding of the True Cross) night. It was the Ethiopian equivalent of fireworks. Lastly, firewood was paid as tax for use in the imperial kitchen (*Ibid*, pp. 311, 305).

Honey Tax

Depending upon regional and local variations, tax paid in honey was quite widespread. The annual tax in honey was about four pounds. The honey collected thus was used for making *tej* (mead).[14] If the people of a region did not produce honey, they had to pay its equivalent in kind or cash (*Ibid*, p. 307).

Ivory Tax

Hunters of elephants were subjected to ivory tax. In the late nineteenth century, it was obligatory for elephant hunters, be they foreigners or subjects, to give Menelik "the first tusk to touch the ground when the elephant was killed" (Pankhurst, *JES*, 5, 2, 1967, p. 51). The law of the land was that the first tusk to touch the ground belonged to the Emperor. In the early twentieth century, a considerable monetary income to the imperial court was obtained from the sale of ivory. In 1904, Emperor Menelik had an income of 201,280 Maria Theresa Thalers from tax on ivory (*Ibid*, p. 52).

Monetary Tax

Monetary tax was paid in Maria Theresa Thalers (Pankhurst, *NEAS* [formerly *Ethiopianist Notes],* 1, 3, 1979-80). The amount of tax paid in money form varied from one region to another. There were four regional classifications for tax collection.

> (1) Regions where the land had been measured
> (2) Regions where the taxes were calculated according to the number of houses or of families
> (3) Regions paying a fixed global tax
> (4) Regions of individual property derived from exceedingly ancient traditions [Mahteme Selassie, *Ethiopia Observer,* 1, 9, 1957, p. 283]

In the first category, gasha (shield) was the unit of measurement. One gasha equals 40 hectares. Qalad (cord) was used for the measurement. In the second, taxes

> were calculated according to the value of the properties, the fertility of the soil, the number of animals possessed by the farmers [i.e., peasants, nomads, and pastoralists] and other indications of prosperity, the number of habitations and families [*Ibid*, p. 287].

The third category was the simplest of all. A general, fixed tax was collected annually from Jimma, Wallaga-Laqamte, Wallaga-Qelem, Beni-Shangul, Aussa, and Guba. These regions submitted to Menelik without a fight. Hence the traditional ruling houses were left somewhat autonomous with their power and wealth, in return for which they paid fixed annual tribute to the central administration (*Ibid*, p. 288). The fourth category was predominant in the *rist* regions.

Lastly, the role of the *naggadras* (head of merchant, derived from the words *naggade*, merchant, and *ras* head). The *naggadras* was the representative of the imperial court. It was his responsibilty to collect taxes at various *kellas* (toll booths) and market places. He also had judicial authority over problems arising from monetary issues, and was himself engaged in commercial ventures (Garretson, IJAHS, 12, 3, 1979, p. 416).

Tribute Payments

> "Man is free, land is tributary." (An old Ethiopian maxim.)

> "For the spiritual and corporal benefits which we derive from the ruler, let us give him tribute and presents in payment for them" (*Fetha Nagast*, p. 272).

Tribute payments took two forms: Labor services, and tribute payments in cash and/or kind.

Labor Services

There were three kinds of labor services:

Hudad. Hudad was land cooperatively cultivated by *gabbars* for the *gultagna*. If *gabbars* did not want to perform labor service on *hudad* lands, they "could pay two [Maria Theresa] thalers if they had a pair of oxen, one thaler if they had but one ox, and half a thaler if they worked their own soil without animals" (Mahteme Selassie, *Ethiopia Observer*, 1, 9, 1957, p. 289).

Yagulbat Eda (Labor Dues). Various forms of labor dues were imposed upon the *gabbars*. They included:

> the construction of a house [for the local official and/or Church], the making of hedges, the mowing of hay, ordered by the Shalaka (military officer) to be executed by a poor peasant either because he was unable to pay his dues to the Government, or to punish him for some other reason [*Ibid*]

Carrying, Grinding, and Repairing. The *gabbar* carried 15 kilos of grain flour tithe to government granaries and firewood to Addis Ababa or the nearest town three to four times a year. He took care of the transport of a mule load of honey, flour, and other similar food items in war times, and looked after government mules during peacetime. He guarded prisoners and escorted them to court. "If the prisoner escaped, the gebbar was fined and had to pay in cash" (Gebre Wold, *Ethiopia Observer*, 5, 4, 1962, p. 306). He built or repaired granaries, houses, and fences for the *malkagna* and other government officials (*Ibid*, pp. 306-7).

Tributes in Cash and/or Kind

Besides labor services, other forms of tribute were paid by *gabbars* to government officials. These included three kinds of tribute payments that were abolished by *Ras* Tafari (later Emperor Haile Selassie) when he became Regent and heir to the throne, but continued nevertheless. They were known as *metin*, called *ilf* when carried by *gabbars*, mashomia (for appointment), and a third one with no specific name.[15]

Other than these, tributes included offering a small jar of *talla* (local beer) or *tej* to the local governor when the *gabbar* had feasts like weddings, baptisms of babies, or other similar occasions. An offer of three kilos of flour yearly, known as *tsom qolo* (roasted grain for fasting periods), was also mandatory upon the *gabbars*. All the above tributes in labor and kind were required in *rist* and *qalad* regions (*Ibid*, p. 307).

Spread throughout the country was an annual payment of about a kilo-and-a-half of honey per beehive to the local or regional notables. There was also payment for *afarsata*, a legal system wherein people of an area where criminal acts allegedly took place paid officials two thalers for investigating the crime (*Ibid*). The entire village was held hostage until the criminal was found.

Gabbars living on Church *gult* paid tribute to the "Church," i.e., to the clergy.[16]

Tributary Relations of the Notables

The relationship among the various ranks of the notables was also tributary. From the lowest rank to the *negusa nagast*, the giving and receiving of tribute was the cement that forged the unity of the various fragments of the tribute-appropriating class. Any breach of payment of tribute on the part of a lower-ranking notable to a higher one could easily lead to his removal from power and expropriation of his title and property. Quite commonly, the refusal to pay tribute was tantamount to rebellion; indeed, it was a declaration of rebellion.[17]

While the relations of hierarchy from the bottom up were cemented by the payment of tribute, the relations from the top down were based on the provision of gifts. The king of kings offered periodic gifts, including members of his own extended family given away as "gifts." The most common "gift" "distributed" and "redistributed" by the Emperor was women in the form of marriage. By "offering" women as wives (the so-called exchange of women in Levi-Straussian jargon), the king of kings and his subordinate notables forged alliances among them (Bairu Tafla, *JES,* 10, 1, 1972, p. 21).

Tributes paid by lower-ranking notables to the imperial court were derived from tribute payments to these notables by peasants, pastoralists, and nomads under their respective domain of rule. In such a way, the tributary relationship formed a chain of command and obedience that tied the various ranks of the *beta mangest-beta kehnat* power bloc, on the one hand, and the producers and the *beta mangest-beta kehnat* power bloc, on the other.

Banquet as Redistribution

Redistribution from the center is to tributary systems what market principle is to capitalism and what reciprocity is to gift economies.[18]

Under the *geber* system, redistribution took three forms: redistribution of consumables (food and drinks), redistribution of possessions (*gults,* titles, slaves, etc.), and redistribution of women as "political wives." In the last case, women were used as pawns in the power plays of the notables, forced to marry and divorce, even after having children from a previous marriage. They were distributed and redistributed among notable men as if they were *gult*. There was some sort of gender gultism at work.

The custom of the state-sponsored banquet falls into the category of redistribution of consumables. It is the least complicated arrangement of the social relations of the *geber* system. From the imperial court of the *negusa Nagast* down to the *chiqa shum*, banquet was the means by which members of the tribute-appropriating class displayed their prodigious wealth in the form of lavish generosity. The physical fights among the common people in order to sit in one of the banquets of Menelik's *adarash* (banquet hall) was depicted well in Haddis Alemayehu's novel, *Feqer Eska Maqaber*. The quality of food and drinks served for the commoners at Menelik's court was not that much better than what they could afford at their homes. It was not a question of eating better food, but of sitting in the same banquet hall with the emperor.

When one of the "big men" or women died, the commoners mourned by invoking the legendary generosity of the deceased. Funeral cries like, *yachomaye geta* (My lord of choma, fatty meat, preferred in Ethiopia), *yateje geta* (My lord of mead), *abba mastat* (Mr. giver), *abba ayalqebat* (Mr. inexhaustible giver), etc., were typical. In the banquet culture of *geber*-system Ethiopia, as in other similar aristocratic polities, notables "competed" to out-generous each other's generosity (Kautsky 1982, p. 194). For Veblen, "Conspicuous consumption of valuable goods is a means of reputability to the gentlemen of leisure" (1945, p. 64); while for Max Weber, "'Luxury'. . . of consumption is for the dominant feudal strata nothing superfluous: it is a means of social self-assertion" (1978, vol. 2, p. 1106).[19]

The lack of "rational" control of consumption was not only a "means of social self-assertion," but also of recruiting clients among the people. Who would fight for a notable that gave no banquet, or one whose banquet was unimpressive. The better the banquet one offered, the more popular he became, the more the number of followers he had. Thus banquets and other forms of redistributive generosity were "rational" in their own social-relational context.

Now let us turn to the details of Emperor Menelik's banquet at Addis Ababa. Our discussion is drawn from Harold Marcus' excellent study of the banquet offered at Emperor Menelik's court, based on interviews he conducted with many of those who were directly engaged in various capacities in the banquet process (*Rural Africana*, Spring, 1970).

A special category of state land was assigned for the provision of the requirements for the imperial kitchen. This land was called *gan-gabb* or *mad-bet* (the latter means kitchen). A ministerial-level office was established for it, the Ministry of the Palace, headed by the Minister of the Palace. It looked after the timely and adequate provision of goods to the imperial court from the various regions of the empire. The *gan-gabb* also included lands where cattle of exceptionally good quality were raised for the exclusive use the imperial kitchen.

Once the raw materials reached the *mad-bet*, the preparation of food and drinks started with a highly sophisticated division of labor.

The imperial kitchen contained four departments: the *sega bet*, (meat house), the *enjara bet* (*enjera* house), the *wot bet* (stew house), and the *tej bet* (mead house).

The meat house had a "maximum of 400 workers" divided into "those who obtained and brought various animals to slaughter, called *weregenuotch* (cattle keepers and drivers), and those who slaughtered and cut up the animals, known as *sigabaitoch* (workers of the meat house)" (*Ibid*, p. 60).

The *enjara* house had 200 bakers, out of whom 10 prepared the best quality *enjara* for Menelik and the high nobility (*Ibid*). The ten bakers worked in the *nech enjara bet* (white *enjara* house). They "had great prestige among women workers, who fought to obtain a coveted job there" (*Ibid*).

The best quality *teff*, known as *magna teff*, was grown, among other places, in Addah and Betcho, in the vicinity of Addis Ababa.

In the *wot bet*, "Of the 30 to 40 working there, only five actually cooked for the more important *makwanent* and Menelik" (*Ibid*). Different kinds of stew were made in the *wot bet*: beef, lamb, chicken, squash, stew with pepper (*barbare*,)[20] or without (*alicha*), *ketfo* (ground beef, raw or cooked), *aiyib* (curd cheese), *brundo* (raw, unground meat), etc. During fasting, different kinds of fasting stew, vegetables, and fish were prepared.

In the *tej bet*, about 30 women worked, "producing two kinds of *tej*: one for the commoners . . . and one fit for the emperor, who never drank it" (*Ibid*). The raw materials for cooking and baking were put in the storage house of the imperial palace, with its own division of labor and respective functionaries (*Ibid*, pp. 60-1).

Now, all the necessary requirements were ready for the banquet to begin. "On a regular basis, the palace fed two to three thousand people daily" (*Ibid*, p. 61). The banquet started at 9:00 A.M. daily.

> The first group to be fed were the palace guards, who, when finished, retired outside to control the waiting crowds and to prepare for Menilek's ceremonial entrance. The next con-

> tingent was the clergy of Addis Ababa, followed by provincial soldiers, merchants, citizens of Addis Ababa, and both male and female palace servants. Menilek was present throughout, and *mekwanint* came and went, each sitting in his own place [*Ibid*].

There were two kinds of food served, one for the nobility, another for the common people. "The *mekwannint* [nobility] ate quietly and usually remained sober, as on these occasions they were on public display" (*Ibid*). Champagne and cognac were provided first, followed by *tej*, "which few ever finished since they preferred champagne and cognac" (*Ibid*). The nobility's preference for champagne and cognac to *tej* shows that they had begun to develop Western consumption tastes. The food and drink served for the commoners, including rank-and-file warriors, was of lower quality. "Whatever food was left after between ten and fifteen thousand people had eaten that day was given to palace workers" (*Ibid*).

All this food and drink for free! Alas, there may be "no free lunch" in America, but there certainly was in *geber*-system Ethiopia.

There was a strict protocol observed in the relations between the nobility and Emperor Menelik during the banquet.

> On arrival in the banquet hall . . . nobles announced their presence to the royal master of ceremonies (*elfin askelkai*), who then presented them to the emperor. Each noble made a very low bow, and a short conversation through the *askelkai* usually ensued. Menilek [as other emperors before and after him] generally talked directly only to his chief advisers and officials; he almost never conversed with an ordinary participant in the . . . [banquet] [*Ibid*, pp. 61-2].

Menelik conversed with the nobility through the master of ceremonies, as if the master of ceremonies was an interpreter of a different language! Indeed, the master of ceremonies was a translator of the language of the Emperor, *the language of power*. As in other patrimonial rules, the very essence of imperial power in Ethiopia was a mediated hierarchy among the different layers of rank, as best exemplified here. For the Emperor to talk directly to a member of the nobility would have been a violation of the imperial law of mediation, a "law" that stipulates that there should be a certain distance, a certain human buffer zone, between the person of the Emperor and his noble entourage. Haile Sellassie perfected this into an art unparalleled in Ethiopian history. This human buffer zone was a means of keeping the nobility in perpetual anxiety about the Emperor's intent. If the Emperor talked directly to a member of the nobility, it was a signal of his good will.

Everybody wished to attend the imperial banquet.

> [P]eople pushed and shoved to enter the . . . [banquet hall], and there were always more people waiting to be fed than could easily be handled. Once inside, however, and in the presence of the emperor, feasters were subdued and polite. Before each took his seat, he bowed to Menilek, who sat in the center of the room at the front on a dais, surrounded by his *mekwannint* [*Ibid*, p. 62].

Concluding his excellent piece on Menelik's banquet, Harold Marcus wrote: "Informants talk about the grandeur of these occasions and of the wealth that Menilek must have had in order to feed so many people. And they complain that the good old days seem to be gone forever" (*Ibid*). Braudel remarked elsewhere that the smell of cooking tells a lot about a civilization. Indeed. The smell coming out of Menelik's banquet hall was the smell of the Ge'ez civilization.

Redistribution was the "socialism of consumption" of the *geber* system, wherein people thought they were getting free food and drinks from a generous *teleq saw* (big man). The *gabbar* who sat in the banquet hall and was offered *tej* hardly thought that the *tej* was the very honey he had offered as tribute, mixed with water. The *gabbar* who devoured raw meat in the banquet hall hardly thought that it was the same cattle he had rendered as tribute that was now being offered to him in the name of generosity. Nevertheless, *gabbars* were hardly visible in the banquet halls of either the imperial palace or that of regional notables. That is why banquet was not tribute extraction from *gabbars* given back to them. It was not unpaid labor paid overdue. Banquets were mostly confined within the dominant class. The mass of producers were left out. The redistributive system, as expressed in banquets, was a mechanism of creating hegemony across the various ranks of the ruling class, and also over the producing classes, although the latter were hardly represented in the redistributive-banquet culture. Banquet was a means of elaborating hegemony throughout the polity.

Banquets were held not only in the imperial court at Addis Ababa but also in the various regions of the country. Although not as sophisticated and glamorous as in the imperial court, the regional nobility had their prodigious banquets offered. In the following accounts, we witness the banquet of Ras Hailu Takla Haimanot of Gojjam.[21]

The sitting protocol and the quality of food and drinks served at the banquet hall varied according to the rank of the host. The notable host welcomed the notable guests, both lay and ecclesiastical, first. Once seated according to their rank — the lay and ecclesiastics of parallel ranks facing each other — the music was played by the *azmari* (minstrels), various *qene* (poetry), mostly *mawades qene* (praise poetry), were given by the *dabtara*, the *denk* (dwarf) engaged in their capacity as entertainers (a tradition that goes back to pharaonic Egypt), the *agafari* (protocol man) selected the wheat from the chaff, those that were to be allowed inside and those that were to be allowed to sit outside, while the *asalafis* (attendants) ran hither and yon to place the food in the right places, fill empty cups, give more to those they liked, and ignore those they did not.

Raw meat and *tej* of different qualities were served at the banquets. The best food and drink was offered to the notables. The clergy belonged to this group. Then came the intermediate level food and drink. Last were the nonproducing poor. They received *talla* (local beer), instead of *tej,* and the leftover food. If *talla* was the only drink served at the banquet, a distinction was made in the quality of the *talla* — the best for the notables, the next best for the commoners, and the leftover for the nonproducing poor. The nonproducing poor were not bound by the etiquette of eating moderately, which they shared with the clergy. In some cases, raw meat and *tej* of the same quality were served for the entire audience in the banquet hall, and the leftover was given to the nonproducing poor. This also happened among the very rich. Besides raw meat, cooked food was also served. As in the rest of Ethiopia, the favorite choice was raw meat. Interestingly enough, modern medicine reinforced this culture of eating raw meat. Ethiopians devour raw meat with merciless appetite, and leave the tapeworm to be taken care of by the *faranj*. The cheapness of the price for the cure of tapeworm added more confidence in eating raw meat, and put more money into the pocket of the pharmacist. The pharmacist and the butcher formed a community of interest. Alas, modern medicine produces cure for this pre-fire-discovery culture of eating raw meat.[22] Or, maybe, it is not that barbaric, after all. What is *sushi* if not raw meat, and yet the favorite of sophisticated cosmopolitans.

Outside the banquet hall were seated lepers, beggars, people with all kinds of diseases — the social refuse of the *geber* system, categorized as *dewyan, nadayan*, and *dekuman* (the miserable, the incapacitated, and the weak, respectively). We called them earlier the "nonproducing poor". W. C. Harris saw them at a religious festival in the early 1840s (their condition hadn't changed a century later), and wrote:

> In the adjacent enclosure a crowd of horrible and revolting objects formed the most miserable of spectacles. The palsied, the leprous, the scrofulous, and those in the most inveterate stages of dropsy and elephantiasis, were mingled with mutilated wretches who had been bereft of hands, feet, eyes, and tongue, by the sanguinary tyrants of Northern Abyssinia, and who bore with them the severed portions, in order that their bodies might be perfect at the Day of Resurrection. The old, the halt and the lame, the deaf, the noseless, and the dumb, the living dead in every shape and form, were still streaming through the narrow door; limbless trunks were borne onwards upon the spectres of asses and horses, and the blind, in long Indian file, rolling their ghastly eyeballs, and touching each the shoulder of his sightless neighbour, groped their way towards the hum of voices, to add new horrors to the appalling picture [1844, vol. 2, pp. 246-47; see also Iliffe 1989, Chap. 2].

"Horrible and revolting," perhaps. "Objects," of course not. These were the beggars of the *geber* system, victims partly of diseases, partly of human cruelty. The most talked about issue among them was where and when food was available, who was giving the feast, wedding, baptismal ceremonies, etc. As beggars, they were not allowed to sit inside the banquet hall while the banquet was in progress. They had to wait outside to be offered the leftover of the food and drink (*terefrafi*). Infighting among these poor souls was part of the scene.

In a separate hall were the socially despised and segregated, but who did not form part of the nonproducing poor: Muslims and outcasts. If meat was served, there were two different "kinds" of meat —*yaislam sega* ("Muslim meat") and *yaamara sega* ("Amara meat," popular term for "Christian meat").

The religious discrimination of food seemed less appealing to the nonproducing poor. They were ready to eat any food. Of course, there were some exceptions, those die-hard "fundamentalists" who preferred death as Christian to life as *erkus* (defiled), for it was considered religious corruption of the worst kind for a Christian to eat

"Muslim Meat."

The banquet order was a microcosm of the social relations of production, appropriation, and distribution of power in the geber system. It was the concentrated expression of the tributary-redistributive arrangement.

Deges (Feast)

Other than banquets which the clergy always attended, there were all kinds of feasts (*degeses*). (Yes, banquet is feast; but not every feast is banquet.) Each day in Ethiopian Christianity is assigned to a heavenly figure. There are supposed to be religious feasts every day. In practice, most of them take place immediately after the harvest season. This season is the heaven of the clergy. Moreover, every time a child is baptized, parents prepare feasts and invite the clergy who took part in the baptismal ceremony. To add insult to injury, not only the living but also the dead pay tribute to the clergy in the form of feasts. As the saying has it, the living pay tribute to the king, the dead pay tribute to the clergy. The feasts are the toll paid by the living relatives so that their dead relatives enter heaven. The will of people on their deathbed included the obligation on their relatives to prepare the best possible feast in their name after their death. What they could not achieve materially in life, they mandated their relatives to do for them after their death. One of the worst insults in Christian Ethiopia is *yaabatun tazkar yalawata* (One who did not prepare feasts in remembrance of his deceased father). Mesfin Wolde Mariam observed, "In Ethiopia, the dead are a tremendous economic burden on the living, for they exact their own heavy taxes in the form of expensive services of remembrance" (1984, p. 17).

There are many feasts for the remembrance of the dead (called *tazkar*) taking place as follows: *sabat* (seven), one week after the death of the deceased; *salasa* (thirty), thirty days after; *arba* (forty) forty days after; *manfaq* (six months) six months after; and *amatat* (years), annually. Of all these, the most important is the *arba*. With the high death rate in Ethiopia, the clergy usually need not worry for their daily bread. And when there are not "enough" deaths, the clergy are compensated by more births. Either way, "nature" is with them. Theirs is a profession with perpetual job security.

Remembrance of dead ancestors is common in African cultures. In *tazkar*, we see the profoundly African foundations of Ethiopian *tabot* Christianity which makes it quite different from the Western missionary Christianity that spread in Africa in the last one hundred years.

In this banquet-and-*deges* culture, the clergy inevitably acquired a "bad name." They were seen as voracious, greedy, and insatiable. The popular expression *yaqes hod* (priest's stomach) relates to the public view of the overindulgence of the clergy in excessive eating and drinking. They consumed a lion's share of banquets and feasts relative to their number. They also made pompous praise poems (*mawades qene*) to those who filled their stomach, and denounced those whose provisions were inadequate by extemporizing *westa waira*, a form of poetry that sounds like praise but is insult.

The non-ordained clergy (the *dabtara*) often engaged in all sorts of astrological and medicinal practices. They acted as *kokab qotari* (star counter, astrologer), *mashaf galach* (book opener, book revealer), and *tanqway* (harm doer). Prior to marriage, couples are advised to consult the *kokab qotari* and the *mashaf galach*, the archaic counterparts of the modern psychiatrist, to see if their marriage was going to work or not. If there was *yakokab magtam* (matching of stars) between the couple, their marriage was declared to be like Abraham and Sarah, long and happy.

The *dabtara* were also engaged in "rain making." When there was either no rain or too much rain, the *dabtara* were held partly accountable for the events (which were believed to be partly due to the sins committed by the people). Indeed, the *dabtara* exacted tribute from the peasants by threatening to stop the rain right before the rainy season, or bringing about heavy rain right on the eve of harvest time. Either way, they used their alleged power of rain making as a threat to get what they wanted. In their capacity as rain makers, they were competing with God, showing that it was not the sin of the people that could bring drought or flooding but the will of the *dabtara*. If a *dabtara* had an enemy, he could wipe out his entire crop by a deluge of rain with such precision that makes laser-precision technology a child's paly that not a single drop of rain would fall on the adjacent fields that belonged to those other than his enemies! People prayed for rain in Church, and offered tribute to the *dabtara* to bring the rain or to put an end to it. Peasants were worshipping two gods, one transcendental, one human, to both of whom they offered tribute. So, if a person could not make it as a priest, he could try as a *dabtara*. Both the priest and the *dabtara* are trained in Church schools. The *dabtara* have more learning than the priests.

In the belief of the *dabtara's* power of "rain making", we are again in the midst of African cultural universe, where "rain making" is one of the highest manifestations of magical power. Here also we discern how profoundly African Ethiopian Christianity is.

The *tanqway* was different. He/she was consulted mostly for seeking vengeance on someone who had done wrong, to get rid of a co-inheritor, an opponent in a litigation case, etc. Amhara culture had it that if a person dies "unexpectedly," he/she is thought to have been poisoned. There was a gender "equality" in being a *tanqway*, women *tanqways* being as revered and trusted in their judgments as their male counterparts. The *tanqway* was mostly without formal Church education. He/she was anti-Christ *par excellence*. If Christianity teaches the morality of turning the other cheek, people turned to the *tanqway* to take care of their enemies. This double standard of fidelity to the Church and to the *tanqway* was based on the duality of the needs of the believer: the Church (priest) takes care of the realm beyond this world; the *tanqway* attends to worldly affairs. Accordingly, a Muslim *tanqway* was not an abhorrence to a faithful Christian, but was consulted just as readily as a non-Muslim *tanqway*. It was all these "pagan" practices that made many European missionaries declare their utmost reservations about the sanctity of Ethiopian Christianity.[23]

Given the unending series of religious holidays and remembrances of the dead (*deges* and *tazkar*) and infant baptisms (feasts that take place almost everyday), it is quite clear that the peasants and small-town dwellers of Christian Ethiopia have been exploited more than their Muslim and "pagan" counterparts.

Our discussion of banquets and feasts won't be complete without considering the question of begging. As the practice was widespread, it needs some investigation.

Begging

Begging under the *geber* system was a form of distribution of "surplus" sanctioned by religious ethics. The history of begging in Ethiopia is yet to be written. For now, we can mention two kinds of begging: lay begging, and religious mendicancy. The former includes people who are physically incapable of working, those on a long journey to a certain destination, recent bankrupts, etc. The latter are from the ecclesiastical establishment. Two kinds exist: *qolo tamari* (Church students who live on roasted grain), and *bahetawyan* (hermits). Hermits are only occasionally mendicant since they spend most of their lives in monastic hideouts procuring their own means of survival, almost exclusively vegetarian.

The *qolo tamari* is the typical religious mendicant. He has to leave his village, go to church school, and survive on begging.[24] Wearing sheep's skin, with a face of Christian pity and utter politeness, these poor souls learn to memorize their studies in Ge'ez, a language they don't understand initially. Only among the higher ranks of the nobility would church teachers go to their houses to teach their children. In all cases of begging, the heavenly figure of the day is invoked, although the most popular is *basema lamaryam sela emaamlak belaw* (In the name of Mary, Mother of the Almighty).

The *qolo tamari* and other mendicants fight their way through dogs that defend what they consider to be their legitimate share been taken away. It is astonishing to see how developed the senses of dogs are when it comes to identifying *qolo tamari*. A calm dog lying down on the ground and letting people pass by suddenly bursts off with anger the moment a *qolo tamari* arounds the corner. The two protagonists in the fight for the share of the "surplus" have been the principal agents in the mendicant/antimendicant showdown: the graduation of *qolo tamari* to the status of deacon and beyond is certified by the seal of dog bites.

Other than these mendicants, who are still with us, were the *amina*, singer mendicants, also known as lalibeloch (see Shelemay, *JAS*, Fall, 1982). Moving in groups, consisting mostly of married couples and children, the *amina* wake people up early in the morning with their songs of begging, adding to the discomfort of sleeping with fleas. They would sing praise-songs in anticipation of offers, and when offers did not come, would insult the household with the most obscene words and curses imaginable. They mostly got their desired result, as the people were terrified of what would happen if the *amina* were not offered what they wanted. Ironically, it was the *amina* who decided what they wanted, while the alms-givers had to bargain for less.

In addition to these, there were the *yaegziabher engeda* (God's guests), people who had to spend the night in someone's home in their long journey to some faraway destination. Without question, they were welcome; there was even "competition" among hosts to welcome them. The guests chose well-to-do homes. The hosts gave up their bed for the guest, the wife washed the guest's feet, prepared dinner and packed *senq* (food for a long journey) for the next day.

The generosity of people receiving guests and giving away to the mendicant was a universal practice prior to the dominance of capitalism. In Ethiopia, as in medieval Europe, almsgiving and receiving guests were moral principles of Christian redistribution.[25]

Beggars and religious mendicants are not the same. People became beggars for all kinds of reasons, including arson, loss of a court case, famine, war, etc. The *qolo tamari* was also different. For him, begging was the medieval form of financial assistance, not from the church school, but from the parishes around the church school.

With the transformation of social relations towards the cash nexus, the economic position of beggars changed. Some grew so "rich" that they became money lenders. Out of their income derived from begging in kind and in cash, they could afford to render the latter superfluous. They gave it away in the form of *arata* (usury).

PART THREE

CREEPING MODERNITY, 1941-1974

CHAPTER 5

THE DEMISE OF THE *GEBER* SYSTEM AND RISE OF STATE BUREAUCRACY

virtue of His Imperial Blood, as well as by anointing which he received, the person of the Emperor is sacred, His dignity is inviolable and His Power indisputable. [Article 3 of the 1955 Revised Constitution of Ethiopia]

> The Ethiopian Orthodox Church, founded in the fourth century, on the doctrines of St. Mark, is the Established Church of the Empire and is, as such, supported by the State. The Emperor should always profess the Ethiopian Orthodox Faith. The name of the Emperor shall be mentioned in all religious services. [Article 6 of the 1955 Revised Constitution of Ethiopia]

The modern bureaucratic state, with its integration into the capitalist world economy, development of commodity production and circulation, rapid growth of urbanization and modern means of communication, establishment of modern educational institutions, dissolution of regional armies — in short, "modernization" — corroded beyond repair the foundations of the *geber* system.

The demise of the *geber* system and its gradual replacement by the modern bureaucratic state took place through two complementary processes: (1) expropriation of the rulers (both lay and ecclesiastical) from the means of rule; and (2) expropriation of the producers from the means of production. Rule by means of repression was carried out by the state, and hegemony through religious moral values by the Church. The political institutions of the modern state and the cultural institutions of modern education ate away the repressive and hegemonic institutions of the old order.

In this chapter, we deal with the historical processes of separation of lay rulers from the means of rule, and the accompanying processes of the rise of bureaucratic state apparatus centered at Addis Ababa. The process of separation of the direct rulers from the possession of the means of administration was a reflection of the parallel process of separation of the producers from the possession of the means of production. The latter is discussed in the next chapter.

Max Weber classified all states into two broad categories:

> All states may be classified according to whether they rest on the principle that the staff of men themselves own the administrative means, or whether the staff is 'separated' from these means of administration. This distinction holds in the same sense in which today we say that the salaried employee and the proletarian in the capitalist enterprise are separated from the material means of production [1974, p. 81].

The disintegration of the *geber* "political" superstructure took place through the integration of political power at Addis Ababa. The anarchy of "free competition" for power — which was the order in disorder of the *geber* system — was replaced by an integrated monopoly of legitimate violence, the modern state in the strict Weberian sense of the term.[1] The basis for the expropriation of rulers from their means of rule was laid down during the 1936-41 Italian occupation.

The Italian occupation played a major role in the centralization of state power at Addis Ababa. This was so in two ways. First, a wide network of roads was built that proved critical for the decline of the power of the regional nobility. The long system of roads built, "the most visible achievement of the Italian presence in Ethiopia" (Sbacchi 1985, p. 199),[2] reduced the spatial distance between the imperial court at Addis Ababa and the various regional notables. Like his Japanese counterparts, Emperor Haile Selassie invited regional notables to his court periodically, especially those whom he suspected of potential conspiracy against him, where they were kept in for a long time under various pretenses.[3] "Once in the capital, the ras became a guest of the emperor for months — even for years — if he was not subsequently banished to some remote mountainous district" (Perham 1969, p. 130).

The other aspect of the reduction of the spatial distance between Addis Ababa and the outlying regions was that it enabled fast movement of troops from the imperial court to areas of regional rebellion. A destination that used to take months for imperial troops to reach now took a few days.

The second major repercussion of the Italian occupation for state centralization was the death of thousands of warriors of the *geber* system, alongside many prominent representatives of regional and centrifugal noble houses. Some of those who survived, like *Ras* Hailu Takla Haimanot of Gojjam, lost prestige due to their collaboration with the Italians, a major crime in the burning nationalism of the Ethiopian resistance. By the time Haile Selassie was back in Addis Ababa on May 5, 1941, within five years to the day of the fall of the city to Italian troops, a major task of his centralizing policies had been accomplished.[4] The Italians rendered Haile Selassie the unintended service for the rise of his autocratic rule. Overall, "the Italian occupation of Ethiopia created a social revolution ruining the dominant classes overnight by taking away all their authority and concomitant financial resources" (Sbacchi 1985, 135).

The separation of rulers of the *geber* system from the possession of the means of rule had three aspects: military, administrative, and judicial. In the *geber* system, the three functions were merged in the person of the ruler. Of the three, the military aspect was the most important, and hence the most critical for the demise of the *geber* system and the rise of state bureaucratic rule (Perham 1969, p. 160).

The anti-Fascist war of liberation was the final war fought by the warrior class of the *geber* system against foreign invasion.

The massive collapse of the Ethiopian army in front of Mussolini's war machine sealed the fate of the warrior class once and for all (Steer 1942). Besides the incomparable gap in military technology between the Fascist war machine and Ethiopia's traditional warrior class, the lack of a modern, bureaucratically organized army contributed greatly to the collapse of the Ethiopian defense line. As Weber noted, "War in our time is a war of machines, and this makes centralized provisioning technically necessary" (1978, vol. 2, p. 981).

Military organization under the *geber* system was based on extensive parcellization and fragmentation of the possession of the means of destruction, from the *negusa nagast* down to the *chiqa shum*. The *negusa nagast* had an army of his own, alongside others, such that in times of war against a foreign enemy, what constituted the "Ethiopian" army was a sum total of the private armies of each notable gathered in one field. Warriors followed the leadership of their respective chief, the death of the chief leading to the disintegration of his army in the case of foreign aggression, and massive defection to the winning side in case of inter-notable conflicts. The army of the *geber* system was made up of regional atoms which, in the aftermath of victory or defeat, broke down into their respective components.

The fragmented nature of the army of the *geber* system was best manifested in the realms of nationalism. Ethiopian nationalism was a popular consciousness in times of foreign aggression. Otherwise, it was the parish, at best the region, that defined one's identity.

Steer, after paternalistically commenting, "I have seen a child nation [ie. Ethiopia] ruled by . . . [Haile Selassie] who was both noble and intelligent, done brutally to death [by the Fascist invasion] almost before it had begun to breathe" (1936, p. 8), went on to remark:

> Defeated only by the Magdhala [Maqdala] expeditionary force of Napier, the Ethiopians were until the end of this war [of the Fascist invasion] one of the most overwhelmingly conceited races that it has been my pleasure to behold. Their conceit did not usually take an offensive outward form: it was simply their spiritual bottom, the bedrock principle which informed invisibly their military theory. The sons of Solomon thought themselves unconquerable; they only had to swoop down like a troop of roaring lions and the macaroni melted.
>
> This view was never shared by the Emperor or by any of his high Ras, but it was the source of the ordinary Amhara's readiness for war [*Ibid,* p. 56].

The Ethiopian warrior was said to lack perseverance in pursuing the enemy, running back to his parish, whether the war was won or lost. Steer wrote, "Indifferent to results, the Ethiopian is incapable of an intense or prolonged effort. He lacks tenacity" (*Ibid*, p. 312). Saying that he heard it from "many serious people in Ethiopia, including

Ras Kassa," Steer quoted their statement that "The Ethiopian soldier, if his assault succeeds, does not go on — he withdraws. And if he loses a position, instead of trying to take another one he withdraws too" (*Ibid*). Mosley made the same observation. Quoting Emperor Menelik, he wrote: "The Ethiopian soldier, if his assault succeeds . . . does not go on — he withdraws. He is capable of great bravery — but only for short periods" (1964, p. 208). Pietro Badoglio, Commander-in-Chief of the Italian army of the Africa Orientali Italiana, described the Achilles' heel of his nemesis:

> An Abyssinian army, whose organization and discipline are normally very feeble and slow-working, when once it is beaten and put to flight, melts away. Each chief, with such fighting men as he has been able to gather round him, and each individual soldier, thinks only of getting back — each for himself and as quickly as possible — to his own village and his own *house*, in the hope of saving whatever can be saved. This kind of army can never be reunited and used again [1937, p. 90].

The Ethiopian warrior had no ration from the state, no salary, no medical supplies, no compensation for his family in case of his death, etc. And the longer he stayed in the war front, the more likely that he would starve. No wonder he "lacked tenacity."

And yet, it would be foolish to agree with the "lack of tenacity" story. How does it square with the fact that the Ethiopian fighter had to walk for months to the battle fronts to fight the foreign enemy if he lacked tenacity? How more tenacious could one be than to fight for one's country under the most difficult circumstances, especially in light of the ridiculously lopsided military balance between Fascist Italy and Ethiopia. If anything, the Ethiopian fighter had all the tenacity imaginable for human contingencies.

Referring to the Ethiopian army of the 1935-36 war, which "resembles so little any other army in the world," Steer noted:

> Dressed each according to his taste, wearing no military insignia; followed by a welter of pack-animals, donkeys and mules, and by their women folk who acted as an Army Service Corps; by their children who carried their rifles and other lumber, and finally by their servants and slaves, this army looked more like the emigration of a whole people [1936, p. 299].[5]

Other than its incapacity of waging war against machines, the army of the *geber* system was a breeding ground for noble heresies of all kinds, the most disastrous of which was collaboration with a foreign enemy. *Dajazmatch* Kassa Mercha collaborated with the Napier expedition against Emperor Tewodros II. Three years after the death of Tewodros, Kassa Mercha was crowned Yohannes IV, and became Emperor of Ethiopia, thanks to the superiority of firearms he had obtained from the departing British forces. While Yohannes IV was busy fighting the Italians in what later became Eritrea, *Negus* Menelik of Shawa was cultivating friendship with them. When Haile Selassie was marching to Mai Chaw to face the Fascist army, *Ras* Hailu Takla Haimanot of Gojjam, and many others, were throwing their lot in with the Italians (Sbacchi, *IJAIIS,* 10, 2, 1977). For many notables, especially those who had claim to the throne, a foreign enemy was a blessing in disguise. If they could not sit on the throne of the "Conquering Lion of the Tribe of Judah," they could at least avenge the Emperor by not lending their mighty hand. It was these two factors of the fragmented nature of the army and noble heresy, more than anything else, that taught Haile Selassie the cardinal lesson: that he either create a national army and destroy the regional private armies of the nobles once and for all, or perish. His defeat at the hands of the modern Fascist army came in the midst of his intense battle against the powerful regional nobility in his attempt to form a national army modelled along Western lines. It was during this process of the formation of a modern army that Mussolini closed in on Ethiopia (Perham 1969, p.167).

The massive frontal attack that was so characteristic of the army of the *geber* system led to disaster when engaging Mussolini's war machine. This was due in part to the contempt the Ethiopian warrior had for lying down on the ground during combat, for that would have been a violation of the law of honor, of masculinity, of the very essence of manhood (*wandenat*) (Levine, *IJSP*, 12, 1, 1966). What is war if not standing up tall, looking the enemy straight in the eye, boast war songs (*fukara*), and hit him right in the heart! From the Italian perspective, this medieval war culture[6] was so convenient that the worst soldier could simply mow down brave Ethiopians with a mere pulling of the trigger of a machine gun (Woolbert, *Foreign Affairs*, 14, 1, October 1935). *Jarbayan latalate alasayem* (I won't show my back to my enemy) — this was the war psychology of the Ethiopian fighter. To retreat from the enemy was considered as cowardly as giving oneself up in surrender. *Ijan latalate alsetem* (I won't give my hands to my enemy) was another.

The army of the *geber* system that faced the Italian war machine despised guerrilla warfare. Steer's point is well taken when he writes, "The Ethiopians translate guerrilla [warfare] with the word *shiftanet,* meaning brigandage" (1936, pp. 317-18). Referring to *Ras* Seyum, whom Haile Selassie advised not to engage the Italian forces in open frontal battle, Steer noted of Seyum's reply, "I am too old and too tired to become a *shifta*" (*Ibid,* p. 318).

After the collapse of the first wave of Ethiopian resistance, guerrilla warfare against Italians spread throughout the country like wild fire (Allen 1943; Pankhurst, *Ethiopia Observer,* 12, 2, 1969). It proved to be easier for the Italians to defeat the imperial army at Mai Chaw than subdue the thousands of guerrilla fighters that sprouted in many parts of the country.[7]

An embryonic national army beyond a mere sum total of regional armies existed a few decades before the Italian invasion. It was Emperor Menelik who saw the need for the formation of a professional standing army organized along modern lines, although Emperor Tewodros also had attempted to do the same previously. Menelik's embryonic modern army was paid partly in cash and partly in kind (Haile Kiros 1978, p. 124).

Although a military school for the training of a modern army was established during Tafari Makonnan's regency, the mass of the Ethiopian army that faced the Fascist war machine was the traditional plunderer army of the warrior class. It was after 1941 that an uninterrupted and ever-expanding formation of a modern army took place, while the decline and disappearance of the plunderer army of the *geber* system entered a point of no return. Thus was born the modern *soldier*, qualitatively distinct from the traditional *warrior class*. The Amharic word *watadar* remains the same, meaning both the warrior class of the *geber* system and the modern bureaucratic army. It is a case of the anachronism of language, its conservative shyness, its failing to catch up with newly-formed social relations. The same conservatism of language can be seen in the word *geber*, which means both tax paid to the modern bureaucratic state, as well as tribute to the warrior class of the *geber* system.

As participants in the war against Italian forces in Ethiopia, the British were instrumental in the re-formation of the modern Ethiopian army. At the time of liberation, Ethiopia came under the control of the British Occupied Enemy Territory Administration (OETA), headed by Sir Phillip Mitchell from Nairobi. The British entertained the idea of establishing a kind of protectorate over the former Italian East Africa (AOI) (Mosley 1964, p. 275). In 1942, the governments of Britain and Ethiopia signed a military agreement that was not different from an "agreement" between a victorious power and a vanquished one (see Perham 1969, Appendix E). Haile Selassie's talent and Britain's immersion into the Second World War enabled the Ethiopian government to slip away from the heavy hand of British domination. In 1944, another agreement was signed by the two powers that recognized Ethiopian sovereignty more seriously than had the one in 1942 (*Ibid*, Appendix F. See also Lipsky 1967, pp. 26-7).[8]

The task of creating the modern bureaucratic army was carried out by Emperor Haile Selassie, which was part of his centralizing and "modernizing" policies. He was the "prince" who "paved the way for the expropriation of the autonomous and 'private' bearers of executive power who stand beside him, of those who in their own right possess the means of administration, warfare, and financial organization, as well as politically usable goods of all sorts" [Weber 1974, p. 82].

It was the American involvement in Ethiopia that brought about drastic changes in the organization of the army.[9] In 1951, the United States replaced Britain as the military patron of Ethiopia by signing a mutual defense pact. In 1953, a Military Assistance Advisory Group (MAAG) was "attached to the Ministry of Defense under the agreement signed in May 1953" (Greenfield 1965, p. 359). In 1963, Ethiopia had received U.S. $73,799,000 in U.S. military assistance, about half the amount given to the rest of Africa (*Ibid*). Under U.S. military support, "The Ethiopian army developed to comprise twenty-three infantry and four artillery battalions, an airborne rifle company and an armoured squadron" (*Ibid*). In return, the U.S. got the Kagnaw military communications center at Asmara.

The modernization of the army went along with the creation of an Imperial Guard of Honor (*kebur zabagna*), a private domain of the Emperor, outside the authority of the Ministry of Defense. Ironically enough, it was the very same *kebur zabagna* that attempted a coup against Haile Selassie in 1960 while he was on a tour in Brazil.[10]

Haile Selassie kept the armed forces separate and suspicious of each other. It was this divide-and-rule policy that saved his throne during the 1960 coup. When his own personal guard rebelled against his rule, the officially Ethiopian Armed Forces and the Air Force suppressed the mutiny and saved him the throne. Fourteen years later, the entire army, including his own guard, forced him out. By keeping the temperature of enmity, mutual contempt, and suspicion among the various sectors of the armed forces high, the Emperor proved to be a master of political intrigue.

By the time Haile Selassie's rule came to an end, there were three basic divisions in the military, as with any other state: the Army proper, the Navy, and the Air Force. Besides these, there were the Imperial Guard of Honor, the Police forces, and the Territorial army. The last was a remnant of the traditional army of the *geber* system, used mainly as reserve for "pacifying" internal rebellions. The core and mass of the military had now become modernized. For the first time in the history of Ethiopia, there was an *Ethiopian* armed force, no more a sum total of regional armies gathered in one field, but a unified, bureaucratically organized national army imbued with state nationalist consciousness and ready for war anytime.

The most "traditional" elements of men-in-uniform were found in the countryside. Working as auxiliaries to the Police Force in times of need, the *nach labash* (white-wearing army), a remnant of the army of the *geber* system, was not dispensed with, especially in times of civil "disturbances." It was, for instance, called upon to put down the peasant uprising in Gojjam in 1968.

The expropriation of rulers of the *geber* system from the possession of the means of destruction took place through a massive shift of military obligations from the warrior class to that of a mass army. As Weber put it:

> Historically, the bureaucratization of the army has everywhere occurred along with the shifting of army service from the shoulders of the propertied to those of the propertyless. Until this transfer occurs, military service is an honorific privilege of propertied men [1978, vol. 2, p. 981].

This shift of the military profession was a class shift. In the *geber* system, the army was a warrior *class* preying upon the producers. From the lowest rung to the highest, the distribution of power relations in society was one of military relations. The *negusa nagast* was king of kings by virtue of the existence of kings below him; the king was king because there were *rases* below him, etc. In the modern bureaucratic army, the identification of army and class came to an end. The army became part of the state bureaucracy, instead of a class of its own. The mass of the modern army is a proletarianized army separated from ownership of the means of production. As more and more peasants joined the ranks of the military, the higher echelons of the defunct *geber* system moved up in the state bureaucracy, mostly in nonmilitary professions.

The replacement of the warrior class by the modern "classless" army also meant a *status* shift.[11] In the *geber* system, military profession, no matter at what level of the hierarchy, had the highest status and prestige. In the modern bureaucratic system, the rank-and-file military came to have low status, while the top brass had high status and prestige. To be an ordinary soldier was considered a lowly profession. Many a soldier and policeman had to wear "civil" garb to gain the respect of the public. As the military profession shifted from the most powerful nobility to peasants-in-uniform, so shifted the status symbol downwards. Overall, the Air Force had the highest status, and the Police Force was the most despised.

The key to the formation of the modern state in Ethiopia was in the realm of the "struggle of expropriation" (Weber 1974, p. 83) of military privileges from the regional nobility and its concentration in the monopoly of legitimate violence at Addis Ababa. Ever since the end of the *geber* system, the proletarianized army became an idle social body "passing time" playing cards while watching over the activities of the "*sheretam sumale*" (loin-wearing Somali!) in the merciless heat of the sands of the Ogaden, or running after the "Arab-bought bandits" of Eritrea.

The expropriation of possession of the means of rule from the nobility was compensated by their being assigned important positions in the civilian sector of the state bureaucracy. With their parcellized sovereignties gone, it was now easier to control and tame them no matter how high the offices they were assigned. In one of the best analyses on the rise of the modern state, Norbert Elias wrote of the replacement of military parcellized sovereignties by centralized ones as follows:

> For all warrior societies with a barter economy — and not only for them — the sword is a frequent and indispensable instrument for acquiring means of production, and the threat of violence an indispensable means of production. Only when the division of functions is very far advanced; only when, as a result of long struggles, a specialized monopoly administration has formed that exercises the functions of rule as its social property; only when a centralized and public monopoly of force exists over large

> areas, can competition for means of consumption and production take its course largely without the intervention of physical violence; and only then do the kind of economy and the kind of struggle exist that we are accustomed to designate by the terms "economy" and "competition" in a more specific sense [1982, pp. 149-50].[12]

The end of the *geber* system and the rise of the modern state bureaucratic institutions took place through what Elias termed "the courtization of warriors" (*Ibid*, p. 258). Elias called this process of courtization of warriors the "inner pacification of society" (*Ibid*). "The concentration of the means of administration" at Addis Ababa, the dissociation of warrior notables from their private armies, the end of tribute extraction from the *gabbar*, the taming, pacification, domestication, and civil-ization of warrior notables transformed them from being warriors into one of being courtiers. Attendance at Haile Selassie's palace, the struggle *to be seen* by him — a process called *dej tenat* (attendance at the gate) — made the once proud notables mere cogs in the wheel of the state bureaucracy.

Before the 1935-36 Italian invasion, there were 34 administrative units in Ethiopia. Each unit was a kind of state within a state, although under the overall authority of the *negusa nagast*. One of the first major political blows Haile Selassie inflicted upon the regional nobility was to liquidate the territorial classification of the *geber* system and reorganize it anew.

In 1942, Ethiopia was reorganized into twelve provinces, *taqlay gezats* (governates-general.) Besides the need for state centralization, the redrawing of provinces had political-power considerations. Shawa and Wallo (the latter was the domain of the Crown Prince Asfa Wossen) expanded their size; the traditional province of Amhara ceased to exist; Tigray was reduced in size, part of it added to Wallo for the Crown Prince; and Hararge was split into Hararge and Bale. Wallo and Hararge had large land holdings of the Imperial family. With the split up of Hararge, and the addition of Eritrea as a province in 1962, the total number of provinces rose to fourteen (Markakis 1974, p. 289).

It was not merely that the administrative units of the country had changed, but also that the power of regional notables was reduced extensively. By redrawing the internal territorial boundaries of Ethiopia, Haile Selassie destroyed the traditional power base of the nobility of the *geber* system.

With the formation of the *taqlay gezat* system, the task of supervising provincial administration was handled by the Ministry of Interior. The head of each *taqlay gezat* was appointed by the Emperor and was known as *endarase* (on my behalf); he was to rule on behalf of the Emperor. To put an end to tribute extraction, restrictions were imposed upon the *endarase*:

> [F]irstly, he was not allowed to receive gifts or bribes of any kind; secondly, he was not allowed to recruit or raise a police force. And, finally, a reminder of his relative independence of the past, the governor-general was not permitted to negotiate or sign treaties with other nations [Haile Kiros 1978, p. 207].

The *endarase* was not the same as the class of warrior notables of the *geber* system. The official title of some of these *endarases* was the same as under the *geber* system. Quite often, Haile Selassie gave people titles of the old *geber* system, although these titles did not correspond to the actual position of the recipients. For example: the traditional titles of *dajazmatch* (commander of the gate), *kagnazmatch* (commander of the right), *gerazmatch* (commander of the left), and *fitawrari* (commander of the front), were generously distributed to various people by Haile Selassie, although none of these titles had any military significance. People were content with the prestige and honor that the titles gave them, although economic gains and military status did not accompany these titles. It was a case where the striving for power was conditioned by the social honor it entailed (Weber 1978, vol. 2, p. 926). The traditional titles continued to be used right up to the revolution despite the qualitative transformations in social relations of production, distribution of power relations, competition vs. monopoly of possession of the means of violence, etc., that had taken place since 1942.

The appointment or demotion of high state officials was the prerogative of the Emperor through the *shum-shir* process. The nobility occupied the highest positions of the civilian administrative bureaucracy, while caution was taken that they not have a critical role in the military bureaucracy. The Shawa nobility had the highest representation in the ruling group (Haile Kiros 1978, pp. 128-29).

Appointment to state office meant power, prestige, status, honor, and access to economic benefits. Aspiring retainers of all kinds congregated around the home of a new appointee like a swarm of bees in a hive to congratulate him for his appointment, while at the same time immediately disassociating themselves from those removed from office. That appointment brings economic benefits, and removal loss of these benefits, is well captured in the saying, *sishom yalbala sishar yeqochawal* (He who does not eat while appointed, regrets it when removed.)

It was those who already had status, honor, and prestige in the traditional social set-up that were the chosen ones eligible for the high posts of state office. Honor went along with bread, although the other way round was not necessarily true. A *jabarti* had all the bread, but hardly any honor. He was in double jeopardy: he was a merchant and he was a Muslim. Either one alone was enough to render him honorless. Hence, when Haile Selassie was running his official prerogative of *shumet* and *shiret*, he looked for those already with honor and prestige, the nobility, for appointment to high state offices.

Although the nobility had paramount position in state administrative offices, those from non-noble backgrounds were not shut out. In what was one of the most interesting aspects of the political process in Ethiopia, as of patrimonial systems elsewhere, it was customary for emperors and those below them to raise people of humble origin to positions of prominence. The practice was known as *katebya asnasto* (raising from the dust). Weber called it "typical" of patrimonial rule, the "rise from rags, from slavery and lowly service for the ruler, to the precarious all-powerful position of the favorite" (1978, vol. 2, p. 1106). Haile Selassie was a master at this. People of very humble background — peasant, servant, even slave — were selected for their loyalty to the person of the Emperor.

Traditionally, the single most important criterion of selection was military heroism displayed in combat. As a result, a slave who proved hero in battle suddenly found himself being awarded high titles.

The rationale behind "raising from the dust" was that the person of humble origin was used by the Emperor as a counterweight to the nobility whose fidelity to the throne was not always dependable. Moreover, the man of humble origin, "Lacking family connections and provincial sources of support . . . represent[ed] the pure retainer type who is wholly dependent on his royal patron" (Markakis 1978, pp. 233-4). The last thing Haile Selassie had to worry about was disloyalty from those whom he had raised to prominent position from the dust. As they had no noble blood in their veins, the only altar they worshipped at was that of the Emperor. Since they reflected back on their humble past, and compared it with their respectable present, the dread of going back to where they started from was such a nightmare that they had to serve their Emperor better than anybody else could.

Even if many of these "types" had established marriage relations with noble families, they were uncomfortable every time discussions of family genealogy came up. Since tracing one's genealogy was the soap opera of the nobility, one of the entertainments they enjoyed was to ask the genealogy of the poor official who had a peasant or slave background. As if they knew nothing about the family background of the person who has been married to their daughter, sister, niece, etc., they asked the notoriously uncomfortable question: *yaman ledj nah?* (Whose son are you?). This simple question was enough to destroy the pride of the official of humble origin. The more the official of humble origin was humiliated by the nobility, the closer he got to the Emperor. For Haile Selassie, this was a perfect balance of power, as he used one against the other to his advantage.

But there is one fundamental problem in relation to the nobility that needs to be addressed. Noble status was a free-floating status in which anybody was a potential candidate for membership. Noble status was not hereditary, any more than *gult* was. Since a noble was defined by his huge *gult* possession and command of a large private army, neither of which was hereditary, a long unbroken line of noble genealogy was nonexistent in Ethiopia. A person like Emperor Tewodros II, coming from a humble background, could seize hold of the throne by simply *claiming* to descend from an imperial line. There was no need to "verify" the claim since it was might that secured right to the throne. If one abided by the sanctity of the *rist* and *gult* systems, protected the Ethiopian Orthodox Church, and claimed to belong to an ancestral line of a royal house, almost anyone could be an Emperor.

The *geber* system was an "equal opportunity employer" in which upward social mobility depended on sheer military strength, as much as on descent from royal line. Descent from royal line alone was not enough. The royal descent had to be protected by armed might. And yet, armed might *created* royal line of descent! It is in this sense that Steer commented, "The Ethiopian system was not a feudal system: it was a tough-man's system" (1936, p. 69), to emphasize the preponderance of military strength as the basis of power. (Needless to say, not to call it feudal because it was a "tough-man's system" is a weak argument.) For Margery Perham, "The power of the [Ethiopian] monarchy may be visualized as a magnificent and lofty throne which was always ready for the dynast who had the military power and ability to climb up into it" [1969, p. 76].

The tradition of detaining members of the royal family at *ambas* (mountain hideouts), the most famous of which was Amba Geshan, while one of them reigned as *negusa nagast*, thereby avoiding competition from other claimants to the throne, the recurrent civil wars that broke out every time a new *negusa nagast* was to be crowned, the fact that the *negusa nagast* had to fight for his throne against all aspirants, including his own brothers, shows the arbitrariness of the rules of succession to the throne.[13] Male members of the royal household were the first "inmates" in Ethiopian history! Theirs was royal serfdom, part-time or for life.

The fact that the nobility could not count their pedigree a long way back, and that any *rist*-possessing person could claim to descend from a royal house that ruled in the remote past, made noble and dynastic narratives murky.[14] It is clear, however, that a hereditary noble status developed in the post-1941 period in lieu of the transformation of tribute into rent, and *gabbar*- lordship into land-lordship. Since land was not the private property of the nobility in the *geber* system, hereditary titles and hereditary status developed simultaneously with the rise of private property in land. The rise of landed private property necessitated the hereditary transmission of property to one's offspring. In this way, the free-floating nobility of the *geber* system became a closed group of hereditary nobles.

When we come to the process of *shiret*, it was the privilege of the Emperor to "grant" it. And since "no appointment can be refused," the official will go "uncomplainingly wherever the *shum-shir* takes him" (Markakis 1978, p. 245).

We discussed earlier that *shiret* was removal from office, and *shumet* was appointment to office. That was indeed so. Nevertheless, the imperial system was such that those who were removed from their previous position were not thrown out in the cold for good. They were assigned to new posts. In some cases, *shiret* meant *gezot* (banning), whereby former officials were not given any new post, but were banned from moving freely. Theirs was noble serfdom, part-time or for life. However, *shiret* normally implied future appointment to another place and another position.

Why *shum-shir?* Why was *shumet* also *shiret* in a different sense? The imperial administration was based on the treatment of political-administrative office as if it were *gult*. The *shum-shir* system was a "political" *gult* system. Like the "economic" *gult* system, the political *gult* system was based on the permanence of impermanence of office-holding, that political office was as ephemeral as was *gult*. It was the privilege of the Emperor to grant political office to whomever he wanted to, just as it was the privilege of the Emperor of the *geber* system to grant *gult* to whomever he wished. In both cases, office and *gult* were granted on a temporary basis, with the proviso that if the client proved loyal enough to capture the confidence of the Emperor, the office or the *gult* could be given permanently, which happened quite rarely. The beauty of this system was that officials became perpetual dependents on the good will of the Emperor, their position always precarious. They could continue with their status only if, and insofar as, they kept their loyalty to the Emperor.

The age-old conflict between the Crown and the nobility throughout Ethiopian history was the pillar upon which the *shum-shir* system was based. Haile Selassie modernized this ancient practice through the help of the modern bureaucratic state apparatus. He made sure that the office always remained occupied, but officials rotated. From one ministry to another, from one *taklay gezat* to another, from home to abroad as ambassador, it wouldn't be exaggerating to say that Haile Selassie's main political function was to see to it that the *shum-shir* system was running well. Haile Selassie gradually eradicated the *geber* system and replaced it by one of bureaucratic rule. In this, he was as much a subject as an object of large-scale historical processes that he had to go along with. If he was a modernizing, enlightened autocrat, it was because he himself was being modernized by global forces of capitalist development.

Both losers and gainers in the *shum-shir* ritual faced the Emperor to thank him for the *shumet* or even for the *shiret*. Who dared to complain of *shiret?* Markakis wrote:

> Those who come in contact with Haile Selassie — the highest officials and dignitaries of the realm not excluded — comport themselves like children confronted by a stern pater familias and are treated accordingly. All proposals, recommendations, suggestions, and advice are put to him as humble requests; and explicit or direct disagreement is unthinkable for those who value their position. Imperial appointments, promotions, grants, and other gestures of favour are bestowed directly by the ruler to deserving subjects, establishing a filial bond and obligation on the part of the beneficiary. All beneficiaries are required to present themselves before the Emperor and kiss his hand. 'What

> can we do for you?' is the question invariably addressed to those who gain Haile Selassie's attention. Those guilty of acts of *lese majeste* face the wrath of paternal disillusionment. 'Who made you what you are?' is the damning question hurled at the culprit. Whatever the nature of the offense, the guilty person is berated for his ingratitude to the person of the Emperor and is given to understand that therein lies the essence of his misdeed [1978, p. 209].

Rarely were officials demoted or punished once and for all, with no chance of a later-day comeback. Markakis noted:

> In accordance with the paternal style, while punishment is meted out as merited, it is never final. The offender is encouraged to hope for forgiveness and restoration of grace, provided he demonstrates his loyalty and devotion during the period of banishment. And more often than not, forgiveness is forthcoming. A coldly rational manipulator of men, Haile Selassie is neither forbearing nor vindictive. He is not really interested in men as such, but in what use can be made of them. Consequently, the use of power to punish or forgive is guided neither by abstract moral criteria, nor by the established legal norm of the state, but basically by the impersonal criteria of power preservation [*Ibid*, pp. 209-10].

It was not uncommon for Haile Selassie to pardon people accused of high treason and condemned to death by the Supreme Court. This pardon was an annual ritual, especially on July 23rd, his birthday, which was a national holiday.

The degree of punishment and forgiveness, and *shiret* eventually being written off by a *shumet* to a higher position, depended mostly on the person and the strength or otherwise of his noble entourage. It was common practice under Haile Selassie not to put to death a man of powerful noble house, even if he was engaged in high treason. The best example was Ras Hailu Takla Haimanot of Gojjam. Notorious for his perfidy against Haile Selassie on many occasions — e.g., alliance with Haile Selassie's arch-enemy, *Ledj* Iyasu; or collaboration with the Italians, in which the *Ras* welcomed the Emperor at Dabra Marqos wearing a full Italian military uniform — *Ras* Hailu was a thorn in the flesh of the Emperor. And yet, the Emperor did not see to it that the *ras* should be executed, despite his being sentenced to death. Rather, *Ras* Hailu was ordered to live in Addis Ababa in *gezot*, his governorship of Gojjam taken away from him. On the other hand, if those accused of treason came from humble backgrounds, with no intricate noble connections, then their challenge to the rule of the Emperor could be punished by death. Such was the case of Balay Zalaqe, the most famous leader of the anti-Fascist resistance in Gojjam. Despite the fact that his treason was a child's play compared to *Ras* Hailu's, he was hanged in Addis Ababa like an ordinary criminal. Alas, how happy Mussolini must have been in his grave! The same fate befell Mengistu Neway in the aftermath of the abortive coup of 1960.

The rationale for the double standard of punishment was that, whereas executing a man of high noble status could endanger Haile Selassie's rule by virtue of the extensive network of relationships among those of the nobility who resent the execution, the death of a man from non-noble background was otherwise. Hence, in the punishment or forgiveness of wrongdoers, social class and traditional status played a significant role.

The same class and status bias worked in the *shum-shir* system. If a person from a noble house was demoted, his opportunities for coming back to the same position or better were open. The demotee would use the sophisticated arsenal of noble connections and political marriages at his disposal to convince the Emperor to change his *shiret* into *shumet*. That was why *shiret* for the nobility was never final. On the other hand, those officials who were in power only by virtue of their personal loyalty to the Emperor, without any roots in the nobility, were done for good once demoted. It was a violation of imperial patrimonialism to lose the favor of the Emperor. The patrimonial client had no power backing him, no prominent noble house to speak on his behalf, no noble to ask forgiveness for him from the Emperor. The loss of imperial favor was the end of his position. As usual, *shiret* for the patrimonial client may also mean *shumet* to another position, but his chance of coming back to a new, higher post and regaining the favor of the Emperor was almost always nil. The best example of this was the career of Wolde Giorgis Wolde Yohannes. *Tsehafe Teezaz* (Writer of Order) from 1941 to 1955, Wolde Giorgis rose to this most prominent position, next only to the Emperor himself, from a humble background. Son of a cobbler from Shawa, Wolde Giorgis started his career before the Italian war as interpreter. His power was so formidable that there was no intermediary between him and Haile Selassie (Clapham 1969, p. 112). In a power structure in which the person of the Emperor was the highest attainable relation, the degree of one's power was measured by the degree of closeness to the Emperor. Other than the Emperor's own family and his confessor, Abba Hana Jima, Wolde Giorgis was the person closest to Haile Selassie. He could reach and touch the Emperor at will, at any time. Since Haile Selassie preferred the typical patrimonial client, Wolde Giorgis was his most favorite. Although this gave Wolde Giorgis extraordinary power, it was also his Achilles' heel. It was bound to be over with him if ever he lost the favor of the Emperor. And he did. In 1955, he was removed from his position as Minister of Pen (the modern term for the ancient office of *tsehafe teezaz*), and demoted to the governorship first of Arsi, and then of Gemu Gofa. He never recovered.[15]

At the apex of the highly intricate system of imperial patronage stood *Atse* Haile Selassie. This "very little great man," as Clapham liked to call him (1969, p. 47), was the head of the imperial bureaucracy. Clapham wrote,

> It is with his ministers and courtiers that [Haile Selassie] should be seen, for the way in which the Emperor dominates the group, not physically but through the bonds of deference which draw the others to him, sums up the working of the central government. Haile Selassie is the very centre of the political system, which radiates out from him to the concentric circles of personalities and institutions which surround the throne; and his domination of the last half-century shows that his delicate features and great personal charm conceal a politician of the greatest skill [*Ibid*].

Markakis accurately summed up the Herculean weight of this diminutive figure as follows:

> Ethiopian emperors have always been surrounded by a mystical aura bordering on the supernatural. There is a strong element of dread mixed in the profound reverence accorded to their emperor by the Ethiopians. Despite the constant exposure of his person to his subjects, Haile Selassie has preserved an aura of awe-inspiring mystery which, instead of dissolving, thickens with the passage of years, and has turned the aging monarch into a legend during his own lifetime. Perpetually frozen into a posture of haughty regal isolation, the sombre figure of the ruler stands across a psychological divide which even his most trusted retainers cannot cross. Seen in the midst of his tense, scurrying

> courtiers, the diminutive Emperor gives the impression of remote aloofness and icy calmness that easily dominate any scene of which he is part. Men of great importance in their own right are reduced to insignificance in the Emperor's presence, and sophisticated Ethiopians who have no illusions concerning their ruler's human and political shortcomings confess to become awe-struck before him. Significantly, after more than fifty years of rule, Haile Selassie remains a mystery to his subjects. Little is ever known about his thoughts, and apparently are shared with no one. Rumors abut the Emperor's role, motivation and interest on decisions abound, but facts about such matters are precious few [1978, p. 208].[16]

Simply put: Haile Selassie was the concentrated expression of Ethiopian politics for over 40 years. He was so autocratically domineering that, according to one informant, "Even if there was a rebellion, he [Haile Selassie] wanted to rule over the rebellion, to command a mutiny, even if it was directed against his own reign" (Kapuscinski 1984, p. 134).

Such was the mechanism of power distribution at the highest levels. The various regions of the country followed the pattern set by Addis Ababa. Below the *taqlay gezat* were *awraja gezat, warada gezat, meketel-warada gezat, atbiya dagna* (village judge), and *chiqa shum*, in descending order. The offices of the *atbiya dagna* and *chiqa shum* were held by traditional authorities. The *chiqa shum* was "expected to possess an intimate knowledge of the people over whom he exercised authority and supervision" (Haile Kiros 1978, pp. 209-10). The *chiqa shum's* functions included:

> (a) representing his village in relations with others and with the hierarchy of the provincial [i.e., *taqlay gezat]* administration; (b) supervising and directing communal work in accordance with orders and directives of the district [*warada*] or sub-district [*meketel-wereda*] administration; (c) taking an active and leading role in the maintenance of law and order in his village. Indeed, his knowledge of local history, genealogy and property rights made him an indispensable administrator, councillor, and witness in local disputes, particularly in matters concerning land. As a link between the people and the provincial administration, he transmitted all information and orders issued by the gov-

> ernment concerning the people in his area. He was involved in the assessment and collection of taxes, for which he was rewarded 2 to 3% of those taxes collected from his area [*Ibid*, p. 210].

Since the modern bureaucratic state began as an extension of the imperial court, the further away a region was from Addis Ababa, the more traditional the patterns of rule remained, and vice-versa.

The third aspect of expropriation of rulers from the possession of the means of rule, other than the military and administrative realms discussed earlier, was the judicial system. The growth of the modern judiciary system accompanied the bureaucratization of the military and administrative apparatuses. Four levels of judicial hierarchy were formed: the Supreme Imperial Court, the High Court, the *awaraja gezat* court, and the *wereda gezat* court.

The Supreme Imperial Court was a court of appeal. It "has always exercised only appellate jurisdiction, hearing appeals from cases originating in or varied by the High Court" (Redden 1968, p. 134). However, ministers could be tried only by the Supreme Court in matters pertaining to their respective ministry. "Such prosecution may be initiated either by order of the Emperor or by a majority vote of both houses of parliament. In such a case the [supreme] court would exercise original jurisdiction" (*Ibid*). The *afa negus* (mouth of the king) was the president of the Supreme Imperial Court. The High Court had jurisdiction on a state-wide level. It had branches in *taqlay gezat* capitals. The hierarchy of the judiciary system was parallel to that of the administrative hierarchy. The *awraja* and *wereda* courts were located in the capitals of each administrative region designated as *awraja* and *wereda*.

Then there were the local courts, the most important being the *atbiya dagna*. The jurisdiction of the *atbiya dagna* did not exceed an equivalent of $10.00 (*Ibid*, p. 136). There were also Islamic courts with jurisdiction over Muslims. The Sharia was represented "as a branch of the supreme Imperial Court" (*Ibid*, p. 138). On the other hand,

> The Ethiopian Orthodox Church was deprived of all jurisdiction in civil matters in 1942. Thus, a Church court is not a court within the meaning of the Constitution and cannot bind private persons in civil matters, though in practice, it may function as a court in ecclesiastical matters and in cases that parties voluntarily submit to [*Ibid*, p. 139].

Another judicial process was the Imperial Chilot. A very ancient institution, the Chilot was the prerogative of the Emperor. As the Emperor was considered the ultimate source of justice, righteousness, and sovereignty, the Chilot continued to exist right up to the end of Haile Selassie's reign. Technically not part of the modern court system, the Chilot was the sphere the Emperor passed judicial decisions that were contrary to the formal rules of the established legal process. In Chilot,

> the Emperor is not bound to decide the case in accordance with the provisions of the formal law, but may base His decisions on principles of "justice and fairness" without reference to the law. He may mitigate the rigors of the application of the strict law in a particular case [*Ibid*, pp. 147-8].

In this way, the formal regularities of the law could be bent in either direction by the Emperor, who was himself above any law whatsoever, constitutional or judicial.

The abstract rules of the legal system are blind when it comes to particular situations. The poor and the defenseless may be treated unfairly. Accordingly, there may be "undue harshness," and "the proper application of the law in a particular case may produce an unjust result" (Sedler, *JAL*, 8, 2, 1964, p. 65). It was here that His Imperial Majesty "interfered" in the internal affairs of the formal law. He could pardon people sentenced to death or long prison terms according to the rules of the formal law. Normally, if the Emperor took a case already decided by other courts, it was to mitigate the punishment. In this way, he could live up to his projected image of being the source of ultimate justice and righteousness.[17]

The contradiction between abstract formal law and its application to particular cases was the rationale for Plato's justification of the rule of philosopher kings in his *Republic*. Ethiopian emperors have played the role of philosopher kings in judicial matters, overriding either the *Fetha Nagast,* the traditional source of judicial legitimacy, or the modern legal codes. More often than not, the judicial intervention of emperors had been for the good of the accused. Many lives condemned to death had been saved thus.

As the modern judicial system took more of a bureaucratic form, the old agents of fusion of military, administrative, and judicial power lost their monopoly of passing *qetat* (punishment) or rendering *mehrat* (forgiveness). The personal element in the judicial process was gradually replaced by impersonal rules of abstract law. In a social relation that made litigation second nature to many Ethiopians, the formalism of the law process brought about the loss of the arbitrariness of justice and replaced it with the impersonality of the rules of abstract law.

The Herculean weight of the Emperor in the legal system was captured in the adage *negus kemote beman yimuagatu* (If the king dies, whom to invoke for litigation?). The Emperor was so dominant a figure of legal-judicial legitimacy that all one needed to do to stop anyone for alleged wrongdoing was to say *ba Haile Selassie amlak qum!* (In the name of Haile Selassie's God, stop!)[18] The person had to stop instantly. If one dared to violate this veto against movement, it was tantamount to violating the divine right of kings, and the authority of the Emperor thereby.

Judicial and legal legitimacies, like their political counterpart, were dominated by the immense reverence given to the Emperor. The national pledge of the people was to say Haile Selassie *yimut* (May Haile Selassie die, i.e., I swear by the name of Haile Selassie). God knows how many times Haile Selassie was "condemned to death" by his loyal subjects in their show of fidelity to him.

Having made a detailed discussion of the expropriation of rulers from the possession of the means of rule and its replacement by a centralized state bureaucracy, how shall we categorize this bureaucratic organization? What conceptual terminology can we use to describe it: patriarchal, patrimonial, or legal-rational? The first two are varieties of traditional rule, while the last one is the modern ideal. Which type was Haile Selassie's bureaucracy?

The concepts of patriarchal, patrimonial, and legal-rational rule do not correspond to the actual historical relations. (They are what Max Weber calls "idea types.") Elements of each can be found, with one being dominant. The popular American saying: "It is not what you know, but whom you know that counts," is a far cry from the impersonal rationalism considered to be the characteristic of modern bureaucracy. In discussing the state bureaucracy under Haile Selassie, we should keep in mind that the real historical conditions could only approximate the abstract concepts of political science.

The bureaucratic organization under Haile Selassie was an amalgam of patrimonial and legal-rational forms, with a distinct division of labor accorded to each. The power relations among officials, especially higher officials, were patrimonial. Fidelity and unwavering subservience to the Emperor was the primary criterion for holding office. On the other hand, the technical aspects of running the day-to-day affairs of the state bureaucracy were according to formal rules, legally binding to those entrusted with state office. To this extent, the bureaucracy was legal-rational. In other words, officials were appointed and demoted by the Emperor patrimonially, while the offices were run by salaried professionals legal-rationally. The two forms were intertwined (Weber 1978, vol. 2, p. 1028, 1028-29).

The dominant position of Haile Selassie in the *shum-shir* system had restricted the possession of office by the patrimonial official as his personal property. On the other hand, however, Haile Selassie himself treated the *shum-shir* process as his personal property. It was in the relation between Haile Selassie and the various officeholders in the higher echelons of the state bureaucracy that the patrimonial nature of the power relationship was clearly discernible. Weber remarked:

> In contrast to bureaucracy . . . the position of the patrimonial official derives from his purely personal submission to the ruler, and his position vis-a-vis the subjects is merely the external aspect of this relation . . . . For the patrimonial official's loyalty to his office . . . is not an impersonal commitment . . . to impersonal tasks which define its extent and its content, it is rather a servant's loyalty based on a strictly personal relationship to the ruler and on an obligation of fealty which in principle permits no limitation [*Ibid*, pp. 1030-1].

It was in this patrimonial capacity that state officials functioned — to serve honestly their Emperor and country. Emperor and country were never separated in the rituals of pledge. To serve Haile Selassie loyally was to serve the country; to be disloyal to him was to be disloyal to the country. Ethiopia and Haile Selassie became identical expressions; *Ethiopia was Haile Selassie*. In his style of rule, Haile Selassie was a patriarchal-patrimonial emperor, who, in a masterful fashion, played notable against notable, and notables against the people, while he always pictured himself as "the father of the people."

The image of "father of the people," called by Weber "the ideal of patrimonial rule" (*Ibid*), was well captured in Ethiopia by the notion of *tsehayu negus* (the sun-king), an analogy between Haile Selassie and the sun, the former being as indispensable as the latter.

The emperor as the ultimate source of legitimate authority —

political, judicial, military, and ecclesiastical — had been an ancient tradition of the Geez civilization.[19] What made Haile Selassie's reign different was that this tradition was grounded on modern, bureaucratic, centralized rule.

If the relationship between Haile Selassie and his officials was patrimonial, so too were the relationships among the various hierarchies of the officials in the bureaucratic ladder. The patrimonial "norm" was reproduced at lower levels, each minor official acting as a minuscule Haile Selassie in his own domain. The best example of this patrimonial relationship is captured in the saying *mangad kaagar ledj sedat kashum ledj* (When travelling, go with one who knows the country; when fleeing from home, go with the son of an appointed official) (see Haile Kiros 1978, pp. 129-30].

Patrimonial clientalism was deeply rooted in the political culture. Former retainers and clients deserted their official patron en masse the moment the official was demoted or transferred to a remote place. Clapham called it "the Ethiopian tendency to follow a leader only so long as he is successful" (1969, p. 96). (Of course, there is nothing exlusively Ethiopian about this. It is normal of patrimonial relations.) The same "traitorous" people prostrated themselves in front of the newly-appointed official (who has brought with him his own entourage of clients, giving him free lectures on the culture of the new region he has been appointed to) hand him over a list of who's who, his possible enemies, the mass psychology of the people of the region, etc. Every aspiring retainer appeared before the newly-appointed official as a social psychologist of the area he lived in, offering his knowledge in anticipation of a deferential repayment by the newly-appointed official in the form of recruitment to state jobs. The more sophisticated and believable the presentation, the higher the chances of recruitment. Other than social-psychological information, the aspiring retainer did all kinds of physical labor in the household of the newly-appointed official, anticipating payment of his labor in the form of recruitment to the civil service. Since the number of people freely offering their labor was always greater than the number that could possibly be hired, the newly-appointed official had immense accumulation of unpaid labor in the form of services in his household or outside. It was an additional means of income to the salary he was paid. Together with bribes and "gifts," the standard of living of a minor official was well beyond his monthly salary.

When we turn to the legal-rational aspect, we find that the technical aspects of state administration were run by trained experts drawn from the modern educational establishment. Since "the objective basis of bureaucratic power is its technical indispensability founded on specialized professional knowledge" (Weber 1978, vol. 2, p. 1007), the training of the human power necessary to run this apparatus was the prime rationale for the development of the modern educational system (Grey 1970).

A systematic attempt to rationalize the bureaucratic apparatus was made in 1961, when the Central Personnel Agency (CPA) was established. Its purpose was to centralize the administrative process according to an all-pervasive national standard of employment based on individual merit. Despite the establishment of the CPA, Haile Selassie himself was "the greatest violator of CPA regulations" (Haile Kiros 1978, p. 157); his status as the supreme authority of the land contradicted the processes of legal-rational rule. The very essence of the *shum-shir* system was contrary to the working of a modern bureaucratic administration. And yet, the greater the number of people that joined the civil service came through the educational process, the more the patrimonial order was challenged.

What was perhaps most striking change in the bureaucratic administration was the demise of the nobility in the highest echelons of the administrative apparatus. In 1967, it could be stated that "The noblemen have disappeared: there are none among the twenty ministers today . . . almost every minister has a university education, quite a number of them since the war" (Clapham 1969, p. 101).

The decline of the power of the nobility and the rise of the educated elite was not in itself the decline of patrimonialism *per se*. The Emperor shifted his patrimonial weight from the nobility to the educated elite, whom he always called "our children." Although the new breed of educated elite were related to the Emperor patrimonially, they were also the very foundation of bureaucratic rationalism and the gradual erosion of imperial patrimonialism. The contradiction between these two forces was to prove deadly for the imperial order in 1974 when the state apparatus cultivated so patriarchically-patrimonially by Haile Selassie "deserted" him en masse.

The development of the modern state bureaucracy underneath patrimonial rule was also run in part by foreign experts. In their quest for technical efficiency of administration, Emperors Menelik and Haile Selassie, especially the latter, sought help from foreign experts of different national origins. With the balance of global power in mind, they drew expert help from Britain, Germany, India,

Yugoslavia, France, Italy, Sweden, Israel, Japan, China, Poland, the Soviet Union, and the U.S. (Haile Kiros 1978, p. 151; for Swedes in Ethiopia, see Halldin 1977). Differences in political and ideological systems were not primary concerns, as the list of countries from which foreign experts were drawn shows. It was technical expertise in rationalizing the bureaucracy that was sought after. Military affairs were dominated by the U.S., while the Israelis had a strong presence in intelligence and training of Air Force pilots and airborne divisions. Experts from Eastern Europe were mostly engaged in preparation of budget, tax, and accounting. Others were in the ministry of health. Great caution was taken not to put them in any capacity as advisors in political matters.

Unlike the rest of colonial Africa, the foreign experts had to work under the control of Ethiopians, whom "they have to guide from below" (Clapham 1969, p. 103). Remarking on the position of foreign experts in Ethiopia, Clapham wrote:

> The guiding principle has generally been that foreigners have been treated on their merits as individuals, and freely used where they have been useful, so long as they possessed the patience and discretion essential for them to fit into the Ethiopian system; but any undue influence on Ethiopian affairs, especially by organized groups of a particular nationality, has immediately aroused hostility. Ethiopians have been jealous of their independence, and have welcomed foreigners only so long as they stayed in what has been regarded their proper place [*Ibid*].

Despite the transfusion of the new blood of modern bureaucratic personnel into the old body of the patriarchal-patrimonial order, the culture of abstract and impersonal norms hardly took firm root in the state bureaucracy. This was primarily due to the slow progress towards "dehumanization" of rule (Weber 1978, vol. 2, p. 975). The predominance of the personal, overlapping jurisdictions, the heavy weight of the Emperor in the *shum-shir* process, ethnic, regional, and personal favoritism, nepotism — such were some of the practices that impeded the development of rational bureaucracy. Throughout Haile Selassie's reign, the state bureaucracy was run akin to a master-servant relationship; the patrimonial norm continued right up to the end of our period (Haile Kiros 1978, pp. 134-5).

A good example of the personal nature of the bureaucratic apparatus was the mass culture of belief in personal, face-to- face communication with officials. There was a public mistrust of written communication: people thought that their cases would find the right solution only when they addressed the issues in person to the responsible official.

Overall, the state bureaucracy was an amalgam of patrimonial and legal-rational rules, with the former dominant in the realms of interpersonal relations, and the latter present in technical organization (Ricci in McEwan ed. 1968). The patrimonial aspect was a continuation of the "traditional" pattern of rule, while the legal-rational aspect was that of "modernity." It is the transition from the former to the latter that is known as "modernization", the so-called "passing of traditional society," as Daniel Lerner called it [1965].

CHAPTER 6

THE DESTRUCTION OF OLD AND FORMATION OF NEW CLASS RELATIONS

Separation of Producers from the Means of Production

The separation of rulers from the means of administration in Ethiopia proceeded simultaneously with the separation of the producers from the means of production. This process of economic separation — the complement of the military, political, and judicial separation of rulers from the means of administration discussed in Chapter Five — can be studied from two angles: *rist*, and non-*rist* regions. In *rist* regions, the separation resulted in massive prostitution, begging, urban unemployment, employment in urban households as maids and servants, and employment in the army. In non-*rist* regions of the South, it led to rural proletarianization. Let us look at these two processes more closely.

Separation in *Rist* Regions

There were three basic reasons for the separation of producers from the means of production in *rist* regions: (1) economic bankruptcy due to loss of legal cases; (2) commoditization of *rist* land; and (3) demographic pressure on land and exhaustion of soil fertility.

Court Cases

It is said that litigation is second nature to Ethiopians.[1] Perhaps so. The intricacies of the *rist* tenure, the names and genealogies that need to be recited from memory, the inability to read and write, etc., were some of the hurdles peasants faced. Some people, especially retired men, started court cases just to pass time! Winning litigation was as heroic as winning battle. After all, what is litigation but pacific war.

In this culture dominated by litigation, peasants were almost always the losers. Not knowing even their age and birth dates, every step of the modern legal process was a trap for them.

Peasants know their age through big events. Time is counted as the passage from one big event to another. Hence when a judge asks a peasant how old he is, the normal answer the peasant gives is that during the Italian invasion, during the battle of Sagale, during the peasant uprising in Gojjam, during the great famine, etc., he was just beginning to plow the land, or he was married for a year, etc. Since the time the big events took place is known, and since the age in which a boy becomes a man (called *nafs mawaq*, coming of age) or begins to plow is known, the age of the peasant can be known thus. There are human calendars, professional memorizers of big events, the human computers of peasant culture, who know not only the dates of the big events, but also the major and minor protagonists of these events, especially war events. Events are, hence, no ephemeral vapors of Braudel. For peasant culture, events are calendars of historical time, both societal and individual. The clergy, as opposed to the peasant, know their birthdays and those of their kin. Even here, it is in the name of the Gospels — Luke, Matthew, Mark, and John — that the year is counted. *Zamana Matewos* (period of Matthew), etc., is how years are counted, such that after a four-year cycle one comes back to the same *Zamana Matewos*, etc. But still, the clergy know the exact year, day, and hour of birth.

To start a legal case, the peasant had to hand over a written complaint to the court which he chose to go to. He had to pay for the *tsahafi* (writer). In urban areas, it may be required for the letter to be typed, hence the peasant had to pay the typist. In front of every court were gathered a coterie of professional writers who knew not only how to write, but also how to write in the language of the law. By the time the peasant reached the court with his letter, he might discover that the writer had not quoted the right article of the legal code to which his case pertained to. For this, he had to find a *tabaqa* (lawyer). Mostly without legal training, a good many ex-churchmen, these were self-taught lawyers who had memorized the articles pertaining to all cases, since many of the cases had to do with land, homicide, theft, or arson. The peasant had to consult the lawyer to get a written letter of complaint, with the necessary articles of the legal code cited. For the service of the lawyer, the peasant had to pay.

Every rank of modern professional legal experts the peasant came into contact with, to whom he had to pay his way through, were so many steps towards his ruin. At the same time, the road of the ruin of the peasant created so many divisionings of labor and their functionaries. The ruin of the one was the condition for the existence of the other. Since there was no fixed amount to be paid to the lawyer, it was the peasant who normally lost, since he could not pay as much as his antagonist who was usually an urban dweller with "lots" of money. By the time the peasant reached the court, a good part of his possessions had been sold off for the payment of legal professionals.

Not knowing how to read and write, the peasant "signed" letters with his fingerprints, letters whose contents he did not know. It was not uncommon for a peasant to "sign" statements in police stations that were read to him differently from what was actually written. Interestingly enough, though, when the actual letter was read in the court, which had the "signature" of the peasant, the peasant would scream loud that he had nothing to do with the letter, withdraw his "signature," and tell the court that he "signed" an oral letter written differently. Since such cases happened often, the right of the peasant to disclaim his "signature" was recognized. Despite Spinoza, ignorance was a sufficient argument.[2]

The peasant was notorious for not giving straight answers to questions raised in court. Knowing quite well that if he gave a direct answer to a question he would not be given the chance to explain why he did the things he was accused of doing, the peasant always started with the circumstances that led him to the alleged illegal act, rather than with the act itself. The judge was interested in the act; the peasant in the conditions that led to the act. That was why peasants needed more time than allotted to them to explain their case. For the judge, facts speak for themselves; for the peasant, facts need circumstantial interpretation. Legal "rationalism" and peasant "traditionalism" were expressed through their respective approach to the relation between act and the social conditions that led to the act.

The courts were notorious for their *qataro* (postponement of hearings). Every additional postponement put more burden on the peasant who had to leave his work to go to towns where the courts were located. Since he may need to pass a few days in town, he needed to bring food and some money with him. The more postponements there were, the more the peasant was pauperized. For some judges, postponements were the means of lengthening time in order to accumulate as much bribe as possible from both sides of the litigation divide. Since the peasant could not compete with his urban counter-litigant in the offering of bribes to judges, he had to bring his sheep to be offered to the judge as a bribe. Normally, sheep as bribe were given to judges on market days, mostly Saturdays, so as to give the impression that the sheep had been bought at the market, not offered as bribe. A rustic, half-naked, rag-tag peasant pulled the sheep that took him years to raise to the house of the judge, telling the wife or the maid that this sheep was bought by *getoch* (the wealthy man.) The sheep was received with politeness, everyone in the transaction knowing the filthy business quite well. Butter, grain, labor-service, etc., almost anything was offered as bribe.

This was not the end of the case, though. Friends and relatives of the peasant would advise him to go for *yegbagn* (appeal), an appeal that could take him all the way up to the Imperial Chilot. So began the horror of appeal, with the same hierarchy of professional writers to be consulted, new articles to be cited, etc. It was not uncommon for people to pursue a legal case for decades, and in the event of death, pass it on to their children who inherit court cases from their parents alongside *rist*. Losing a court case was, among other things, dishonorable and shameful.

The contradiction between the numerous hurdles of the legal process and the economic resources at the disposal of the peasant resulted in utter pauperism. Selling whatever was left of his possessions, the losing peasant had two options left: sell his labor-power to a prosperous peasant nearby, or leave his parish for the glittering towns. Whichever way he decided, his separation from the possession of the means of production had now reached a point of no return.

One of the fundamental causes of litigation was *gafahagn* (You pushed me), i.e., one is pushing his territorial domain into someone else's. Trees, ditches, fences, etc., were used to demarcate one's territorial sovereignty from others. Normally, it was in the name of erecting new fences that the push would take place. A mere one-foot push would unleash the notorious process of *muget* (litigation) that may not end even in one's lifetime.

Land was the fundamental bone of contention among litigants. Belonging in the same *rist* kin group, or even the same family, did not in the least help avoid conflict among members of the group. The degree of animosity among relatives is indicated in the saying, *esatena zamad karuqu naw* (Fire and relatives should be handled from a distance.) A kin was the closest relative, but also the closest enemy. The relationship among members of the kin group was first and foremost a relationship of subjects linked to each other by a common claim to *rist*. They were relatives because they shared *rist*; they shared *rist* because they were relatives.

In the *rist* regions, the modern court system spelled the ruin and pauperization of the peasant. It was one of the most important factors of depeasantization.

Commoditization of *rist* Land

The second main reason for depeasantization was commoditization of land. It had three aspects. First, *rist* claimants living in towns wanted their share of *rist* to be sold and the money given to them since they could not use the land themselves or did not want to arrange share-cropping with their co-*rist* possessors in the countryside. Given the rapid expansion of commodity production in the post-Italian period, *rist* itself came more within the commodity circuit. Second, peasants themselves began to sell their part of *rist* to pay for litigation cases, market transactions, taxes, etc. Third, an entire category of people excluded thus far from possessing *rist* land in the *geber* system now started to get access to land ownership.

Muslims and craftsworkers were landless tenants in the *rist* regions under the *geber* system. With the development of commodity-money relations, they could now buy land as private property. And since they were "forced to be free" of the entanglements of the *rist* system, they owned the land they bought with relative peace of mind. In less than three decades after the end of the Italian occupation, a good many of the big land and real estate owners in the towns of the *rist* regions were Muslims and former craftsworkers. As they had been engaged in commodity production and exchange for centuries, the demise of the *geber* system opened up fortunes for them in transforming their hoarded money into capital. Their success in capital accumulation was such that in Dabra Marqos, capital of one of the most conservative Christian regions in Ethiopia, the richest man was Sheta Leyaw, a former craftsman, who was on his way to buying almost all the land of the town. Next to him were Muslim merchants engaged in grain trade. One of the grievances of peasants in the 1968 uprising in Gojjam was that Muslims and craftsmen were allowed to buy land from Christians.[3]

Peasants in *rist* regions were thus conducting two battles simultaneously. One, against each other, the war of all against all that the *rist* system engendered, which got worse as commoditization of land intensified; and, two, peasants as such fighting in defense of their *rist* rights from being destroyed by the intrusion of private landed property (see Schwab 1972, Chap. 8). Thus, the same *rist* system that tore the peasants apart also united them. The defense of the *rist* system was peasants' class struggle against proletarianization, their last stand to maintain *rist* possession rights. Overall, peasants succeeded in slowing down the process of transformation of *rist* land into large private holdings. This, however, did not prevent them from being depeasantized on a massive scale.[4]

Population Growth and Soil Exhaustion

The population of Ethiopia was not known until a few years ago, when a relatively accurate census was taken through the thousands of peasants and urban dwellers associations. For more than a decade under Haile Selassie's reign, the population was said to be twenty million, with no growth. Although the official population growth rate was frozen for years, its increase could be seen from the fragmentation of *rist* land into increasingly shrinking sizes as new households were formed. The demographic pressure on *rist* land was reduced in part by migration of peasants into urban areas in search of jobs. A peasant hardly ever return back to his parish once he left for town. *Men yetzhe lemalas?* (What do I have to take back?) was the cumbersome realization of urban pauperism that weighed upon the recent ex-peasant. Heading off for town in anticipation of a better life and not finding it, the return to his former parish was blocked by the barbed wire called shame.

Prostitution as a Vocation

> Of all human relationships, prostitution is perhaps the most striking instance of mutual degradation to a means, and this may be the strongest and most fundamental factor that places prostitution in such a close historical relationship to the money economy, the economy of 'means' in the strictest sense [Georg Simmel 1978, pp. 376-77].

Prostitution was one of the most important indicators of depeasantization in *rist* regions. The disintegration of peasant households led to massive female migration to towns. In 1970-71, there were 51,312 people employed in the manufacturing industry in Ethiopia. In 1974, there were 80,000 prostitutes in Addis Ababa alone, 25 percent of the adult female population of the city! (Laketch Dirasse 1978, p. iv). It is shocking to compare the number of prostitutes in Addis Ababa *alone* with that of civil servants in the whole country. In 1968, there were 132,000 civil servants, excluding the military personnel (Haile Kiros 1978, p. 138). If we add the number of people working in the civilian bureaucracy to that of the industrial manufacturing proletariat, it was still less than the number of women engaged in prostitution! In 1974, the total number of prostitutes in the country was estimated at 335,000 (Laketch 1978, p. 1). Simply put: by the end of Haile Selassie's reign, the number of women engaged in prostitution in Addis Ababa alone was one-and-a-half times the number of the industrial manufacturing proletariat of the whole country put together!

A prostitute is known as *setagna adari* (one who spends the night as a woman, i.e., without a husband.) Prostitution on a massive scale started during the 1936-41 Italian occupation (see Sbacchi 1975, pp. 311-30; Laketch 1978, pp. 35-37). Prior to that, there were women known as *qemet* (kept-woman) and *yachen garrad* (thigh-servant) whose clients were the notables (Laketch 1978, pp. 10-11).

There were over 300,000 Italian men in Ethiopia during the occupation, of whom more than 90 percent did not have their families with them (Sbacchi 1975, p. 311). Hence, prostitution by Ethiopian women was the only means of keeping the "sanity" of Italian men. Sbacchi wrote:

> There were never enough white prostitutes to meet the needs of the Italians in Ethiopia. Thus, Lessona, Terruzzi and Mussolini all proposed setting up houses of prostitu-

> tion with Ethiopian females for use by Italians only. Itinerant companies of prostitutes visited forts, villages and the most isolated Italian outposts. From the very beginning, while Italian troops were advancing into Ethiopia from the north, Italian authorities were busy establishing brothels to meet the needs of the soldiers and also facilities to prevent the spread of venereal disease. Ethiopian females could exercise their profession only if they attached a special sign to their homes. Houses for officers had a yellow flag; for Italian soldiers and workers, the house was marked by a green flag; and for colonial troops, a black flag. Those females who would not subject themselves to the bi-weekly medical visits or who operated outside their assigned quarters were fined 30 to 200 lires [*Ibid*, pp. 312-3].

The dependence of Italian troops on Ethiopian women was "disturbing" for the Fascists. "Some [of the Fascists] felt that the Italian conquerors were conquered by the Ethiopian 'weaker sex' . . . . the Italian allegedly debased himself spiritually and sank morally to the lowest point" (*Ibid*, p. 308).

Although prostitution on a massive scale started with the Italian occupation, it did not die out with the end of the occupation. In the postoccupation period, prostitution gained a life of its own and spread like wild fire.

The history of prostitution in Ethiopia remains yet to be written (Pankhurst, *JES*, 12, 2, 1974). The most comprehensive study yet is Laketch Dirasses's Ph.D. dissertation, "The Socio-Economic Position of Women in Addis Ababa: The Case of Prostitution" (1978). Her basic thesis is that prostitution is "a means of maximizing economic and social opportunities under extreme labor market constraints, [and that it] has provided a livelihood for thousands of Ethiopian women" (*Ibid*, p. vi). Our interest here is not in prostitution per se, but rather in the process of female depeasantization that ended up in prostitution.

Based on Laketch's work, we can offer the following analysis of the class, ethnic, and religious backgrounds of prostitutes in Addis Ababa in 1974.

Class Background

According to Laketch's survey of prostitutes in Addis Ababa, which constituted 25 % of the prostitute population of the whole country in 1974, the largest percentage (42%) of prostitutes came from households that had peasant fathers. Of this, 77.3% were tenant peasants. The next highest percentage (30%) of fathers' occupations was made up of clerical workers, soldiers, and guards; 23.5% of fathers' occupations varied from priests to merchants and day laborers; 4.5% of the sample did not know their fathers (*Ibid*, p. 62).

As to their mothers' occupations, 93.5% of the prostitutes had mothers who were "housewives"; 1.5% were petty-traders, 1% maids, and 3.5% brewers. "None in the sample reported that they had mothers who were prostitutes" (*Ibid*). Looking into the previous occupation of the prostitutes sampled, Laketch came up with the following distribution: housewife, 54%; student, 27%; domestic servant, 7.5%; factory worker, 5.5%; and never employed before, 5.5%; and 67.5% percent of the women were married at least once.

Ethnic and Religious Background

Ninety-six percent of the prostitutes in Addis Ababa belonged to the Ethiopian Orthodox Christian faith, 2.5% were Muslim, while the remaining 1.5% belonged to Catholic or Protestant persuasions (*Ibid*, p. 63). In a country where Muslims are estimated to be about 40% of the population, it is surprising that almost all the prostitutes in Addis Ababa were Ethiopian Orthodox Christians. As far as ethnic identification goes, 60.5% of the prostitutes reported that they were Amhara, 19% Oromo, 10% Tigrayan, and 3.5% Eritrean. Since the ethnic identification of prostitutes is of critical importance for our discussion of depeasantization in *rist* regions, we reproduce below Laketch's table on the ethnic distribution of the prostitutes.

Since Gojjame women are famed for their sexual prowess, for they do not undergo clitoridectomy, many non-Gojjame prostitutes identify themselves as Gojjame, thereby raising their price.

Given that the percentage of Amhara women engaged in prostitution was well above the percentage of Amharas to the total population, it seems that poverty, continuous fragmentation of *rist* land, freedom of mobility, environmental degradation, famine, starvation, and lack of cash crops like coffee are some of the factors that rendered Amhara regions most prone to disintegration and women to prostitution.

Table 1.
Frequency distribution of reported ethnic identity of prostitutes in Addis Ababa.

Ethnic Group	Relative Frequency (%)
Shoa Amhara	25.5
Wolloye Amhara	17.5
Gojjame Amhara	11.5
Gondare Amhara	6.0
Tigre	10.0
Eritrean	3.5
Shoa Galla	12.5
Arusi Galla	2.5
Harrar Galla	2.5
Wollega Galla	0.5
Adere	1.0
Gurage	3.0
Italian Ethiopian	0.5
Amhara & Galla	1.5
Gurage & Amhara	0.5
Amhara & Tigre	1.5
Total	100.0

[*Ibid*, p. 67].

Another case is the negligible presence of prostitutes from the southern regions. Over half of the peasants in southern regions were tenants (Cohen and Weintraub 1975, p. 51). In 1975, there were 285,200 people living in the ten major urban settlements of the southern regions, of whom close to half were found in the two cities of Dire Dawa and Harar alone (Mulatu and Yohannes 1988, p. 139). The population of the three largest cities of the South — Dire Dawa, Harar, and Jimma — together add up to to 189,400, i.e., well over half of the entire population of the ten largest southern cities put together. On the other hand, the entire population of the ten largest southern cities constituted only about 25 % of the population of Addis Ababa alone. The number of prostitutes in Addis Ababa alone was 30 % of the population of the ten largest southern cities. In other words, the population of prostitutes in Addis Ababa was equal to the population of the largest southern city, Dire Dawa. A good many of the prostitutes found in the cities of the South were migrant prostitutes, mainly from Addis Ababa, and other cities like Nazareth.

During the coffee harvest season in January, a large labor force of male, migrant, part-time proletarians from Northern and Central Ethiopia moved to the coffee regions of the South, especially Kaffa, in search of jobs. They were followed by a large coterie of prostitutes who moved to such towns as Jimma and Agaro to exchange sexual service for money. Saving their money, some of the migrant prostitutes became bourgeois prostitutes.

Prostitution in Ethiopia has become a means of livelihood for hundreds of thousands of women. These women raise families, send their children to schools, attend church, and participate in other civic affairs. From the smallest town of a few hundred people to the largest city of over a million, prostitution has penetrated deep into the very fabric of urban Ethiopian society. Prostitution is to urban Ethiopia what apple pie is to America.

Prostitution in Ethiopia, as elsewhere, has its own hierarchy, its own stratification. There are prostitutes for every class in the country. In a "class analysis" of prostitution, we find four categories of prostitutes. The first category consists of "proletarian prostitutes," those who sell their labor power to bar and restaurant owners as waitresses as well as sexual service to the public. This group is engaged in full-time prostitution. The second category can be called "petty bourgeois prostitutes." Living mainly in small towns, petty bourgeois prostitutes are engaged in the production and/or sale of *talla* and *katikala* (household beer and household hard liquor, respectively). They engage in prostitution as an additional means of income. This group is engaged in part-time prostitution. The third category consists of "bourgeois prostitutes." They own bars and restaurants and hire women to work as waitresses and prostitutes. To this extent they are bourgeois. On the other hand, they are also engaged in prostitution themselves, "reserved" for the well-to-do.

The bourgeois prostitute, alongside the nonprostitute bourgeoisie engaged in bar and restaurant business, pay the proletarian prostitutes an extremely low wage. The rationale behind this is that the proletarian prostitute is not just a proletarian, but also a prostitute, so that the meager wage she gets as a proletarian is compensated by the "lots of money" she makes as a prostitute. The prostitute's economic situation is not much different from that of the part-time agricultural workers who supplement their low wages by keeping a small farm around their households.

A fresh young woman from the countryside works for the bourgeois prostitute for free as long as she gets "free" food and sleeping place in the bourgeois prostitute's house. There she learns the profession of her lady. The urban "big men" turn their eyes to the fresh country woman, away from the rather "used-up" madam. That is when the poor woman is thrown out of the house, for she is now competing with the madam in her own home. The thrown-out woman may end up as independent prostitute, maid, beggar, or give her former profession a second try.

In the process of recruiting fresh country women for the booming prostitution market, the ex-peasant-turned-bourgeois prostitute plays a significant role. Her glittering gold rings, necklaces, shining shoes, lubricated face, soft hands, beautiful clothes, hair as straight as the horse's, and polished Amharic are temptations hard to resist for the country woman. In all her material success, the ex-peasant-turned-bourgeois prostitute need not utter a word to convince the country woman about the beauty of urban life and the profession of prostitution. The glitter on her speaks for itself. The only question she finds difficult to answer is the question of customers. (Sleeping with a Muslim? Who knows who is who in big cities?) If she can win over her potential candidate on the Muslim question, then hundreds of customers will beat a path to her door. Successful ex-peasant prostitutes return to their birth place quite often since they do not have to worry about the question, "What do I have to take back?"

Ex-peasant-turned-bourgeois prostitutes have contributed a great deal of money for the building of churches, thereby "fighting the good fight" against the forces of Satan. The churchmen appreciate this Christian duty. As to the sin of prostitution, they can absolve it with a mere "May God forgive you!"

The fourth category of prostitutes is the "independents." Not selling their labor power to capital, not engaged in the production and/or sale of *talla* or *katikala*, crowded in hovels, available and ready for anyone, not choosy, charging the cheapest rate, these are the souls identified in Marxist theory as belonging to the class of lumpenproletarians. These prostitutes, some of whom known as "street girls" and not found in smaller towns, render Addis Ababa a city of lumpenproletarians.

These four classes of women engaged in prostitution constitute perhaps the largest employer of Ethiopian urban women outside the household!

As there is a hierarchy in the status and price of prostitutes, there are also differences in the social backgrounds of prostitutes. Almost all low-income prostitutes are recent migrants from rural areas. The chance of climbing up the ladder of the hierarchy of prostitution depends, in most cases, on how beautiful and attractive one is. The most difficult hurdle for a new recruit in the business of prostitution is to reject her peasant humanism and accept the civilization of bourgeois reification. If she passes the test of reification, the ex-country woman becomes a "civilized" citizen of the world. She becomes a modern Stoic, a secular Christian, a liberal cosmopolite who accepts the equality of all humans in front of the impartial jury, money.

"Upper class" prostitutes are mostly recruited from urban areas, from those who already have an urban taste and "civilized" manners. Nevertheless, the possibility of a "lower class" prostitute rising up the prostitution ladder is not closed. Since prostitution is "rational," it does not have a hereditary or religious bias against social mobility. All one needs is excellence in the profession.

Prostitution has its own logic of disenchantment and rationalization. To the degree that prostitutes become reified in their social relations, so are they "rational". After all, what is Weberian rationality if not the replacement of humanism by the impersonal institutionalization of the cash nexus? The process of commodity fetishism and impersonalization is developed in prostitution more than in any other sphere of social relations. It is quite revealing to see hundreds of thousands of women selling their bodies piecemeal as a commodity in the midst of one of the most devout Christian countries in the world. Alas, it was easier for Ethiopia to be "modernized" through prostitution than through any other sphere.

The massive engagement of women in prostitution is a manifestation of the deep structural crisis in the position of female labor power in the countryside. Women fled from the drudgery of a male-dominated countryside to urban areas. Some became prostitutes. For female sexuality, prostitution is a radical transition from monogamy to public sex, *from personal dependence on one man to absolute independence from one man and total dependence on all men*.

Female rural emigration was most pronounced in lower-middle and poor peasant households. For the well-to-do peasant household, no profession is more respectable than agriculture. It is to the lower-middle and poor peasants that the glitter of urban life is attractive. Not that they do not prefer agriculture, but because they can hardly make ends meet. Peasants rarely leave their household unless life reaches a negative point of no return. In that case, the household breaks up, the wife runs to an urban area and may end up as prostitute or maid, while the husband either hires himself out to a nearby rich peasant or moves to urban areas and may end up as a day laborer, guard, servant, etc.

Hardly a male adult grows up in urban Ethiopia without knocking at the door of a prostitute, which is always open. The transition from boyhood to adulthood in urban Ethiopia now takes place through the modern initiation rite called prostitution. Armed with tetracycline tablets, the urban adult male is the most reliable customer of the prostitute. Tetracycline tablets have made the young men feel invincible. And yet, millions have become devout customers of venereal diseases transmitted through prostitution.

Prostitution is the most concentrated expression of the disintegration of the Central Ethiopian social structure and the magnitude of depeasantization. Tenancy and Muslim polygamy[5] in the South kept female labor power relatively immobile, while the freedom of movement of peasants of *rist* regions enabled them to run away wherever they wanted to. The easiest job available for women in towns is prostitution.

If such has been the fate of depeasantized women, it is otherwise with men. Their employment is coterminous with jobs available. And yet there is an equivalent of prostitution for men — begging. Like prostitution, begging is a profession without limits, and it has been run by people of mostly Central Ethiopian extraction. It is these two professions of begging and prostitution that gave Amharas their "bad name." Alas, the Amharas were found at both ends of the social divide: at the topmost, personified by the "Conquering Lion of the Tribe of Judah," and at the bottom, engaged in such professions as begging and prostitution.

It has been argued that prostitution among the Amhara has a lot to do with their liberal attitude towards sex, as opposed to other groups, that concubinage was normal among Amhara men, especially the notables. It is, however, in the material social relations that the phenomenon of prostitution should be studied, not in some psychological-cultural explanation or so-called value systems. Humans do not live on values alone; if they do, the values are coded signifiers of their material needs.

If such were the processes of separation of the producers from the means of production in *rist* regions, how different were they in the non-*rist* regions of the South? To discuss this, we now turn to the formation of new class relations.

The Formation of New Class Relations

Landlord-Tenant Ratio

The landlord-tenant ratios in the South are scematized in the following:

Table 2.
Tenant population as percentage of total ruarl population in private tenure areas.*

		Tenant population					
		With Wholly		Part-Owned &		Total	
	Rural	Rented Land		Part-Rented Land			
Province+	Pop.	No.	%	No.	%	No.	%
Arussi	690,600	307,764	45	50,724	7	358,488	52
Gemu Goffa	583,300	249,412	43	21,633	4	271,045	45
Hararge	1,435,570	703,429	49	71,778	5	775,207	54
Illubabor	515,375	376,224	73	10,307	2	386,531	75
Keffa	969,100	571,769	59	29,073	3	600,842	62
Shoa	3,585,000	1,828,350	51	573,600	16	2,401,950	67
Sidamo	1,987,590	735,408	37	39,751	2	775,159	39
Wollega	1,064,100	574,738	54	49,715	5	624,453	59
Wollo	2,061,800	341,586	16	330,396	16	671,982	32
Total	12,892,435	5,688,680	46	1,176,977	9	6,865,657	55

*Source: Central Statistical Office, National Survey Sample of Arussi, Gemu Gofa, Hararge, Illubabor, Kefa, Shewa, Sidamo, Wellega and Welo (Addis Ababa: Central Statistical Office, 1963-1967).
+The province of Bale was not included in the National Survey Sample. Low population figures indicate problems in survey (cited in Cohen and Weintraub 1975, p. 51).

With the exception of Wollo (Wallo) and Shoa (Shawa), all the provinces in Table 2 above are southern regions. And yet, with the exception of Illubabor, the highest rate of full and partial tenancy is from Shawa. The absolute number of peasants who lived under tenancy in Shawa was larger than those of the provinces of Arsi, Gemu Gofa, Hararge, Illubabor, and Keffa combined.

By comparison with Shawa, whose Amhara part was *rist* region, those of Begemeder, Gojjam, and Tigray — the other *rist* regions —

had much lower percentages of peasant tenancy, as shown in Table 3. The distribution of cultivated areas between owners and tenants in privately-held non-*rist* regions is shown in Table 4.

Table 3.
Tenant population as percentage of total rural population in communal tenure areas.*

Subject	Province+		
	Begemeder	Gojjam	Tigre
Rural Population	1,087,200	1,344,500	1,410,800
Tenant Population			
Wholly Renters	97,848 (9%)	172,785 (13%)	98,756 (7%)
Part Owners and Part Renters	65,232 (6%)	95,024 (7%)	257,218 (18%)
Total	163,080 (15%)	267,809 (20%)	355,974 (25%)

*Source: Ethiopia, Central Statistical Office, National Survey Sample of Begemidir, Gojam, and Tigre (Addis Ababa: Central Statistical Office, 1963-1967).
+The provinces of Bale and Eritrea were not included in the National Sample Survey (cited in *Ibid*, p. 52).

Table 4.
Distribution of total cultivated area between owners and tenants in private-tenure non-*rist* areas.*

Province+	Owned		Rented		Partially Owned/Rented	
	No.	%	No.	%	No.	%
Arussi	84,789	38	114,178	51	25,542	11
Gemu Goffa	29,246	48	28,592	46	3,855	6
Hararge	117,312	39	136,690	46	45,647	15
Illubabor	26,055	34	47,718	62	3,433	4
Keffa	58,278	29	135,246	67	8,225	4
Shoa	314,826	28	618,409	55	191,144	17
Sidamo	125,728	64	68,453	35	2,302	1
Wollega	102,905	46	110,291	49	10,792	5
Wollo	239,654	61	56,438	14	96,267	25
Total	1,098,793	39	1,316,015	47	387,207	14

*Source: Ethiopia, Central Statistical Office, *National Survey Sample of Arussi, Gemu Gofa, Hararge, Illubabor, Kefa, Shewa, Sidamo, Wellega and Welo* (Addis Ababa: Central Statistical Office, 1963-1967).
+The province of Bale was not included in the National Survey Sample (cited in *Ibid).*

The degree of development of private landed property in Ethiopia is best manifested in the holdings of one who was considered to be the biggest landlord in the country, *Ras* Masfen Selashi. He was supposed to have owned 50,000 gashas of land in Kaffa and Illubabor, plus substantial estates in Shawa and Hararge (Gilkes 1975, p. 120). In Hararge province, "25 people or 0.2 percent of the total landowners have under their control 74.6 percent of the land" (cited in Schwab 1972, p. 71). Since landlords used to register their holdings under various names to reduce taxes, the exact amount of their ownership could not be known. Of these landlords, the incidence of those who were absentee and lived in towns can be seen in Table 5.

Table 5.
Extent of absentee ownership in private-tenure area.*

Province	Absentee Owners as percentage of Total Owners	Percentage of Total Owned Area Held by Absentee Owners	
Measured land		Unmeasured land	
Arussi	28	27	-
Bale	15	12	-
Gemu Goffa	10	42	8
Hararge	23	48	-
Illubabor	42	42	-
Keffa	18	34	16
Shoa	35	45	22
Sidamo	25	42	5
Wollega	29	28	-
Wello	26	13	27

*Source: Ethiopia, Ministry of Land Reform and Administration, *Reports on Land Tenure Survey of Arussi, Bali, Gemu Gofa, Hararghe, Illubabor, Kefa, Shewa, Sidamo, Wellega and Welo* (Addis Ababa: Department of Land Tenure, 1967-1970) (cited in *Ibid*, p. 40).

Twenty five percent of the landlords in these provinces were absentee landlords owning 33 % of the land (Gilkes 1975, p. 120). A good many of these landlords turned the rent they extracted from peasants into capital to be invested in urban areas. The distribution and mode of rent payment in landlord-dominated regions was as follows (Table 6).

Table 6. Distribution of tenancies in private-tenure areas according to province.*

Province	Mode of Payment			
	In Crop & Cash	In Cash Service	In Crop	Labor/and/or/
Arussi	92	7	1	-
Begemder	66	30	3	1
Gemu Goffa	15	70	5	10
Gojjam	70	24	2	4
Hararge	47	42	11	-
Illubabor	25	66	9	-
Keffa	31	64	5	-
Shoa	82	15	3	-
Sidamo	12	84	4	-
Tigre	90	5	5	-
Wollega	37	48	12	3
Wello	84	9	6	3

*Source: Ethiopia, Central Statistical Office, *National Survey Sample of Arussi, Begemdir, Gemu Gofa, Gojjam, Hararge, Illubabor, Kefa, Shewa, Sidamo, Tigre, Wellega, and Welo* (Addis Ababa: Central Statistical Office, 1963-1967).
+The provinces of Bale and Eritrea were not included in the National Sample Survey (cited in Cohen and Weintraub, 1975, p. 54).

The transformation of tribute into rent, and *gabbar* into tenant, took place on the backs of the peasants. The tenants did not know that they had long ceased being *gabbars*, that they were now paying rent, not tribute, until they were about to be evicted from the land by the landlord (Pausewang in Hess ed. *PFICES*, 1979, p. 706). While the labor process remained the same, the social relations of appropriation had changed. That is why to continue referring to the ex-*naftagna* as *naftagna* and the ex-*gabbar* as *gabbar* is a mistake.

The transformation of tribute into rent and *gabbar* status into tenant meant a fundamental shift of importance in the human/land equation. In the *geber* system, people were more important than land, for land without people working on it was useless. It was the *gabbars* that paid tribute, not the land. In the tenant system of landlordship, land became more important than peasants, since not only can land be sold at a higher return than *gabbar*-tribute, but also, for anticipated rent, land could be left empty waiting for a price rise in the future. Land had become capital. The landlord is the personification of this landed property.

There were three forms of rent extraction: *erbo arash, siso arash,* and *ekul arash* (one-fourth cultivator, one-third cultivator, and one-half cultivator, respectively), meaning that rent extractions were 1/4, 1/3, or 1/2 of peasants' produce paid in cash and/or kind. In all three cases, the tenant had to pay an additional tithe, i.e., 10 % of his produce to the landlord (Cohen and Weintraub 1975, p. 53). As more land became alienable, *erbo* arrangements declined while *ekul* rose. *Siso* arrangements were the most widespread. As can be seen from Table 6, in the coffee-growing regions of Sidamo, Gemu Gofa, Keffa, and Illubabor, well over 64 % of rent payments were in cash, followed by Wollega and Hararge, also important coffee-growing regions. The lowest percentage of cash payments for rent was from Tigray. Overall, with the exception of Arsi, all the other places that paid rent in crops were *rist* regions of Northern and Central Ethiopia. Although tenancy and private landed property were the weakest in *rist* regions, the main reason for the low percentage of payment in cash was due to the relatively slower development of commodity production. It is no accident that the coffee-growing regions, the most integrated to the world economy, happen to be the most commoditized.

The development of commodity production and the transformation of land into commodity spelled tremendous growth of utter poverty and destitution. The Enlightenment-cum-Marxist faith in progress aside, the introduction of bourgeois commodity relations into the countryside brought about *more* misery and poverty for the peasant, not less. Mesfin Wolde Mariam concluded from his detailed empirical study, *Rural Vulnerability to Famine in Ethiopia, 1958-1977* (1984) that "more than 81% Ethiopian peasants live under abject poverty, *not relative but absolute poverty*" (*Ibid*, p. 90; emphasis added).

> [These peasants] starve three to six months every year when natural conditions are said to be normal, that they periodically sink from their precarious subsistence level into the abyss of famine, and that they are unable to sell their labour seasonally for some cash or grain are not exceptional but regular conditions of existence. Especially during the critical 'hungry season', the daily affirmation of their penury and helplessness in the face of the humiliating misery and suffering of their wives and children drives them into debt [*Ibid*].

The extent of debt in rural Ethiopia and the degree of peasant exploitation by money lenders is described by Mesfin:

> Rural Ethiopia had become a fertile ground for people who had some cash reserves, to double or even quadruple it in less than a year. Lending money, or grain, at extortionate rates of interest that might often reach 200% or more a year was becoming a very lucrative business. . . .
>
> . . . about 46% of the indebted peasants were landowning peasants, 32% were tenants, and 19% were partly owners and partly tenants. The most important single purpose of these loans was for purchasing food [*Ibid*, pp. 90-92].

The fact that land-owning peasants were more indebted than tenants, that the main reason for their need to borrow money was to buy food, is an additional pointer to the observations made earlier that owning land by peasants like in *rist* did not imply better living conditions than that of tenancy arrangements.

The Formation of the Proletariat

As elsewhere in the capitalist world economy, the formation of the proletariat in Ethiopia followed the same "laws" and patterns of separation from the means of production. As elsewhere in peripheral capitalism, this proletarian labor was not totally dissociated from possession of the means of production.

Looking at the industrial proletariat engaged in manufacturing in 1970-71, there were 51,312 workers with a total gross value output of a little over 300 million U.S. dollars (Markakis and Nega 1978, p. 47). The average daily wage of unskilled laborer in Addis Ababa until the mid-1970s was between 1 and 1.25 Ethiopian dollars (about U.S. $ 0.50) (*Ibid*, p. 45). In 1970, out of a total of 466 industrial establishments, 223 were located in Shawa, 165 in Eritrea, 42 in Hararge, and 10 in Wallo. The remaining 26 plants were distributed in the six provinces of Begemidir (9), Sidamo (8), Kaffa (4), Gojjam and Tigray (2 each) and Arsi (1). Bale, Gemu Gofa, Illubabor, and Wallaga had no industrial plants at all (Gilkes 1975, p. 146). Shawa alone had close to half of the plants in the whole country, and more than half of all industrial workers (*Ibid*). The combined number of industrial plants in Shawa and Eritrea was 84 % of the whole country, while Addis Ababa and Asmara alone had 70 % of the total (*Ibid*, p. 147). This is an excellent indicator of what Samir Amin called peripheral capitalism. Ethiopia has been a peasant ocean with pockets of industrial islands.

Proletarianization as separation from the means of production was the highest in *rist* regions, some of the reasons for which were discussed earlier in the chapter. A major part of this proletarianized mass, especially women, ended up in nonproletarian occupations. The gap between proletarianization as separation from the means of production and proletarianization as a class relation to capital defines the limit of pauperism. This gap was the widest among the Amhara people of the *rist* regions. Hence, their overrepresented presence in the company of pauperism.

The Awash valley, which became a center of capitalist plantations and sugar industry, was inhabited by pastoralists. When the land was given as concession to the HVA, the pastoralists were evicted. This pastoralist group was the Gile, an Oromo group. The Gile disintegrated and disappeared as a community (Markakis and Nega, 1978, p. 56). Further up north, the Afar pastoralists were evicted from their grazing areas (Harbeson, *Rural Africana*, 28, 1975). The Tandaho Plantation Share Company, a subsidiary of the Mitchell Cotts Group, started cotton plantations in the Awash valley. Italian and Israeli firms joined the venture. Plantation capitalism changed the lives of the Afars. The Afar Sultan of Awsa, Ali Mirah, recognizing "the economic potential of cotton production, as well as the danger of being dispossessed by foreign capital,"

> . . . began to block the latter's expansion by setting up his own plantations in the path of the foreign firms. A number of Afar chiefs followed his example, and set their people to work on their plantations for little or no pay. Impoverished highlanders also descended to the valley to work as sharecroppers.
>
> . . . By 1973, about one-third of the total irrigable land had been put under cultivation. The grazing area was correspondingly reduced, and the Afar were forced to congregate on less fertile land, with overpopulation and overgrazing as the result. Dispossessed by capitalism and betrayed by their traditional leaders, the Afar were doomed when the drought hit the region in 1973 [*Ibid*, pp. 56-7; see also Bondestam, *JMAS*, 12, 3, 1974].

At Setit Humera, the northwestern side of the Ethiopian plateau, a large capitalist agricultural venture was being developed by a new breed of Ethiopian entrepreneurial bourgeoisie. A good many of them having been educated at the agricultural college at Alam Maya, this new breed of energetic bourgeoisie engaged itself in the production of agricultural commodities, soybean being the most important, for the world market.

Notorious for its malaria infections, the Setit Humera region absorbed tens of thousands of part-time proletarian converts, most of whom came from the *rist* highland regions.

> By the end of 1971 [Setit Humera] contained some 500 farmers and about 700,000 hectares were occupied; and a further 50,000 [farmers] were being employed as seasonal workers, largely from the depressed areas of Eritrea and Tigre [Gilkes 1975, p. 129].

Setit Humera became the Awash of the northwest. Close to the Sudanese border, Setit Humera opened another front of Ethiopia's link with the world economy.

Another region of proletarian labor concentration was the southwest. The coffee-growing regions of Kaffa and Illubabor were centers of attraction for thousands of part-time proletarians needed during the picking season. The declasse elements of the *rist* system living in towns filled this labor demand. Many a peasant of *rist* regions threw off his plow and headed for Setit Humera or Jimma. Those who went to Setit Humera were lucky to return back alive. A good many of them died, unable to resist the forces of extreme heat, hunger, and malaria. As elsewhere in peripheral capitalism, part-time, migratory proletarian labor was the norm in agricultural capitalism in Ethiopia.[6]

The Formation of the Bourgeoisie

Following the trajectory sequence of feudalism-transition- bourgeois revolution, Addis Hiwet wrote:

> Unlike their European counterparts the Ethiopian feudal monarchists did not have to promote capitalist development as long as Imperialism could afford them an organized state that could maintain them in power and as long as their own social-economic needs were more than sufficiently catered for by the goods of the world-capitalist sys-

> tem the promotion of internally generated capitalist relations were tasks they would never undertake, i.e. their own liquidation as a class. . . . Feudalism would definitely be disrupted by a host of capitalist relations . . . but its conscious disintegration was not called for by the monarchists [*RAPE,* 1, 1975, pp. 78-9].

Furthermore, Addis Hiwet commented:

> Unlike its European (and Japanese) and so much like its Tsa*rist* counterpart, the modern state arose in Ethiopia not as an agency of social-economic change but as a method, as an apparatus of administration and government with tremendous resources and capacity for repression [*Ibid,* p. 79].

And Bahru Zewde noted that, "the political impotence and economic strength of the nobility became the hallmark of Ethiopian absolutism, of advanced feudalism" (1991, p. 230). These remarks of Addis Hiwet and Bahru Zewde were typical of the Ethiopian left intelligentsia. To these views, Patrick Gilkes added his weight:

> The growth of a national bourgeoisie has been stifled at birth and the feudal landowners have acquired two other groups to strengthen their position — the *comprador* and bureaucratic bourgeoisie. Both have been infiltrated thoroughly by feudal elements. They have assisted the landowning class to invest in capitalist development through mechanization on the land, and thus provided for a mechanized feudalism [!], rather than any true development of capitalist modes of production [1975, pp. 169-70].

Addis Hiwet's "feudal lord" ruling class, Bahru Zewde's "advanced feudalism," and Patrick Gilkes's "mechanized feudalism" notwithstanding, it can be seen from the discussion we had so far that the label "feudal" attached to the social system of 1974 Ethiopia is a misnomer. The monarchist ruling class had committed class suicide and become born-again bourgeois to the extent of becoming "advanced" and "mechanized." The fact that the Ethiopian noble bourgeoisie did not duplicate the accomplishments of their Western or Japanese counterparts is not to be explained by their feudal nature but rather by Ethiopia's position in the capitalist world economy. Yes, the Ethiopian bourgeoisie were engaged in the so-called tertiary sector. They did not carry out an industrial revolution. They invested in land, real estate, bars, hotels, transport, small-scale industries, and, belatedly, large-scale capitalist agriculture. But all this was not due to the existence of feudal relations of production becoming a "fetter" on the development of bourgeois productive forces. A mere look at the rest of independent Africa shows a similar pattern, although there was no feudalism there. What is explained as due to feudalism is due rather to peripheral status in the capitalist world economy.

The formation of the Ethiopian bourgeoisie started from the imperial court. After all, who was more bourgeois than Haile Selassie? Bourgeois does not just mean one engaged in production, as opposed to circulation or distribution. A person engaged in the restaurant business, insurance, or real estate is no less bourgeois than the one engaged in the production of shoes. These are different sectors of bourgeois relations, or else one has to assume a bourgeois class that excludes bankers, landlords, real-estate developers, insurance agencies, airline owners, hotel and restaurant owners, etc. And yet a production-centered bias, a la Althusserian Marxism, has been the blind spot of the Ethiopian left on the class identity of the bourgeois. The bourgeois is more than just confined to the "abode of production" (see Teshale Tibebu 1990).

As elsewhere in peripheral capitalism, the state in Ethiopia has been a means of capital accumulation, giving rise to a class identified as bureaucratic bourgeoisie in Maoist literature, recoined as "state bourgeoisie" by Charles Bettelheim (1975). The state became a terrain of "substitute accumulation" in which state financial resources were transformed into means of private enrichment. Whether the money was used for productive investment or for the accumulation of Mercedes Benzes of different colors, the bourgeois class identification is not altered thereby.

"Development plans" such as road construction, building of schools, hospitals, clinics, churches, etc., were also used as means of accumulating capital. It was quite interesting to listen to the national radio about the various "development projects" in the country, and the amount of money contributed from the regions where the development was supposed to take place. A good part the money collected from the people went into the pockets of state officials and was converted into capital, mostly used for buying urban land, construction of houses for rent, or buying of rural land to start large-scale capitalist agriculture. In Ethiopia, as elsewhere in peripheral capitalism, the state is not only an "instrument" of oppression, but also a source of capital accumulation and formation of the bourgeois class. Frantz Fanon called it the state of the "bourgeoisie of the civil service."

Looking at the pattern of formation of the bourgeoisie, two groups stand out most: Eritreans and the Gurage. Both have been internal migrants from their home areas to cities, mainly Addis Ababa. Contemptuous of "dirty jobs," the Amhara aristocratic "mentality" admires the Gurage for doing any kind of job. Eritreans have a derogatory saying about the Amhara, that they prefer begging to hard work. Indeed, one hardly sees Eritrean or Gurage beggars on the streets of Addis Ababa or other cities.

Learning their "protestant work ethic" from Catholic Italians during colonial rule, Eritreans moved to the rest of Ethiopia with their business expertise. Their business acumen gave them a sense of superiority over first and foremost their ethnic brothers and sisters on the other side of the Marab. As Eritreans moved south, companies of destitute Tigrayans descended on Asmara and other cities looking for menial jobs. Hence the notorious Hamasien/Agame stereotyping.

If the Gurage and Eritreans became bourgeois through "hard work" and upward economic mobility, a good many of the Amhara ruling elite made it in a different way: they became bourgeois in and through the state. As they were dominant in the political realm, their capitalism was "political" capitalism, state capitalism, as opposed to the "real," "economic" capitalism of the Eritreans and Gurages. From the beginning of the twentieth century up until the 1960s, the terms Gurage and coolie were synonymous. When one needed a coolie, all one had to do was shout, "Gurage, Gurage!"

Terrified of the court system, quick to pay their way out of trouble that may take them to the police, the Gurage never understood the rationale for why the Amhara spent years in litigation that ultimately ruined them. The "rationality" of the Gurage "mind" can be best expressed by their avoidance of the litigation process. Cost/benefit analysis is the closest to their heart, but not to the Amhara. For the latter, winning a court case, no matter what the cost, is at least as important as saving money in the bank, if not more so. For the Amhara, man is not yet *homo-economicus;* man is *homo-respectus*. The Gurage, on the contrary, bought themselves the distinction of being the "Jews of Ethiopia" for their enterprising spirit.[7]

Despite their economic success, the Gurage economic bourgeoisie were looked down upon by the Amhara political state bourgeoisie. Civilized manners on the part of the Gurage economic bourgeoisie were thought to be lacking. They were perceived as economic animals who measure the worth of a person by the size and content of his pocket. They were rich, but rude.

Contrary to the Gurage bourgeoisie were the Amhara state bourgeoisie. As an outgrowth of the nobility of the geber system, the dominant Amhara aristocratic bourgeoisie perceived themselves as "cultured" and trained in the "civilizing process," in the elaboration of "civilized manners" (Elias 1978). Their model was the English aristocratic-bourgeoisie — rich, cultured, well-mannered.

In the midst of this "civilizing process," things began to change fast. The Amhara aristocratic bourgeoisie and other sectors of the state bourgeoisie started to give their children names that were uncommon under the *geber* system. Amharic names are meant to be meaningful such that when a person's name is put with his father's name, the combination has meaning. Amharas should be addressed with their full name, i.e., their given name together with their father's name, in addition, sometimes, to the grandfather's name. To address a person by his/her given name alone is an insult, as if saying that the person is a slave or illegitimate. Some Shawa Amhara names under the *geber* system included Asfa Wassan (Expand the frontier), Ashanafi (Winner), Mandafroh (Who dares to challenge you), Asagadach (for female, She makes them bow), Damesaw (Destroy it), Atlabachaw (Cast your shadow upon them), Letyebalu (Let them prostrate themselves in front of you), Yechanaqu (Make them worry), Andargachaw (Unify them), Aytanfesu (Make them not breathe), Afenie (Suffocator), Ashaber (Terrorizer), Manyazehal (Who dares give you order), Shawaragad (for female, One who makes Shawa tremble), Yayahyerad (Let him who sees you tremble), Balachaw (Hit them), Gezachaw (Rule over them), Astateqe (Arms provider), etc. (See Reminick 1973, p. 112). My favorite is the name of a famous official, Million Naqneq (Million shaker.)

With the transformation of the warrior nobility of the *geber* system into an aristocratic bourgeoisie, Amharic names of the children of this class of people started to lose their aggressive, expansionist, and domineering character. *As the nobility got civilized, their children's names became soft, pacific, and meaningless.* Moreover, those with Western education started to give their names Western forms. Accordingly, Dawit became David, Endereyas became Andreas, Yeshaq became Isaac, Yohannes became John, Tewodros became Teddy, etc. In modern Addis Ababa Amharic, the imperialism of Shawa names lost ground to meaningless, impersonal, and unmatching names. Names became "rational."

As opposed to this "rationalistic" scramble for name change, the more "backward" Amhara regions retained their original custom of giving meaningful names. In Gojjam, for example, people take their time debating about the name to be given to a newborn child such that when it is put in front of the father's name, it becomes meaningful. Names in Gojjam are given mainly on the basis of events of personal tragedy or happiness, the former being quite the norm. Names like Tsagaye (My grace), Alalegn (He is for me), Banch Amlak (for female, By your God), Irq Yehun (Let there be reconciliation), Kassaye (My compensation), Tasfaye (My hope), Dasta (Happiness), etc., express feelings of social needs articulated in precisely thought-out processes of name giving. Behind the formalism of names is the substantive concern over household labor, as well as the fear of eternal damnation in the afterlife. In Gojjam, as elsewhere, a name like Tasfaye Taddesse (My hope is renewed) refers to the renewal of hope of parents in seeing a new baby boy. The happiness is for having a new helping hand in production, as it is for seeing the fruit of one's "seed." As elsewhere in patriarchal cultures, baby boys are preferred to that of baby girls.

By and large, Amhara names in Gojjam, both under the *geber* system and later, are not like the imperialist names of Shawa — aggressive, expansionist, domineering, missionary. The fact that not a single Gojjame ever became *negusa nagast* (Emperor Susenyos was coronated in Gojjam, but he was not Gojjame), the fact that Gojjam had only one *negus* in its entire history (Takla Haimanot) partly explains this. On the other hand, Shawa had been the center of Amhara state power for centuries since 1270.

The change or retention of "traditional" Amhara names was an expression of the degree of the progress of the "civilizing process." The more "civilized" one became, the more names moved in a meaningless direction, and vice-versa. For rural people, meaningful names were psychological compensations for their material deprivation.

Other than Muslims, who retained their Islamic names, the exception to all this scramble for adopting "civilized" Amharic names were the Tegreans on both sides of the Marab divide. The children of Aksum stood fast to their names, and hardly looked at Amharic names for adoption. If there were similarities between Amhara and Tegrean names, it was not because the latter adopted the name of the former, but because many Amharic and Tegrean names are similar.

With oppressed nationalities of the South, it was otherewise. They adopted "civilized" Amharic names, for who would dare to introduce themselves with such names as Qalbesa, Magarsa, Tenker, Lapiso, Chaltu, Jalata! Names like these were the object of ridicule and scorn by the Amhara-Tegrean couplet. Hence, urban dwellers of southern nationalities gave their children "civilized" Amharic names, followed by a southerner father's name, as in Tasfaye Magersa.[8]

To sum up our discussion on the formation of the bourgeoisie in Ethiopia, Zoltan Gyenge's remarks are worth quoting:

> The developing Ethiopian bourgeoisie was subject to a twofold influence. Firstly, that of the commercial and industrial layer of foreign origin living in Ethiopia. It could acquire capital and wage its initial ventures under the influence of this group, from which it took over its "specialized" knowledge, connections and capitalist exploiting practices. Secondly, by serving the social layer of the nobility and developing connections with the state, it came under the influence of this layer too. In order to further develop and expand its business ventures it has to pass on some of its profits to the families of the nobility sitting in government offices. This bourgeoisie then come to be interwoven with the corruptly bureaucratic administration by the gentry. In its majority it engaged in non-productive ventures, bought houses and lands, and strove to get rich fast under the conditions of the feudal system [1976, p. 16].

The Tentacles of Peripheral Capitalism

One of the manifestations of the impact of state sovereignty on the processes of incorporation and peripheralization is in the realm of the multinationality of foreign capital. Under colonial rule, the colonial power has a monopoly of exploitation of its colonies, while this is not the case under political sovereignty. The best case of incorporation-peripheralization without colonization in Africa is that of Ethiopia. The Ethiopian ruling class played its political card well, such that those foreign powers that were heavily represented in capital investment had little, if any, political weight, while the U.S., the most important political-military patron, had a meager economic role. American interest in Ethiopia was primarily strategic, not economic.

Besides the relative autonomy Ethiopian rulers had, the fundamental processes of incorporation and peripheralization in Ethiopia were not much different from those of colonial Africa. Perhaps the most important result of Ethiopia's state sovereignty lies in blocking the possibility of massive land alienation. Mussolini's plan of settling five million Italians in Ethiopia would have changed the political economy of the region beyond recognition, and making Ethiopia the largest colonial settlement in Africa.

The processes of peripheralization in Ethiopia took place in an original neocolonial relationship, which makes Ethiopia, alongside Liberia, the oldest neocolonized state in Africa. The need for a neocolonial solution to the "Abyssinian problem" was the motive of the 1906 Tripartite agreement entered into between Britain, France, and Italy. In this agreement, signed on December 13, 1906, the three powers divided the country into separate spheres of influence, "the Blue Nile Basin for Britain, the hinterland of Eritrea and Italian Somaliland that would connect the two territories to the West of Addis Ababa to Italy and the then under construction Djibouti-Addis Ababa zone to France" (Legesse Lemma 1979, p. 120). The significance of this treaty lies in the fact that none of these powers attempted direct colonization, jointly or individually. The relative autonomy of the Ethiopian state enabled it to exploit the contradictions among these powers. Marcus wrote:

> Although Ethiopia had not been a participant in the negotiations, she gained considerable stability from the agreement. It ended the active imperialism of France and England in the Horn of Africa and eliminated for a time the possibility for Italian expansion [*JES*, 2, 2, 1964, p. 40].

Other than this treaty, the American Consulate in Aden, Arabia, in a February 6, 1922 dispatch, observed the necessity of a neocolonial approach to the exploitation of the mineral and human resources of Ethiopia:

> The desirability of discovering a peaceable solution to the problem of exploiting the mineral resources of Abyssinia is great, but it will be by no means easy. National jealousy between the French, Italian and British, the nations most closely interested in the surrounding territory and not keenly aware of the possibilities of Abyssinia, is already intense, and an abrupt or strong move by any one of them or of their subjects seems certain to precipitate very grave inter-

> national complications, if not actually lead to war. . . .
>
> The military difficulty of subduing the country would be tremendous, because of the spirit and fighting ability of the inhabitants and the difficult nature of the topography. . . . The Abyssinians have displayed an ability to maintain a fairly stable government capable in general of maintaining public order and it is believed they are in fairness entitled to retain and enjoy their own country, but it is exceedingly doubtful if they will long be permitted to do so, unless some way is found to permit the peaceful exploitation of the resources of the country [Steffanson and Stanret eds. 1976, vol. 3, p. 5].

That Ethiopia was not first colonized, then decolonized, and at last neocolonized, as was the rest of Africa, does not change the nature of the neocolonial relations.

Looking more closely at the national origins of foreign capital investment in Ethiopia, we find that Dutch capital engaged in the sugar industry was the largest foreign capital in the country. Indian, Japanese, Italian, American, French, British, Greek, Israeli, and Swiss capitalists invested in various fields.[9] These included sugar, cotton, coffee, textile, cereals, canning, fruits and vegetables, banking and insurance. Multinational corporations were actively involved in Ethiopia (Bondestam, *African Review*, 5, 1975).

Foreign investment in Ethiopia started in the late nineteenth century through concessions granted to foreign companies by Emperor Menelik, the most important of which was the railway line construction from Djibouti to Addis Ababa given to the French (Christopher 1942). Greek, Armenian, French, and Arab capitalists were actively involved in capitalist ventures from the very beginning of the twentieth century (see Garretson 1974). This continued up to the present, only interrupted by the 1936-41 Italian occupation.

Peripheral capitalism in Ethiopia of the 1960s is shown in Tables 7 and 8.

Table 7. Major Exports (Eth.$M).*

Commodity	1966	1967	1968	1969	1970
Coffee	155.7	139.2	153.3	173.9	181.3
Hides and skins	35.7	29.8	24.9	29.2	24.5
Pulses & cereals	23.7	20.7	21.7	24.2	18.9
Oilseeds	21.7	22.7	21.4	23.2	28.4
Others	40.7	40.3	44.7	47.6	52.7
Total	277.5	52.7	266.0	298.1	305.8

*Source: Africa Development, Nov. 1971, p. 11

Ethiopia's world trade was dominated by a single commodity, coffee. "In 1973 . . . 96% of the country's exports by value was agriculture, while 3.7% was accounted by manufacturing (excluding manufactured food, beverages and tobacco) and only 0.3 by mining and quarrying" (Legesse 1979, p. 217).

While exports were agriculturally monocultural, the composition of imports by item for the years 1962, 1967, and (projected) 1972 was as shown in Table 8.

Table 8. Composition of Imports 1962/67 with 1972 Projection Eth. $M).*

	1962	%	1967	%	1972	%
Capital goods	58.5	25.1	109.6	27.6	233.0	33.4
Intermediate goods (includes fuel)	47.8	20.4	137.1	34.5	218.8	31.4
Consumer Goods	127.6	54.5	150.4	37.9	245.3	35.2

*The province of Eritrea was not included in the National Sampe Survey. Low population figures indicate problems in survey (*Africa Development*, Nov. 1971, p. 11).

The preponderance of an extroverted economy of coffee,[10] hides, and skins; the feeble development of bourgeois class of producers, concentrated instead in the tertiary sector; the massiveness of the proletarianized, relative to the proletariat proper; the extremely low level of wages, despite high productivity; the regional unevenness of capitalist development — these were some of the characteristics of peripheral capitalism in Ethiopia (see Assefa Bequele and Eshetu Chloe 1969).[11] They defined the level of “development” of the country by the time the old order died of senility in 1974.

Epilogue

THE UNMAKING OF ETHIOPIA

ON September 12, 1974, the Conquering Lion of the Tribe of Judah, Haile Selassie I, Elect of God, Emperor of Ethiopia, His Imperial Majesty, King of Kings, the 225th direct descendant of Menelik I — son of King Solomon of Jerusalem and Queen Saba of Ethiopia — was deposed (Legum 1975).[1] So ended the lineage of the oldest Christian monarchy in the world. So ended the sixteen centuries of Christian theocracy in Ethiopia. (Since then, God was no more allowed to interfere in the internal affairs of the State. Secularism in Ethiopia is barely two decades young.) So ended the concentrated expression of the power of the Ge'ez civilization.

Renowned by the world, revered by Africa, and reviled by students at home, Haile Selassie died in 1975, buried in an unmarked grave in Menelik's palace. Exhausted by historic anachronism and physical senility, the "Conquering Lion of the Tribe of Judah" was finally conquered by a handful of his own men-in-uniforms who broke their oath of allegiance to protect him. Their guns, meant for keeping Ethiopia safe from enemies, found Haile Selassie to be Ethiopia's number-one enemy. Ethiopia was divorced from her marriage with Haile Selassie.

The Provisional Military Administrative Council, otherwise known as the Derg, that replaced Haile Selassie was made up of 120 young officers with zealous passion for the development of their country. With the slogan *Ityopya Teqdam* (Ethiopia First), the Derg called upon the people of Ethiopia to rise up from their long slumber of poverty and backwardness. The Derg carried out what it thought was the peoples' will — to depose the aging monarch and lead Ethiopia into the twenty-first century.

The Derg was as much a product of the revolution as it was an active participant in it. The February 1974 revolution was triggered by the 1973 oil crisis, the covered-up famine in Northern Ethiopia, the bleeding revolution in Eritrea, and many other factors. A detailed discussion of the post-1974 period needs a book of its own. The attempt here is to skim through the last two decades and draw some lessons from them.

In the seventeen years of its iron-handed dictatorship, the Derg carried out a *social revolution*.[2] The revolution destroyed the power base of the ruling class of the Ge'ez civilization. By daring to declare Christians and Muslims equal, by separating State and Church, by expropriating land from the landlords and making it available to the peasants, and by using a new state language — the language of Marxism — the Derg indeed accomplished a revolution.

At the head of this revolution was Mengistu Haile Mariam. Like Tewodros before him, he came from a humble background. Like Tewodros, his was a fiery passion of Ethiopian state nationalism. Like Tewodros, he was an implacable enemy of the status quo, of the powers that be. Like Tewodros, he was hated by the people. Like Tewodros, he was the nemesis of the Church. Like Tewodros, he fell by the weight of his incalculable cruelty. His murderous reign was unequalled in modern Ethiopian history. And yet, he had succeeded in one area: He dealt a mortal blow to the old order of lordly leisure. How happy he must have been to spit at those whom he once was forced to prostrate himself in front of, those who saw in him nothing but a *barya*. For Mengistu, as for Stalin, oppression was a lived experience. Perhaps that may explain his obsessed hatred for the old order.

As a destroyer of the key arsenals of the Ge'ez civilization — from its land base (*gult* and big landed property) to its air defence (the divine rights of kings) — the Derg changed the political landscape of Ethiopia beyond recognition. The most important outcome of the Ethiopian revolution was the rise of the people of the South to public visibility. Ethiopia was no more the land of Solomonic rulers with divine mandate to rule. To make the revolution even more deadly, it was personified by that phenotypical refuse of the old order — Mengistu Haile Mariam. He "looked like" a "*barya*." Nay more, he came right after Haile Selassie — that mesmerizing, charismatic, frail, "Arabic-looking," petit Solomonic giant!

I am not indulging myself in a psychological profile of one of the most ruthless leaders Ethiopia has ever seen in its history. Nor I am trying to infuse a biographical element into such a critical issue as the Ethiopian revolution. But it would be scholarly treason not to write about how the people saw Mengistu and felt about him, that he was not just a murderer for them, but also a *barya*. This double negativity in the public perception of Mengistu should be part of our construction of the history of the Ethiopian revolution. Mengistu was more than just a killer; he was also a cultural representative of denigrated phenotypes.

Mengistu was the first leader in Ethiopian history of the last seven centuries — beginning from the so-called restoration of the Solomonic dynasty in 1270 — who did not claim Solomonic lineage. Had, for example, Endalkatchaw Makonnan been, by some miracle, a revolutionary leader like Mengistu, it would not have been that profound culturally, for he was of "Solomonic" descent. The Ethiopian revolution led by Mengistu Haile Mariam was of tremendous *cultural* significance in that the Ge'ez civilization was also a cultural civilization articulated in the phenotypical superiority of people that "look like Ethiopian" (*ityopyawi yamimasel.*) Mengistu did not "look like Ethiopian." He was thought to be a phenotypical refuse who belonged more in the company of his "brothers" like Idi Amin than sitting in the revered majesty of Menelik's palace. The public gossip that Mengistu could pass for a brother of the Liberian Samuel Doe, when the latter was on a visit to Ethiopia, was just part of the phenotypical prejudice that runs deep in the many cultures of the Horn of Africa.

This epilogue is not an attempt at a comprehensive discussion of the many facets of the Ethiopian revolution. Nor is it one of comparing the virtues and vices of the different revolutionary organizations. One thing we are certain about is that the Ethiopian revolution was one of dual competition: competition of revolutions, and competition of nationalisms. Every organized political group throughout Mengistu's reign of terror, from the Ethiopian Peoples Revolutionary Party (EPRP) to the Eritrean Peoples Liberation Front (EPLF), called itself "revolutionary." Each was also nationalist, or at least labelled so by others.

Since I cannot discuss the various aspects of the simultaneously dual revolutions — class and national struggles — of the post-monarchic period, I focus on my metaphorical query "The Unmaking of Ethiopia?" Since we now are living in an age of unbridled nationalism worldwide, I deal in the remaining pages with what has been referred to as the "national question" in the discourse of the Ethiopian left intelligentsia. For this intelligentsia, as for Ernest Gellner, "The Amhara empire was a prison-house of nations if ever there was one" (1992, p. 85). To this "prison-house of nations," we now turn.

What do we mean when we say that one nationality oppresses, dominates, imposes its culture upon, and exploits another nationality? In considering these questions, it is instructive to look at two historical situations: the racial structures of countries like South Africa, the U.S.A., Australia, etc., or Western democracy in the global colonial context, on the one hand, and precapitalist polities and empires, on the other.

In the first case, national/racial oppression means that the dominant race/nation denies the dominated racial/national groups the same rights that it enjoys. For example, it gives democratic rights to all those defined as white, but forbids the oppressed racial/national groups to have access to these rights. Race/nation sets the boundary that separates those who can enjoy democratic rights from those who cannot. This is racial democracy, as the history of the U.S.A., South Africa, Australia, etc., shows.

In racial democracy, we can indeed talk of racial or national oppression in that the entire "white race" has some tangible social, political, economic, and cultural advantages over the entire "black race" by the mere fact of being white. Apartheid is the most extreme expression of this. There are certain fundamental privileges that even the poor white enjoys that a black person cannot. The "poor white" thanks God for not making him a "nigger." This gives him a sense of superiority over blacks. Racial/national laws keep the oppressed groups as far separate and down as possible. A bureaucratic power structure enforces a racial/national pattern of segregation. In sum, it is a situation of all-round dominance.

In the second case, precapitalist empires, relationships were quite different. In imperial rule, the sovereign's unquestioned authority was such that he appointed his favorites to the highest positions of state power. Merit and personal loyalty to the person of the sovereign were the basis of recruitment and promotion. Ethnic ties and royal blood were less of a factor.

The Ottoman Empire, Imperial China, the Abbasid Caliphate, the

Ethiopian polity, etc., were in one aspect or another and to varying degrees, examples of this meritocratic system. Their political systems provided for a great deal of political and social mobility. A slave captured in war could become a general if, in subsequent service, he proved himself courageous and resourceful, and personally loyal to the sovereign. For example, the Mamlukes, a ruling military corps in Egypt, were originally slaves. In Ethiopia, where there was no tradition of hereditary aristocracy, the *negusa nagasts* often raised to the highest positions of rank and influence people from the humblest background. This practice was known as "raising from the dust" or "lifting from the dust," as Emperor Tewodros described his ascent to power. Being non-Amhara was no barrier to such appointments. For example, during the latter part of Emperor Menelik's reign and in the period after his death, *Fitawrary* Habte Giorgis was one of the most powerful men in Ethiopia. Yet not only was he from a humble, non-Amhara background; he was brought to Menelik's court as a young war captive. Haile Selassie used to great political advantage this ethnic-blind system of recruitment. His appointments to high offices hardly showed any ethnic preference. He was as comfortable (even more so), with Oromos from Wallaga as he was with Amharas from Gondar. He only made sure that the appointee was personally loyal to him.

In this context, we should raise what I call the "Amba Geshan syndrome." Ethiopian emperors, as elsewhere in Africa and the Ottoman, Byzantine, etc., empires, believed that to rule their polity undisturbed, the most potent sources of challenge to their rule, their brothers, had to be politically neutralized. Hence the practice of putting younger brothers in prison at the various ambas (secluded mountain hideouts), the most famous of which was Amba Geshan (hence the name I give to this phenomenon). The practice entailed the detaining of imperial relatives, their legs tied — as befit their royal persons — with gold chains. The consequence was that brothers of reigning emperors had less chance of upward social mobility than ordinary retainers who might have won the emperor's favor through loyal and competent service.

Moreover, Ethiopian sovereigns, like their precapitalist peers elsewhere, forged political ties by giving their sons and daughters in marriage to even defeated enemies across ethnic and regional lines.

The tradition of ethnic-blind incorporation in Ethiopian history was even more pronounced among the Oromo. Through what

Mohammed Hassen called the "Oromo genius for assimilation," conquering Oromos on their path of expansion assimilated those whom they conquered, thereby enlarging their number.

Contrast this with Western racial policies. With the intent of preserving white dominance, the modern Europeans, wherever they established their rule outside Europe, made it a point to declare inter-racial marriage illegal. The Mixed Marriages and Immorality Acts of apartheid South Africa are simply recent reminders of a long tradition of the modern West's obsession with racial narcissism, exclusivism, and purity in its "contact" with "people of color."

The Ethiopian system tried, however, to achieve the opposite: to prevent ethnicity from becoming a base for political supremacy by arranging interethnic marriages. This policy was sometimes pushed to extremes. For example, Muslims were forcibly baptized and brought into political and matrimonial bonds. Emperor Yohannes IV's wife, Halima, an Afar, and *Negus* Mikael of Wallo, are cases in point. Both were Muslims before converting to Christianity. Because personal loyalty to the person of the Emperor was what kept the imperial system running, it was frequently an advantage for an aspiring court retainer to be of nonroyal background. Gabreye of Tewodros, Alula of Yohannes, and Gobana of Menelik — to mention the three emperors' most outstanding military leaders of the nineteenth century — all came from humble backgrounds. The last two were non-Amhara. Ethiopian emperors — like their Ottoman, Byzantine, African, etc., peers elsewhere — preferred those without royal connections since they were less likely to have aspirations of ascending to the throne, and would therefore serve them more loyally than those with imperial blood. (The immense power held by the chief eunuch at the Ottoman Porte is just one case in point.) Historically, this process helped to create an interethnic mix at the center of imperial power. In addressing the national question in Ethiopia, the cumulative effect of such appointments should be closely examined. Regrettably, it has been ignored by the modern Ethiopian intelligentsia.

The biggest mistake the Ethiopian left intelligentsia made on the national question — with no intent of malice, but rather out of heroic, good-will naivete — was to read Ethiopia as if it were Western Europe or America. This has been the main problem in the discussion on the national question. Yes, Ethiopia was seen as different from the West, as a semifeudal, semicolonial entity. And yet, this was more of theoretical sloganeering than an assessment based on a detailed study of Ethiopian history.

With this background in mind, and the distinction between the Ge'ez civilization and the South as a constant given, I believe the national question in Ethiopia should be addressed as follows.

There are *two sets* of national questions in Ethiopia. The first set is the highland core of the country. The second set is the hot lowland areas along Ethiopia's international borders with the Sudan, Djibouti, and Somalia. These regions were more neglected than oppressed or exploited, since the hand of the central government and the ruling class stretched thin. The climate helped them as a protective shield against the power of the highland dominant class. The highland has been the main source of the ruling class's power, and hence the main center of national oppression. We can divide it into two main categories, with two different national questions: Tigray, on the one hand, and the South, on the other. Although there may be varying dimensions of national oppression in all, the underlying factors in each are complex and encompass elements pertaining to ethnicity, class, historical patterns of acculturation at the power center, religion, the role of Amharic as a language of assimilation, etc.

The position of Tigray in the terrain of power arrangement was *qualitatively* different from that of the South. Under Haile Selassie and before him, Tigray was on average one among equals, sometimes more, sometimes less equal than others. Contrary to the myth propagated by Tigrayan nationalists (and, of course, there is no nationalism without myth), Haile Selassie handled Tigray with deference and sensitivity. He established political bonds with the Tigrayan aristocracy through royal marriages. Tigray was left with a wider margin of regional autonomous space than any other, save perhaps Afarland. It may seem paradoxical, but one of the reasons why Tigray exhibited such nationalist passion is because it had autonomous space for nationalist exercise. Addis Ababa might have ruffled Tigrayan feathers sometimes, but a systematic policy of dismantling the political and cultural foundations of Tigray was never a policy; nor could it have worked had it been attempted.

Thus, when the leaders of the Tigrayan Peoples Liberation Front (TPLF) argue that class oppression can sometimes be manifested in national oppression, they may have a point. Moreover, when they say that at certain historical junctures, the national question can be more important than that of class, they may be right also. The irony is that the former does not apply to Tigray at all. It applies only to the South. And even there, there were cases like Wallaga where the power of northern settlers was weak. It is therefore not accidental that the area with the most pronounced Oromo nationalism is Wallaga — the Tigray of the South.

As to the second claim, it is purely ideological. With equal passion and justification, the national question can be replaced by religion, gender, class, environment, etc., as *the* most important question to be addressed. How else can a feminist, for example, be a feminist without putting gender as the primordial question of all questions, or a "fundamentalist" religion? Let us not forget that nationalism is patriotism, i.e., a male domain. A starving peasant in Wallo does not give a damn about the ethnic identity of the person sitting at Menelik's throne.

What, then, is the nature of Tigrayan nationalism? It is a compound of aspirations for hegemony and struggle against *Amharic* linguistic oppression.

For a good part of Ethiopian history, Tigray and Shawa were the two most powerful regional rivals for power. Emperors from Shawa were coronated at Aksum. The Amhara invoke Aksum with pride. Aksum Tseyon has always been the most revered shrine of Christian Ethiopia. The most heroic place in the annals of Ethiopian defiance of European expansion is Adwa, which made Ethiopia a symbol of black pride throughout the world. All these and others have sustained in the Tigrayan a sense of superiority-in-seniority over their historical juniors, the Amhara. The Tigrayans feel that they are the direct descendants of Aksumite civilization, as opposed to the Amhara who have been "bastardized." As Harold Levine put it, the Tigrayans are the cultural aristocrats of Ethiopia. Whatever acrimony there may be between Tigrayans and Amharas, it is a sibling rivalry, or a quarrel between cousins. This can mean either skin-deep hostilities or ugly hatreds, since in the culture of the Ge'ez civilization relatives are the best friends but can also be the deadliest enemies. Although the TPLF has presented its struggle in the new political language of fighting against national oppression, what has been unfolding before our eyes is the resurgence of the power of Tigray one hundred years after the death of Emperor Yohannes IV. It should come as no surprise that after the collapse of Shawa power in the South during the revolution, the most "logical" candidate for replacing Shawa was Tigray.

The tradition of power struggle between Tigray and Shawa was also complemented by competition between Aksum Tseyon and

Dabra Libanos. The Neburaed of Aksum was revered as that of the Echage of Dabra Libanos.

In the historical setting of the Ge'ez civilization, Tigray had acted as a regional power broker, not as a national-ethnic entity. The competition between Tigray, on the one hand, and Shawa, on the other, was not an ethnic competition between Tigrayans and Amharas. However, two main factors — the beginning of modern education, and centralization of power at Addis Ababa — led to the transformation of Tigray from a regional entity into a national-ethnic one; hence the rise of the national question in Tigray.

In the modern educational system, Amharic became the language of instruction throughout Ethiopia. This was perceived as the language of the Amhara becoming dominant over that of Tigrayans. And yet, Tigrayan notables, including Emperor Yohannes IV, used Amharic as their secular language, as the TPLF-dominated Ethiopian Peoples Revolutionary Democratic Front (EPRDF) is doing now. Interestingly enough, in Church education, Ge'ez was the language of neither the Amhara nor the Tigrayans but of the Church. No *qolo tamari* complained about Ge'ez being the language of instruction as opposed to his mother tongue, any more than a modern student complains about English. It is the usage of Amharic as the sole language of instruction *in the modern educational and administrative system* that unleashed other vernacular nationalisms.

Furthermore, the autonomy of Tigray under Haile Selassie was eroded even more by the ever-centralizing forces of the revolution, which in turn alienated Tigray further.

So, on top of the base of the old regional identity of Tigray was imposed a national-ethnic identity, a combined regional-ethnic awareness called the national question. This is the origin of the national question in Tigray. Tigrayan nationalism is articulated by the modern educated elite. As elsewhere, nationalism in Ethiopia is the "invention" of the modern educated elite; and as elsewhere, it flourishes on a systematic "invention of tradition" (Hobsbawm and Ranger eds. 1983) and "imagined communities" (Benedict Anderson 1991).

It is by looking at such historic aspects that we can address the national question in Tigray. We should remind ourselves that no matter how much we may think that history is behind us or that we have gone beyond it, it always leaves behind a pattern, a residue. And in a country like Ethiopia, where things move at a snail's pace, the footprints of history are even more pronounced. This despite the revolution. As the French love to say, the more things change, the more they tend to remain the same.

When we come to the South, things are quite different. Here were *kattamas* of Christian warrior-settlers of predominantly Amhara extraction that were imposed on the local population. The *chawa/balagar* class distinction of the Ge'ez civilization was exported to the South with the vengeance of the rifle. It became part of the *naftagna/gabbar* system. But *naftagna* was nothing but *chawa* with rifle, and *gabbar* nothing but a newly conquered *balagar*. Class and nationality *almost* merged in the form of an Amhara nation-class, but there were Tigrayans and Shawa Oromos in Menelik's army that settled as *naftagna*, too.

It is a mistake to put the people of the South and the Tigrayans together under the singular rubric of national oppression and Amhara dominance. (By South here is meant not a *geographical* South, but a *cultural* South. Accordingly, the Raya and Azabo, Oromo Muslims living in Wallo and Tigray, are the cultural South of Dabra Libanos, although they are geographically north of it.) *National oppression in Ethiopia is not Amharas oppressing non-Amharas. National oppression in Ethiopia is the imposition of the cultural hegemony of the Ge'ez civilization over those outside its embrace.* Those who were national oppressors happened to be so not by virtue of being Amharas, but by virtue of being the personifications of the Ge'ez civilization, its carriers, its functionaries. The chief protagonists of the Ge'ez civilization, the Amhara-Tigrayan couplet, were the Adam and Eve of the Original Sin that was national oppression. They ate the same forbidden fruit together, although the Amhara may have eaten more. They ruled jointly — as senior and junior partners — exchanging seats according to their respective strength. What we are now witnessing under the rule of the EPRDF is the passage of senior partnership from the Amhara to the Tigrayans.

What then is Amhara oppression? What do we mean by it? What does the theory that casts the ruling class in Ethiopia as Amhara mean? Can we talk of Amhara national oppression without also assuming that all Amharas have somehow benefitted from this oppression, no matter what their class, gender, or religion?

In the various discussions on the national question among the Ethiopia Left, the standard reference was the writings of Lenin and Stalin. For example, the argument that although the overwhelming majority of the Amhara are oppressed and exploited, belonging to the dominant nationality has given them a privileged position vis-a-vis other nationalities, is taken straight from Lenin's and Stalin's theory that says although the Western working class is an exploited class, it benefits from colonial and neocolonial exploitation. The Leninist thesis was also extended by the EPRP to include the verbatim transplanting of Lenin's call to transform World War I into a civil war such that when Somalia invaded Ethiopia in 1977, the EPRP thought that it was the Derg that was the main enemy, and not the Somali invaders. That, among others, proved to be its undoing.

Lenin's argument was that the Western working class enjoys a higher standard of living due in part to the super exploitation of the workers and peasants of the Third World. This means there was an economic trickle-down effect of imperialist domination to the Western working class.

Now apply this to Ethiopia and see how did the trickle-down effect worked: Did Amhara workers and peasants benefit from Amhara domination, and if so how? One index is standard of living. Did they have a higher standard of living compared with other nationalities? The answer is an emphatic no. Not only was there no trickle-down effect, but actually, other than Tigray, the overwhelming majority of the Amhara have been more poverty stricken than their non-Amhara counterparts. Some of the reasons for this have been discussed in earlier chapters.

In rural development, there has been no trickle down either. In Shawa, for example, the most "backward" regions in schools, roads, health centers, etc., are the Amhara areas of Menz and Geshe, Tegulet and Bulga, and Merha Bete. To add insult to injury, many an Amhara in rural Shawa lives under cliffs and gorges, competing with monkeys for space, and practicing the back-breaking horror of terracing. Compared to this, Selale or Ambo are Gardens of Eden. In the other Amhara areas of Gojjam, Gondar, and Wallo, development indices have been by far worse than in the South.

If there was no economic trickle down, what about a political one? This can be discussed in the framework of what political rights Amharas enjoyed that others did not. Non-ruling-class Amharas have been in the same political position of lack of political rights as other nationalities. The political establishment in Ethiopia has never been representative of anyone save the powers that be. Haile Selassie's government was not an Amhara government, any more than Mengistu's, unless by Amhara government one simply means head-counting of those in government that were Amhara. Even then, a good many of them, beginning from Haile Selassie and Mengistu

Haile Mariam themselves, were "interesting compromises," to use Bereket Habte Selassie's apt expression of Mengistu Haile Mariam. Haile Selassie was more of an Oromo than Amhara, fluent in Oromogna language, which he spoke in private. His paternal grandfather was Oromo, as was his wife Empress Mannan, a Wallo Oromo, thereby making his children even more Oromo. Haile Selassie's royal family was one of assimilated Oromos. What was denigrated by the Ge'ez civilization was not the Oromo people *per se* but Oromo culture, for it was thought to be uncivilized and unchristian. Hence the very assumption that the Ethiopian ruling class represents a certain ethnic group is a misnomer, perhaps something taken from the American experience where the state represents white Americans as opposed to "minorities."

How about psychological trickle-down, i.e., that the Amhara feel superior to the non-Amhara? This is perhaps the most intriguing aspect of the issue. What makes it so is that the overwhelming majority of the Amhara people, i.e., peasants, do not know that they are Amhara! How can they feel supremacy about something that they do not even know? For the Amhara peasant, and for many who live in small towns, the word "Amara" is contrasted with "Islam," as the quite common Amharic expression *islamna amara* (Muslim and Amhara.) Amhara is a term of religious reference, not of ethnicity. Hence when people identify themselves as "Amara" they mean Christian. When "Amara" is contrasted with "Galla," as in the saying *amarana galla* (Amhara and Galla), the term "Galla" is understood as meaning "pagan," not as an ethnic name. Given the Ethiopian ruling class's ethnic blindness, this was even more so for the peasant. Hence the assumption that even the poor Amhara feels superior to the non-Amhara is a wrong reading of the reality. As in other cases, it is an assumption taken from other experiences that simply do not apply to Ethiopia.

Other than Amhara meaning Christian, the "traditional" Amhara literati identified themselves along lines of *beher*. *Beher* does not mean "nation," a la Stalin. Those who thought so and translated nation as *beher* made a mistake. *Za behere* (of the *beher* of) Dima, Lasta, Sayint, Bulga, Manz, etc. — this is how the "traditional" Amhara intelligentsia identified themselves. *Beher* means land. While the "traditional" Amhara intelligentsia define their identity as *beher*, the Amhara peasants refer to their *qaye* (locality) of their birth. Both *beher* and *qaye* refer to natal places and ancestral graves. This was the double identity of the Amhara, religious and natal.

As to Muslim Amharas, they also have the same religious and natal double identity as the Christian Amhara. The only difference is that instead of being Christian ("Amara,") they identify themselves as "Islam" (Amharic for Muslim).

If, indeed, the Ethiopian ruling class could hardly be defined in ethnic terms, as I argue, what was it then? Since the so-called restoration of the Solomonic dynasty in 1270, the Ethiopian ruling class has been marked by a triple identity: *tabot-Christian religion, Amharic state language, and multi-ethnic origin*; multi-ethnic in the double sense of its ethnic makeup, and also in that the most powerful in it, like Haile Selassie and Mengistu Haile Mariam, were interesting compromises. In terms of policy, it has been an ethnic-blind, theocratic, and militaristic powerhouse that trampled upon any manifestation of popular dissent. No Ethiopian leader felt companionship to his ethnic basis as opposed to others. If Tigray was bombed by Haile Selassie, so was Gojjam. The massacre of civilians at Hawzen in Tigray by Mengistu Haile Mariam's regime was preceded by that of Bichena in Gojjam. If the Ethiopian Air Force bombed open markets in Tigray, so did it in Gondar and Gojjam. The "Red Terror" was perhaps the most ethnic-blind campaign the Mengistu regime ever accomplished so "successfully." And most of its victims were Amhara. The Ethiopian state has been a dictatorial machine that crushes anyone that dares to challenge it with force. To give it an ethnic interpretation is a serious mistake.

It is quite revealing that while anyone from any ethnic origin could climb to the highest positions of political power, this was closed off to non-Christians. *Ledj* Iyasu was driven out of power for his liberal attitudes towards Muslims. As the son of *Negus* Mikael, his alleged conversion to Islam was difficult to disprove. Without any doubt, Muslims have been second-class subjects. John Markakis's Biblical remark that "In imperial Ethiopia . . . it was easier for a non-Christian, who also did not speak Amharigna, to pass through the eye of a needle than to enter the charmed circle of power and privilege" (1987, p. 274) may not be that exaggerated.

If, indeed, the overwhelming majority of the Amhara have not benefitted in the form of economic, political or psychological advantages over the non-Amhara, and given the identity of the Ethiopian ruling class discussed earlier, what then is Amhara domination? We should look at two aspects to answer this question: an all-Ethiopia level, and a regional level.

On an all-Ethiopia level, what is identified as "Amhara domination" is a misnomer for the cultural hegemony of the Amharic language over other languages. As such, the only singular reference to the national question in Ethiopia is the question of language. Although Ethiopian emperors since 1270 A.D. came from different ethnic backgrounds, the division of labor between Amharic and Ge'ez remained unaltered to this day. It was one's facility in the Amharic language rather than actually being Amhara that was necessary for upward mobility. That is why there has always been so many "Amharicized" non-Amharas at the highest positions of state power. Generals Aman Andom (Eritrean) and Tafari Banti (Oromo) and Colonel Mengistu Haile Mariam ("*barya*") were such cases.

Other than the cultural hegemony of Amharic, there is no common, country-wide reference for Amhara oppression. On a regional level, however, the very expression "Amhara domination" can be applied to the South. Here the personifications of the triple dominance of the dominant class — nationality, religion, and language — merged in the person of the *naftagna*. Besides, there were thousands of Eritreans, Tigrayans, Gurages, etc., in the South who were seen as Amharas by the local population.

Ethiopia has been in the midst of crisis of civilizational senility. Unable to extricate itself out of its historic inertia, and yet eager to "catch up" with modern civilization, the tension between her "glorious past" and her miserable present turned the heart of her Ge'ez civilization into a huge expanse of free firing zone, a killing field. The epicenter of this crisis had been along the Marab line. With the collapse of the largest army in Black Africa — thanks to the cumbersome load imposed upon it by Mengistu Haile Mariam, and exhausted by the multiplicity of its enemies — the EPLF and EPRDF entered Asmara and Addis Ababa, respectively, in May 1991. Thus ended the thirty-year war in Eritrea. Two years later, Eritrea became a sovereign state. With that, an episode in the history of modern Ethiopia was closed, and a new one opened. Ethiopia is back to its Menelikan boundary, and Eritrea back out of Ethiopia, a century after its creation by Italian colonialism in 1890. Baptized as EPRDF, the descendants of Emperor Yohannes are presiding over Emperor Menelik's Ethiopia, saying farewell to *Ras* Allula, to Emperor Yohannes, and fighting to keep the Ogaden and "Oromia" within Ethiopia. Alas, how true it is that the more things change, the more they tend to remain the same!

The national-question-comes-first wing of the Ethiopian Students' Movement had won out over that of the class-question-comes-first. And, of course, the former read their victory as a vindication that they have been right all along; and their AK-47s gave them the might to be right.

Let me depart the scene with a reminder and a closing statement. First, the reminder. Next time we write about Ethiopian history, let us start with Kaffa and end with Aksum. Second, a borrowed closing statement:

> It is hoped that Ethiopia will one day be able to transform itself radically and create a democratic system which will right the old wrongs, redress the old injustice, heal old wounds and, more importantly, ensure the genuine equality of all Ethiopians in every facet of life — political, economic, social, and religious, which in turn will guarantee its survival [Mohammed Hassen, 1990, p. 200].

Notes

1. Bahru Zewde's, *A History of Modern Ethiopia, 1855-1974* (1991) is an excellent introduction to modern Ethiopian history. It is a descriptive account of events centered around the deeds of *teleq sawach* (big men). This despite the author's otherwise excellent grasp of theoretical history.
2. Edward Said wrote: "Almost without exception, every Orientalist began his career as a philologist" (1979, p. 98). For Ethiopic as a "pure Semitic speech," see Dillman (1974, p. 3); for the study of the Semitic classification of Ethiopian languages, see Robert Hertzron (1975).
3. Ludolf learned Ge'ez from the Ethiopian ecclesiastic Abba Gorgoriyos of Makana Selassie (of Amhara) who was then living in Rome. See Pankhurst ed. (1965, pp. 56-66).
4. For a bibliography of Ullendorff's works on Ethiopia, see Simon Hopkins, *JSS*, 34, 2 (Autumn 1989), pp. 253-289.
5. Wolf Leslau produced an encyclopedic study of the Semitic languages of Ethiopia. He wrote dictionaries for almost all the Ethiopian languages classified as Semitic — Amharic, Gurage, Harari, Gafat, etc. Some of his works include, *An Annotated Bibliography of the Semitic Languages of Ethiopia* (1965); *Arabic Loanwords in Ethiopian Semitic* (1990); *English-Amharic Context Dictionary* (1973); and *Etymological Dictionary of Gurage* (1979). The last work consists of three big volumes, with a total of over 2,802 pages. Monica Devens was right to call him "the father of Gurage Studies". For a list of Leslau's works on Ethiopia, see Monica Devens in Stanislav Segert and Andras J. E. Bodrogligeti eds. (1983, pp. 1-37).
6. For a theoretical discussion of European traveller discourse of the non-European "Other," see Mary L. Pratt, *Imperial Eyes* (1992).
7. When he saw a sign reading: "Mussolini Invades Ethiopia," in

London, Nkrumah said: ". . . it was as if the whole of London had suddenly declared war on me personally . . . . My nationalism surged to the fore. I was ready and willing to go to hell itself, if need be, in order to achieve my object [of ending colonialism in Africa]" (quoted in S. K. Asante 1977, p. 201).

8. For an excellent critique of Mazrui's views, see Hailu Habtu, (*Issue*, 13, 1984, pp. 26-29). See also Molefi Asante (1990, pp. 114-17).
9. Whether the migrations might have taken the opposite direction, from Ethiopia to Arabia, seems not to have attracted much attention. This was in part due to the so-called Hamitic thesis of the time that argued that civilization was introduced in Africa by "dark-skinned Caucasians" called Hamites who came from the Asian side of the Red Sea. For the African elements in the South Arabian population, see R. B. Serjeant (in *PTICES*, 1969).
10. Sergew Hable Selassie commented on the Gibbon statement: "It is a fact that Ethiopia was surrounded by unfriendly neighbours, but when a man finds himself in such circumstances, he rarely falls asleep" (1972, p. 209).
11. For a dissenting view on the geographical paradigm, see Sven Rubenson (1976, pp. 1-5)
12. Clause four of the *Fetha Nagast* prohibits the Ethiopian Orthodox Church from having her own Patriarch. Tekle Tsadik Mekouria commented: "What is strange is that the [Ethiopian] *Beta Mangest* and the *Beta Kehnat* accepted this racist clause [clause four] with equanimity and for such a long time" (1981 Eth. Calendar, p. 90; my translation from the Amharic original).
13. For Georg Simmel, secrecy is "the hiding of realities by negative or positive means, [and] is one of man's greatest achievements" (1969, p. 330).
14. The noted African American scholar, Chancellor Williams accused Ethiopians (alongside the Sudanese) of "maintain[ing] a privileged class society based on color," and that "their discriminatory practices are just as subtle and real as those of the whites" (1987, p. 29). That Williams should have known better goes without saying.
15. Interestingly enough, the image of Ethiopia as the anomaly of Africa was also applied to Italy as being the anomaly of Europe. In Barclay's words: "It has become a truism to say that Italy is the enigma of Europe" (1973, p. 9). Like Italy, whom Croce

called "at once old and young" (1929, p. 27), so was Ethiopia. Like Levine's Amhara, for whom deception is allegedly second nature, the Italians were referred to as "a gang of thieves and beggars," as the "blue-bottle flies of International politics: always buzzing when one wants to be quiet. Happily they do not stay" (quoted in Bosworth 1979, p. 7). Like Levine's Amharas, who are "untrustworthy," so were Italians: "For many a European statesman the Italians could never be relied to live up to their past, or even, ironically, to their present" (*Ibid)*. For a parallel between Ethiopia and Italy, see Dugan and Lafort (1973, pp. 3-4).

16. Said wrote: "The West is the actor, the Orient a passive reactor. The West is the spectator, the judge and jury, of every facet of Oriental behavior" (1979, p. 109).
17. For a discussion on Absolutism, see Teshale Tibebu, *Review*, 13, 1 (Winter 1990), pp. 49-151.
18. Polanyi wrote: "We shall call `archaic' such economic institutions as are absent in `primitive', kinship-organized society and emerge only in state societies, but fade when money as a means of exchange becomes widespread" (1966, p. 173).
19. There is a considerable Western literature stating active Ethiopian participation in the European Scramble for Africa. Some of it includes Arnold Toynbee (1965, p. 44); Schwab (1985, p. 5); Tidy and Leeming (1981, vol. 2, pp. 104, 105); Gann and Duignan (1981, vol. 1, p. 16).

    In their book, *The Invention of Ethiopia* (1990, pp. xv-xvi), Bonnie K. Holcomb and Sisai Ibssa came up with the strange idea that Ethiopia was "invented" by European powers, thereby ignoring the immense sacrifice of the Ethiopian people against European colonial expansion. That some old white men in late nineteenth-century Europe gathered around a table and said: "Let us invent a state in our image in North East Africa, and let that be Ethiopia" might be entertaining for some crowd; as an historical undertaking, it is at best misleading, at worst mean-spirited. Ethiopia was neither "invented" nor "imagined" (Sorenson 1993). Ethiopia was *struggled for* by its people. Ethiopia was not left alone to be free. It became free of European colonialism thanks to the heroic struggle and unflinching defiance of her people (Haggai 1973; 1986; Rubenson 1975; Caulk, *TAJH*, 1, 2, 1971). What else were Dogali, Metemma, Adwa, Amba Alagie, Mai Chaw, etc. Dinner parties celebrating the patent of the "invention of Ethiopia"?

Interestingly enough, Liberia, the only other Black sovereign state in Africa besides Ethiopia, was called a black colonialist state (see Akpan, *CJAS*, 7, 2, 1973).

CHAPTER 1

1. *Tabot* is the Ethiopic word for the Ark of the Covenant. According to Graham Hancock's etymological linkage, the word *tabot* is Ethiopic for *tapet*, the ancient Egyptian word for Thebes. The word *tebah* was used in Biblical Hebrew for Noah's ark and for Moses's ark of bulrushes (1992, p. 557). *Tabot* is also known as *tselat*.
2. What I call the *geber* system is referred to as tributary mode of production by Samir Amin (1980), and redistributive system by Karl Polanyi (1966, 1971). It is also called feudalism in Marxist circles (Addis Hiwet, *RAPE*, 1, 1975). The fusion and confusion of production, tribute\tax, and banquet under the same Amharic term *geber* shows that the modern distinction between *state* and *civil society* was not yet elaborated.
3. See Catherine Coquery-Vidrovitch (1988, p. 159); Jack Goody (1971, p. 30). Montesquieu wrote:

   > It is the Christian religion that, in spite of the extent of the empire and the influence of the climate, has hindered despotic power from being established in Ethiopia, and has carried into the heart of Africa the manners and laws of Europe [1949, vol. 2, p. 29].

4. The word *zalan* was used during the Gondarine period to refer to a group of pastoralists in the Gondar region, alongside with that of the Wayto, Beta Israel, Qemant, and "Shanqellas." As usual in the Ethiopian tradition, people's place in the division of labor was identified by their ethnicity, and vice versa. Hence Barya for slave, Gurage for "coolie," etc. See James Quirin (1992, p, 32, 87). Later on, the term *zalan* lost its occupational connotation and came to mean rude in social etiquette.
5. Charles L. Gesheketer noted on the Christian Ethiopian image of the Muslim, the Nomad, the Somali as follows:

   > With the veneer of imperial went a chauvinist vocabulary of supercilious, condescending terms used by high-

land residents to contrast the lowlands and its people with their own cool, mountainous homeland. Somalis were called barias (slaves), shiftas (bandits), or shiretam (from shiret-loin cloth), which inferred a characteristic cowardice or feebleness among men (Somalis) who wore long cotton garments from their waists. The Somalis were seen as simple despoilers, as unruly disobedient children [IJAHS, 18, 1, 1985, p. 12].

6. On the nomadic origins of aristocratic life, see Kautsky (1982, p. 178). We don't know whether the Ethiopian aristocracy had nomadic origins or not. What we do know is that at least for the last sixteen centuries, the aristocracy had been established as a social class, or, more fittingly, a social order, in the midst of an agrarian civilization. Whether the custom of the emperors moving from one place to another, the so-called wandering capitals of Ethiopia, had anything to do with a nomadic origin is not clear either. What is clear is that these "wandering capitals" were the only viable means of tribute appropriation from the *gabbar* in the absence of even a modest degree of monetary circulation, commodity production, and urban centers of administration. This was the case especially after the demise of Aksum. Even during Aksum's glory, the kings were busy travelling through their domain, fighting wars against opponents, and collecting tribute from their subjects.

   Moreover, as Taddesse Tamrat correctly remarked, a mobile imperial court with thousands of warriors was the only means of putting down the various intermittent regional rebellions by the nobility or by newly-subjugated peoples (in Niane ed. 1984, pp. 436-37). Hence the mobile nature of the imperial court, and the warrior class at large, was basically conditioned by the two circumstances of tribute extraction and the "maintenance of law and order." As to the nomads' contempt for agriculturalists, the rather well-known pride of the lowland nomadic Afars and Somalis and their utter contempt for their highland agriculturalist counterparts is a case in point — a mutual contempt of modes of production, as of religions.

7. *Chawa* was initially a name given to "a colony of imperial soldiers stationed in a particular region or locality as a defensive or controlling force" Atsme Giyorgis (1987, translated from Amharic by Bairu Tafla, p. 193). Several places in Northern Ethiopia have names with the word chawa in them, like Addi

Chawa in Adwa.

On the *chawa/balagar* dichotomy, see Merid Wolde Aregay (1971, p. 81; Atsme Giyorgis 1987, p. 201).

8. See Elias (1978, p. 5). Jacques Le Goff wrote that in 13th-century "Germany," there were "six declensions for the word 'peasant'—villain, rustic, devil, robber, brigand and looter; and in the plural - wretches, beggars, liars, rogues, trash and infidels" (in Carlo Cipolla ed., 1972, vol. 1, p. 71).
9. The era Before Christ (B.C.) is called under various names like *Amata Kunane* (Era of Damnation or Sin), *Amata Feda* (Era of Suffering), or *Amata Alam* (Era of the World.) The Era after the birth of Christ (A.D.) is called *Amata Mehrat* (Era of Forgiveness.)
10. See also the *Fetha Nagast*, p. 13
11. James T. Bent wrote that the argument of Judaic presence in Ethiopia prior to Christianity "may be relegated to the chapter of myths" (1983, p. viii). The "dedication to Mars [in pre-Christian Aksum] shows the influence of Greek paganism, and the legend of the existence of Judaism as the religion of the country prior to the introduction of Christianity is worth nothing" (*Ibid*, p. 181.)
12. For the philosophical aspects of Hebraic-Jewish elements in the culture of the Ge'ez civilization, see Ephraim Isaac (1969).
13. For an excellent account of the Beta Israel and their relations with Christian Ethiopia, see Quirin (1992). See also Gamst (1969).
14. Since the conversion of King Ezana of Aksum to Christianity in the fourth century A.D., the identity of the ruling class of the Ge'ez civilization can be divided into two main historical epochs: from the fourth century to the demise of the Zagwe dynasty in the thirteenth century, and from the so-called restoration of the Solomonic dynasty in 1270 (the coronation of Yekuno-Amlak), to the end of Haile Selassie's reign in 1974. In both periods, Christianity was the State religion and Ge'ez was (and still is) the language of the Church. The difference between the two periods is that before the thirteenth century, the language of both the State and the Church was Ge'ez, while in the post-thirteenth century period, Amharic became the language of state (*lesana negus*, king's language) while Ge'ez remained the language of the Church.

Sergew Hable Selassie reminds us that Christianity in

Ethiopia started with the "upper" classes and descends down to the "lower," contrary to its Greco-Roman counterpart which started with the "lower" classes and moved "up." "Consequently, this different way of expansion of Christianity in Ethiopia implies a different relationship between the Church and the State" (in *PTICES*, 1969, p. 5). For the most recent work on Aksum, see Munro-Hay (1991).

15. According to Abd El-Samei Muhammad Ahmad, the *Fetha Nagast* is a translation from Arabic of a thirteenth-century Egyptian Coptic work, *Al-Majmou as-Safawi*, which was a collection of ecclesiastical and civil laws of the Egyptian Coptic Church. See his thesis (1965, p. 3).
16. Budge wrote of the *Kebra Nagast*:

    > The Kebra Nagast is a great storehouse of legends and traditions, some historical and some of a purely folklore character, derived from the Old Testament and the later Rabbinical writings, and from Egyptian (both pagan and Christian), Arabian, and Ethiopian sources [1932, p. xv].

17. Ullendorff wrote:

    > Emperor Menelik's polity, into which Lidj Tafari [later Haile Selassie] was born in 1892, was further removed from the so-called socialist republic of Colonel Mengistu . . . than it was from Ezana's Aksumite Empire, 1,600 years earlier [1988, p. 235].

18. For a detailed discussion of the Beta Israel, see Quirin (1992). See also Sterns (1968).
19. See, for example, Haberland (*JSS*, 9, 1, Spring, 1964).
20. Zewde Gebre Selassie's "cultural core" concept is the same as that of Donald Levine's concept of greater Ethiopia (1974). See also Lord (1970).
21. Quirin wrote of the *Kebra Nagast*:

    > Though it [the Kebra Nagast] did not receive its final written form until the early fourteenth-century reign of Amda Seyon, it has often been assumed that it was created in at least oral form soon after the Aksumite conversion to Christianity, and in written versions later [1992, p. 18].

22. According to Budge, the Aksumite scribe Yishaq who wrote the *Kebra Nagast* in its final form, made three claims that are cen-

tral to the *Kebra Nagast*:

> That the lawful kings of Ethiopia were descended from SOLOMON, King of ISRAEL. 2. That the Tabernacle of the Law of God, i.e., the Ark of the Covenant, had been brought from JERUSALEM to AKSUM by MENYELEK, SOLOMON'S firstborn son . . . . [and] 3. That the God of ISRAEL had transferred His place of abode on earth from JERUSALEM to AKSUM [1932, p. xvii].

23. In his influential work, *Civilization: A Personal View* (1969, p. 4), Kenneth Clark distinguishes between "real" barbarians, like the Huns "who were totally illiterate and destructively hostile to what they couldn't understand" and the not-so-real ones like the Germanic people that overrun the western flanks of Roman Empire.
24. "*Ayhud*" means Jew, while *ayhuda* or *yihuda* refers to either an unbeliever or a traitor, as in Judas, or both. In popular Amharic, *kehadi yihuda* means "traitorous Judas."
25. For an account of "pagan" resistance to Ethiopian *tabot* Christianity in the fourteenth and fifteenth centuries, see Taddesse Tamrat (*JES*, 10, 1, 1972).
26. Jan Vansina wrote: "In the period between 1500-1800, the Oromo mass migration and expansion, with attendant movements by communities belonging to other cultures, was the only fully fledged mass migration in Africa" (in Ogot ed. 1992, p. 58).
27. Atsme Giyorgis wrote: "A ["Galla"] man who kills a man of Sawa [Shawa] or an Amhara should not shave his head nor should he wear a Quncho [both signs of bravery] for, although they [the Amhara] speak like people, they are animals" (1987, p. 465).
28. The thesis of pastoralist and nomadic "barbarian hordes" spreading havoc and destruction into civilization has been used as an explanation not only to the Oromo vis-a-vis the Christian kingdom during the sixteenth and seventeenth centuries, but also to the great devastation of China and Russia by the Mongol "hordes" (the so-called Golden horde, as the Russian literature calls them), the overrunning of the Roman Empire by Germanic "barbarian tribes," the nomads of Anatolia riding over the Byzantine Empire, Arab Bedouin neophytes of Islam subduing the grandeur of ancient Egypt, etc. One of the most celebrated

authorities on nomadic-pastoralist "hordes" destroying sedentary-agrarian civilizations is Ibn Khaldun. See his *Muqaddimah* (1958, in three volumes, translated and edited by Franz Rosenthal). Recently, Tessema Ta'a attacked this approach in relation to the Oromo expansion for its civilizational chauvinism (1986, p. 25).

29. There is nothing Ethiopian about "barbarism" beginning at home. See, for example, Eugene Weber's excellent discussion of the image of the peasant as barbarian in France (1976). It was quite commonplace in the writings of Marx and Engels to refer to peasants as "barbarians in the midst of civilization."
30. Ernest Gellner wrote that the Somali view the Oromo as "a kind of human population without a set form, a pre-ethnic raw material, waiting to be turned either into Amharas or into Somalis by the turn of political fortune and religious conversion" (1992, p. 84). Sure enough, the Somali government of Ziad Barre formed the Somali Abo Liberation Front in an attempt to Somalize the Oromo.

CHAPTER 2

1. For a comparative global study of modern state formations, see Ali Kazancigil ed. (1986). See also J. Anderson ed. (1986).
2. For a definitive discussion of the concepts of incorporation and peripheralization, see Wallerstein, with W. G. Martin, in Wallerstein (1986, pp. 139-40).
3. For a revisionist interpretation of the rise of capitalism, see Janet Abu-Lughod (1991).
4. For Addis Hiwet, "The same historical forces that created the 'Gold Coast' and the 'Ivory Coast', the Sudan and Kenya, were the very ones that created modern Ethiopia too." This makes modern Ethiopia "no older than these African states." "What makes Ethiopia's creation as a 'modern state' formally different is the way the same historical forces evolved" (*RAPE*, 1975, p. 1).
5. Referring to preindustrial Europe, Carlo Cipolla made a distinction between "voluntary transfer of wealth" and "compulsory transfer of wealth," and classified taxation, plunder, raids, robbery, and theft as belonging to the category of compulsory transfer of wealth (1976, p. 24).
6. Intermittent destruction of productive forces is not unique to predatory exploitation. Under capitalism, economic crises, wars,

de-industrialization, destruction of handicrafts, annihilation of entire peoples, etc., are even more destructive than that of the pre-capitalist predator. However, there is one major difference: for capitalism, destruction of productive forces is seen as a means for a further, faster, and better development of productive forces. The Enlightenment idea of progress through conquest of nature is its secular religion. The pre-capitalist predatory relation is innocent of this idea of progress. It does not know it; it cannot achieve it. What is destroyed is replaced by the same as the one destroyed. The life mechanism of pre-capitalist predatory relationship is enclosed in the envelope of the "recurrence of the same"; the "organic cycle of simple peasant existence," as Weber called it (1964, p. 242). For a cursory look at society and technology in Ethiopia, 1500-1800, see Merid Wolde Aregay (*JES*, 17, 1984).

7. Referring to the noncombatant retainers in the mobile army, Almeida wrote, "when ten thousand soldiers march, the number in the encampment is usually over thirty thousand souls, and when the Emperor marches with his entire force the whole multitude is over a hundred or a hundred and twenty thousand" (in Beckingham and Huntingford ed. 1967, p. 78).
8. Although predatory exploitation was overall done away with in the post-Italian period, it was widely practiced in times of internal uprisings. Two well-known cases are the Weyane uprising in Tigray in 1943, and the rebellion in Gojjam in 1967. In both cases, the territorial army, a militia force recruited from peasants, was sent to these areas to restore "order." It resorted to the old-style practice of looting, burning crops, raping, driving away cattle, and consuming the peasants' foods and drinks. (See Gebru Tareke, 1977, pp. 202-204, 406.)

   In Tigray, those who were suspected of participating in the Weyane uprising or thought to be sympathetic to it were "often tied against pillars with salted ropes so that they suffered from bleeding, forced to sit on hot pans or had boiling water thrown at their faces. Women had their hair shaved off" (*Ibid*, p. 204). Forcing peasants to sit on hot pans was a typical punishment both by the warriors and the *shefta* (Pankhurst, *Ethiopia Observer*, 7, 2, 1963).
9. For a revealing personal observation of the practice of hiding food in the nineteenth century, see Nathaniel Pearce's *Life and Adventures* (1831, vol. 1, pp. 183-34).

The custom of putting food in deep pits outside the homes continued long after the end of predatory exploitation, in some places to this day. It is a means of saving food from enemy attack, which normally takes the form of arson.

10. For an excellent study of the political and military traditions of the Ethiopian peasantry, see Tsehai Berhane Selassie (1980).
11. Peter Garretson wrote of a departing governor in the 1920s, *Dajazmach* Mekuria, who "raided Maji and its surroundings and made off with some 18,000 cattle and 50,000 sheep. His wife, *weyzero* Asselefech, carried out at least one raid against the Tishana, obtaining 93 slaves" (in Donham and James ed. 1986, p. 205).

    The removal of a governor from his territorial jurisdiction was often accompanied by extensive raids, since this may be the last time he will be able to plunder the region. The border regions along the Sudan were sources of slave hunts up until the 1930s. See Darley (1969).
12. The phrase "*agar maqnat*" is similar to the Roman concept of the Latin term *colere*. As Charles Verlinden said, *colere* means "to cultivate," "to put to use," "to make of value." "Therefore it is not surprising that the first meaning of "colonization" and of "to colonize" should be agricultural" (1970, p. ix).
13. Donald Levine wrote:

    > Part of the explanation for the resurgence [of Amhara power in the late nineteenth century] must certainly lie in the fact that the Amharas carried in their heads a picture of the world in which a divinely charged Solomonid monarch of Ethiopia played a crucial role, even though no such monarch had been on the scene for generations [1974, p. 156].

    Gellner "compared" the Afrikaners of South Africa, who possessed "the Book, the wheel and the gun" as opposed to the Africans, with the Amharas and Somalis, as opposed to the Oromo, and wrote: "In the Horn of Africa both the Amharas and the Somalis possessed both gun and Book [the Bible and the Quran] . . . and neither bothered greatly with the wheel" (1992, p. 84).
14. See, for example, Tekle Tsadik Mekouria's passionate defence of the occupation of Harar by Menelik as reunification, that Hararge was the land of Emperors Amde Tseyon, Zara Yaqob,

etc., in his *Atse Yohannesna Yaityopiya Andenat* (*Emperor Yohannes and Ethiopian Unity*, 1982 Eth. calendar, p. 296).

15. That some of the territories of southern Ethiopia like Enarya and Dawaro were part of the tribute-paying network of the post-Zagwe Christian kingdom before the Oromo expansion cut off the link is accepted among historians. See Huntingford's, *The Historical Geography of Ethiopia, From the First Century AD to 1704*, edited by Richard Pankhurst (1989, pp. 86-88). Even such a serious critique of the Aksumite paradigm as Mohammed Hassen agrees with this (1990).
16. Getahun Dilebo wrote, "Menelik's military policy against these people [of Southern Ethiopia] was flagrant imperial conquest and consolidation, not 'unification,' let alone 'reunification' (1974, p. 124).
17. For an excellent summary of the different forms of hegemony in Ethiopia, see Mantel-Niecko (1980, p. 134).
18. The sixteenth-century Ethiopian monk Bahrey, who witnessed the massive Oromo migration, made an interesting "class analysis" about how the Oromo defeated the Amhara. He argued that the Christians were divided into "ten classes, nine of which take no part whatever in war" while among the Oromos these "nine classes . . . do not exist; all men, from small to great, were instructed in warfare, and for this reason they ruin and kill us" (Bahrey, in Beckingham and Huntingford ed. 1967, pp. 125-26). Mohammed Hassen wrote: "the so-called 'Galla invasion' destroyed . . . [the Muslim power at Harar and the Christian kingdom] and by so doing destroyed the very dam that had checked the migration of the pastoral Oromo for many centuries" (1990, p. 20).
19. Marx wrote:

    > In all cases of conquest, three things are possible. The conquering people subjugates the conquered under its own mode of production . . . or it leaves the old mode intact and contents itself with a tribute . . . or a reciprocal interaction takes place whereby something new, a synthesis, arises . . . . In all cases, the mode of production, whether that of the conquering people, that of the conquered, or that emerging from the fusion of both, is decisive for the new distribution which arises [1973, p. 97].

    In the Ethiopian case, the first corresponds to the larger part of the South; the second to Jimma, Wallaga-Qelem, and Neqemte; the third to Harar, wherein, as a result of the fusion of Harari urban civilization and Shawan *geber* system, a semi-*geber* system, semibourgeois order evolved.

20. For a discussion of the concept of interstate system, see Wallerstein (1992, Chap. 2).
21. The expression "creative destruction" is used by Joseph Schumpeter in his book, *Capitalism, Socialism, and Democracy* (1950) to refer to capitalism's simultaneous destruction and innovation of productive forces.
22. We cannot get a complete picture of the history of modern state formation in Ethiopia without taking into consideration the various conditions of political life in the southern regions before these areas were incorporated into Menelik's empire. This aspect has not been discussed in detail in this work. It suffices for now to say that simultaneously with the rise to power of Kassa-Tewodros in the North, a process of state formation was taking place in what is now Wallaga. The disintegration of the Gada system, based as it was on the combination of age-set democracy (inside the Gada system, with the exclusion of women) and wars of conquest, and the continued infighting among the various Oromo groups themselves, gradually evolved into attempts by stronger groups to establish firm, centralized authority over larger territories (see Terrefe Woldetsadik, *JES*, 6, 1, 1965, p. 74; Mohammed Hassen 1990, Chap. 3.) There were also the "highly organized despotic Galla monarchies between the Omo and the Didessa" (Abir, *JAH*, 6, 2, 1965, p. 206.) These were the Oromo states of Limmu-Enarea, Guma, Goma, Jimma-Kakka and Gera, all of whom save Jimma "lay in dust" (Mohammed Hassen 1990, p. 200) during Menelik's conquest, as well as the Kingdoms of Walayta and Kaffa.

    The lowland nomads and pastoralists lived in arid lands, always in search of grazing land, water, and salt for their cattle, with sporadic plunder of the highland agriculturalists as supplementary means of subsistence when hard times struck. In the processes of state formation in modern Ethiopia, they were the most difficult to subdue for the extraction of tribute.
23. Keefer wrote that the *nafatgna/gabbar* system was more efficient than that of British colonialism in the "competition for empire" between Great Britain and Ethiopia (*IJAHS*, 6, 3, 1973).

24. Roland Oliver reminds us that "Not all of the Africans tried to found states" (1991, p. 145).
25. For a study of firearms in Africa during the nineteenth century, see (*JAH*, 12, 2, 1971, pp. 173-254; 12, 4, 1971, pp. 517-570). For the role of firearms in Ethiopian culture, 16th-20th centuries, see Pankhurst, (*Journal des Africanistes*, XLVIII, 2, pp. 131-44.
26. In his book, *Oromia and Ethiopia* (1993), Asafa Jalata wrote that "there was no inherent superiority [of Ethiopians over that of other Africans] to prevent [them] from being colonized militarily and technologically" (p. 7). Like Holcomb and Sisai Ibssa (1990), Asafa argues that Ethiopia's independence had more to do with the will of European powers to let Ethiopia be sovereign than with the strength of Ethiopian resistance. As in Holcomb and Sisai Ibssa (1990), he passes in silence about the struggles of the Ethiopian people — Adwa, Mai Chaw, the five-year resistance against the Fascist occupation, etc.

    As to Ethiopia's technological backwardness, military might does not have to correspond to technological level of development. Think of North Korea, Vietnam, Iraq, Egypt, etc. Or Mengistu Haile Mariam's war machine, once the largest and best equipped in Black Africa, and compare it with Ethiopia's technological level of development. To be militarily strong in the contemporary world, all one needs is to either make the weapons of war, or get them from those who know how to make them. And Ethiopia did the latter, from Menelik to Mengistu.

CHAPTER 3

1. Patterson distinguishes among what he called personal, sovereignal, and civic freedom (1991, pp. 3-4).
2. For a philosophical analysis of the master-salve dialectic, see Hegel's immortal piece, "Lordship and Bondage" in his *Phenomenology of Spirit* (1977).
3. James Bruce, the eighteenth-century Scottish traveller to Ethiopia, once called the "Shanqella" a "nation of Troglodytes," while Mansfield Parkyns saw in them the living embodiment of the Rousseauistic "noble savage" (1966, p. 181)
4. The phenotypical self consciousness of most peoples of the Horn of Africa — Christian and Muslim — is similar to that of the Arabs. For an excellent discussion of slavery and "color prejudice" in Arabia and the Middle East at large, see St. Claire Drake

(1990, Chap. 5).

5. The word *chawa* in relation to *barya* is different from *chawa* in relation to *balagar*, clergy, and rude, all discussed in Chapter One. The most comprehensive definition of *chawa* is: well-mannered, "free", Christian, warrior, layperson.
6. Almeida wrote of imperial appointments in the seventeenth century:

> The formula of the proclamation: *We have made our slave to reign* will seem strange to any foreigner. In Ethiopia, however, it is so much in use that every time the Emperor bestows an office (which they call Xumete) [appointment] on anyone, even if it is one of his brothers, the honour is always accompanied by this fly in the ointment: *We have made our slave so-and-so Viceroy or Governor of such and such a kingdom or such and such territories.* This is the formula of the proclamation [in Beckinhham and Huntingford ed. 1967, p. 71; emphasis in the original].

7. Describing the Arab demand for Oromo female slaves, M. Lucereau (the French traveller in Zeila in the 1880s) wrote:

> They [Oromo female slaves] fetch a great price, and are much prized by the Arabs, who superstitiously believe that a Galla woman can re-animate and renew the blood of an old man; and as the Arab only lives for his wife and would ruin himself to have one, they always find purchasers at a high price [in Beachey ed. 1976, pp. 60-61].

8. For a discussion on the end of slavery in Northern Ethiopia, see James McCann, in Suzanne Meirs and Richard Roberts eds. (1988).
9. James Bruce wrote of the "Abyssinians's" view of the Wayto as follows:

> [The Abyssinians held the Wayto] in utter abhorrence, so that to touch them, or anything that belongs to them, makes a man unclean all that day till the evening, separates him from his family and friends, and excludes him from the church and all divine service till he is washed and purified on the following day [cited in Hallpike 1968, p. 46].

10. Trimingham wrote:

> Among the Somali, there are three occupational minorities: the Mijan, a serf-caste who are hunters or trappers and also act as hewers of wood and drawers of water for the Somali tribes, amongst whom they are scattered; the Yibir, a sorcerer-caste who exist on the fees they are paid for charms and amulets; and the Tomal who are a smith-caste . . . . These castes, by an Islamic rationalization, are regarded as being in a perpetual state of ritual impurity (Najasa) [1965, p. 224].

The word *Sab* designates the three groups of Tumal, Yibir, and Midgan. The *Sab* cannot have marital relations with the Somalis. See I. M. Lewis (1969, pp. 51-52).

11. The tenacious resistance put up by the Beta Israel against Christian proselytization may not be that anomalous in light of the millennial struggle of Jews against forced conversion to Christianity. Edward Gibbon, who saw the Jews as the "single people [who] refused to join in the common intercourse of mankind" (1977, p. 383), wrote:

> The sullen obstinacy with which they [Jews] maintained their peculiar rites and unsocial manners seemed to mark them out a distinct species of men, who boldly professed, or who faintly disguised, their implacable hatred to the rest of human-kind [1977, vol. 1, p. 384].

Gibbon's statement above smacks of anti-Jewish disposition. The caste-like consciousness of the Beta Israel, a consciousness and practice elevated to the degree of almost fanatical perfection, was unparalleled in Ethiopian history. They came to the aid of "Gragn" in his bid to destroy Christian Ethiopia. Over there in Reconquista Spain, the Grand Inquisition of Catholic Christendom; over here in Ethiopia, Judaic Ethiopians allying themselves with the forces of Islam against *tabot* Christianity. Over there, the Spanish driving out Muslims and Jews. Over here, Judaic Ethiopians coming to the aid of Muslims. After all, was not Islam the most tolerant religion towards Judaism among the religions of the Near East? A Judaic-Islamic alliance against Christianity makes every sense. See Cutler and Cutler (1986).

12. In his comparative historical anthropology, *The Cultural Unity of Black Africa* (1990), Chiekh Anta Diop sees African history, and what he calls the "Southern Cradle of Civilizations" at large, as one based on the caste principle of social organization, as

opposed to the "Northern Cradle."

For the social and historical setting of the existence of "castes" in Africa, including Ethiopia, see Haberland (in Hess ed. *PFICES*, 1979, p. 132).

CHAPTER 4

1. Hoben's work (1973) still remains to be the most comprehensive study of *rist* tenure.
2. For the global processes of housewifeization, see Mies (1984).
3. For the distinctions among lineage, clan and "tribal" relations, see Jacques Maquet (1971, p. 42).
4. See the one hundred documents of land charters from the fourth to the nineteenth centuries collected, translated, and edited by Huntingford (1965). In the fifteen-centuries period covered in the documents, one finds a repetition of the same religious invocations and threats of excommunication (*Ibid*, p. 29).

   Huntingford related a suggestion made to him by a certain W. A. Pantin of Oriel College, Oxford that the origin of the Ethiopian land charters "could be sought in late Roman private deeds of land transfer, and that such deeds could have reached Ethiopia through the agency of monks from Antioch or Alexandria" (*Ibid*, p. 16).

   Granting land charters existed in Ethiopia prior to Saxon England, thereby throwing cold water on Mr. W. A. Pantin's thesis. For Anglo-Saxon England's land charters during the ninth and eleventh centuries, see Robertson ed. (1986, p. 15, 221-23; Maitland 1987; Denman 1958).
5. Taddesse Tamrat suggested that *rist* evolved out of *gult*, with *gult* rights later becoming hereditary holdings. With the ethnic and religious mixing of the original conqueror and conquered, *gults* that resulted from military conquests died out and became *rist*. The distinction between conqueror and conquered, which was the mainstay of the *gult* system, disappeared (1972, p. 3).

   And yet, Taddesse's analysis does not help us explain why *gult* continued to have its firm grip in the Christian regions well into the twentieth century, centuries after cultural and religious assimilation has taken place. It seems more reasonable to argue that *rist* preceded *gult*, that *gult* right was imposed from above on people who already had *rist* usufruct rights. The very fact that *rist* equalizes while *gult* creates class distinctions comes from the imposition of a warrior class upon a prior existing freeholding peasantry.

6. See Barrow (1956, pp. 97-8) for the religious universe of fourteenth-century Britain, which was similar to that of Christian Ethiopia.
7. For Church-State relations in Ethiopia, see Ephraim Isaac (*Ethiopia Observer*, 14, 4, 1971, p. 247). Church and State kept their distinct identities; the one did not collapse in the other, as in Islam (Trimingham 1950, p. 17). For Islam, see Bernard Lewis (1968, p. 20).
8. Jerome Lobo, the Portuguese traveller in Ethiopia during the seventeenth century, wrote: "No country in the world is so full of churches, monasteries and ecclesiastics as Abyssinia" (1978, p. 88). See also Stitz (*JES*, 13, 1, 1975).
9. An iconoclastic philosophical critique of celibacy as being contrary to the laws of nature and God was made by an Ethiopian rationalist philosopher of the seventeenth century, Zara Yaqob (Seed of Jacob). The similarity of his views with that of seventeenth-century Western philosophy of natural law, the debate over his identity and his work, the *Hattata*, are discussed in detail in Claude Sumner (1974, vol. 2).
10. For a detailed description of rights to land and rights to tribute, and the various regional differences, see Mahteme Sellassie (1957).
11. In Oromo areas the office of the *malkagna* was known under various names like *laqo*, *qoro*, and *sanga* (Gebre Wold 1962, p. 314). Other names in other regions like Illubabor, where there were fourteen rank names (*Ibid*, p. 322), were mere variations on the same three basic local offices.
12. The term *garad* was used in the Hararge region and was equivalent to the office of the *chiqa shum*.
13. Mahteme Sellassie gave a detailed explanation on the origins of the tithe in modern Ethiopia (1957, pp. 294-5). The decimation of the cattle population and the subsequent famine, known as *kefu qan* (bad times), brought about a social transformation in the modality of tribute extraction. By 1892, 90% of the cattle had died of the plague. Mesfin Wolde Mariam (1984, p. 33).
14. As in Ethiopia, mead was the most prestigious drink of the Russian nobility. See Smith in Hobsbawm ed. (1980, p. 50).
15. The nameless tribute was "when the government rewarded an official or when a new baby was born to a governor, a gebbar had to give money to the governor to congratulate him" (Gebre

Wold, 1962, p. 307).

16. The Church's power of tribute exaction was derived from the State. See Alan Hoben in Tudena and Plotnicov eds. (1970, p. 214).
17. The first four articles of the Leche Agreement signed by *Negusa Nagast* Yohannes IV and *Negus* Menelik of Shawa on March 20, 1878 exemplified the relations between king of kings and king, and other lower-ranking notables (see Appendix in Wylde 1970, p. 471). The Leche Agreement deals with three essential aspects: (1) The relationship between king and the king of kings was tributary. The tribute had two forms: payment of tribute of goods proper, and manpower tribute, mostly warriors. (2) The king of kings was obliged to come to the defense of the king when a foreign power intruded. In that case, it was not the king's domain that the king of kings defended, but the country as a whole, his overall domain. If the domain that belonged to a king was attacked by a foreign power, it was the responsibility of the king to fight first. It was when the king could not handle the situation by himself that the king of kings came to his aid. (3) Strict observance of the rules of official titles was mandatory. It was not uncommon for the real king of kings to go to war against aspirants who gave themselves that title. To claim that title against an already existing king of kings was a breach of the tributary relationship. Many wars in Ethiopian history were fought between aspirant king of kings and established ones.
18. In his discussion of the archaic system of Dahomey, Polanyi called redistribution that system of "move[ment] of goods and money toward the center and out of it again" (1966, p. 34).
19. Marx called the conspicuous consumption of late Greece and Rome "mad extravagance" (1977, Part I, p. 528).
20. Commenting on the extremely hot pepper consumed by Ethiopians, Gerald Portal wrote: "A long course of burning, extending over many generations, must have made their mouths, tongues, and throats, like leather" (1892, pp. 144-5).
21. For a discussion of *Ras* Hailu Takla Haimanot's banquets in Gojjam, see Hoben in Tudena and Plotnicov eds. (1970, p. 208).
22. *Ras* Hailu Takla Haimanot told an American visitor in 1916 about the historical rationale of the culture of eating raw meat:

    Raw meat eating is not really one of the ancient customs with us, although we have been doing it for a great many years. Our country was invaded at one time — so long ago that I don't know who the invaders were — but the Abyssinians were defeated and driven into the mountains in small bands, where they were forced to hide. But a great many were discovered and butchered, betrayed by the smoke of their cooking fires. It was then that our people began to eat meat raw. We have since kept up the custom and now prefer it raw to any other way. [Quoted in Baum, 1927, p. 262].

Ras Hailu's story makes sense from a military point of view. In Ethiopia, where war-making was second nature to the notables, eating meat raw was quite "rational."

23. Witchcraft, cults, sorcery, etc., were no mere "pagan" residues of Ethiopian Christianity. Medieval Christian Europe was full of them. See Braudel (1972, vol. 1, p. 34). Christopher Hill said of seventeenth-century England that "The best and most authoritative opinions favoured magic" (1986, vol. 3, p. 275).
24. On Ethiopian Church education, see Ephraim Isaac (1967, pp. 37-38); Inbakom Kalewold (1970).
25. Georges Lefebvre wrote of eighteenth-century France: "At least one-tenth of the rural population did nothing but beg from one year's end to the other . . . . In the North, in 1790, about a fifth of the population was so engaged" (1973, p. 14). Wallerstein noted that begging and vagabondage were "a notorious feature of Elizabethan England" (1974, p. 253). Braudel wrote, "In the old days [of medieval Europe], the beggar who knocked at the rich man's door was regarded as a messenger from God, and might even be Christ in disguise" (1979, vol. 2, p. 508). And Cipolla reminds us that "There is no chronicle or hagiography of medieval or Renaissance Europe which does not mention the beggars" (1976, p. 14).

CHAPTER 5

1. With the rise of the capitalist world system, the "free competition" for power of the medieval world — the various intranoble "class" struggles — was pushed out of its domain into the politics of interstate rivalry. As more and more integration and monopoly of legitimate violence took place in individual states, a parallel but opposite process of competition developed in the interstate system. Internally, the modern state is based on the

monopoly of legitimate violence; externally, each state is but a cog in the wheel of fierce competition of states against each other. By the time peace, order, and legitimate monopoly of violence were established in the modern state, a new and systemically entrenched competition based on war, disorder, and parcellized monopolies of legitimate violence were being formed at the level of the interstate system. The two processes are not merely parallel and opposite; they are also complementary. The centralized sovereignty and legitimacy monopoly of each state is defined by the parcellized sovereignties and legitimate monopolies of all states. The so-called principle of international law is an attempt to create a global monopoly of legitimate violence as a "superstructure" corresponding to the unitary world economy. The principle of noninterference in the internal affairs of each state is itself a recognition of the Hobbesian nature of the interstate system, a combined effort of all states to protect their monopolies of legitimate violence at "home" from being infringed upon by "outside" states.

2. The Italians "planned to build about 6,210 miles of roads and tracks and actually succeeded as to 4,347 miles, 2,145 of which were tarred or macadamized" (Perham 1969, p. 182). To this day, a good part of the road network in Ethiopia remains the one built during the Italian occupation (see Pankhurst, *Ethiopia Observer*, 14, 1, 1971).
3. For a discussion of the Japanese *sankin kotai* (alternate attendance) system, which was similar to that of the Ethiopian, see Toshio Tsukahira (1966, p. 1).
4. Angelo del Boca wrote: "The Italian intervention in Ethiopia also led to the centralization of the ruling power and the elimination of the feudal system of the rases, the system Haile Selassie had vainly strived for years to bring to an end" (1969, p. 238).
5. Mosley made similar comment: "The retreating [Ethiopian] army was such a rabble of ragged men, women, children and slaves, that to Konavoloff it looked more like the emigration of a whole people" (1964, p. 199). And Tekle Haimanot Teferi wrote: "One could not watch an Ethiopian army [of the *geber* system] without being reminded of a military museum" (1972, p. 20). On the perception of the army of the *geber* system as an "emigration of a whole people," without any discipline or order, Charles Rey, for whom the "Abyssinian army is in effect prac-

tically the Abyssinian people, for with the exception of the priests and monks every man is an actual or potential soldier" (1923, p. 170), made a different and more real appraisal of the situation. For Rey, the army of the *geber* system followed order and discipline, that "when a halt is called the camp is marked out and arranged in an incredibly short space of time, each contingent seems to know its allotted place, and the apparent disorder of the march is shown to have been disorder merely according to our ideas" (*Ibid*, p. 176).

6. For the war culture of medieval Europe, see Norman (1971).
7. Machiavelli made an excellent comparison between the Turkish and French forms of rule, whose relevance to the Ethiopian situation was astounding:

> All the Turkish monarchy is governed by one ruler, the others are his servants, and dividing his kingdom into "sangiacates," he sends to them various administrators, and changes or recalls them at his pleasure. But the King of France is surrounded by a large number of ancient nobles, recognized as such by their prerogatives, of which the King cannot deprive them without danger to himself. Whoever now considers these two states will see that it would be difficult to acquire the state of the Turk; but having acquired it, it would be very easy to hold it. In many respects, on the other hand, it would be easier to conquer the Kingdom of France, but there would be great difficulty in holding it [1950, pp. 15-6].

The Ethiopian state on the eve of the Fascist invasion was similar to that of Machiavelli's France. The very factor that led to the collapse of the Ethiopian army at Mai Chaw later proved to be its strength. If its weakness led to defeat, it also made Italian rule unrealizable and Ethiopia ungovernable.

8. For a history of British policy toward Ethiopia during the period 1909-1919, see Caplan (1971).
9. For a history of Ethio-American relations, see (Shinn, *Ethiopia Observer*, 14, 4, 1971; Skinner 1969; Robbins, *American Mercury*, 29, 1933).
10. To this date, Greenfield's (1965) account of the 1960 abortive coup is the most comprehensive.
11. For a discussion of status and social change in modern Ethiopia, see Shack (*Africa*, 46, 2, 1976).

12. Elias (1982) referred to "Abyssinia" as the contemporary variant of medieval Europe. Contemporary meant 1939, when the book was first published.
13. For succession wars in African history, see Coquery-Vidrovitch (1988, pp. 63-4).
14. Perham observed: "The lavish concubinage of princely houses in Ethiopia, the frequency of divorce, and the tolerant attitude towards illegitimacy together make the precise tracing of a dynasty almost impossible" (1969, p. 70). William Howard wrote,

    > It was the policy of Ethiopian rulers as far back as the sixteenth century [and beyond] to check the development of great families with local connections by transferring the heads of provinces and by alternating Rases with men of lower rank in the same governorship. In many cases, one had to gain the title on his own merit [1956, p. 53].

15. For a discussion of Wolde Giorgis' career, see Clapham (1969, pp. 110-17).
16. To this day, the best account of Haile Selassie's politics is the chapter, "The Autocrat" in Markakis (1978). For a panoramic view of Haile Selassie's years, see Spencer (1984).
17. The perception of Ethiopian emperors as the ultimate source of justice was similar to that of the kings of England (Robert Sedler 1964, pp. 61-66). Moreover, like the Ethiopian, the English kings were seen as the caretakers of the poor (see Spence wrote quoted in *Ibid*, p. 64).
18. To say, "in the name of Haile Selassie, stop!" is not that different from saying "in the name of the king" by which English policemen stop and arrest a person. In Ethiopia, however, anybody could say "in the name of Haile Selassie, stop!" to any person, stop the person, and take him to a police station. Everybody functioned as an unpaid policeperson.
19. For an excellent synopsis of the traditional legitimacy in Ethiopia, see Markakis, (*Presence Africaine*, 66, pp. 79-97). For the modernization process of the Ethiopian autocracy, see Hess (1970).

CHAPTER 6

1. C. F. Rey, among others, commented: "The Abyssinian is extremely fond of litigation," (1969, p. 127).

2. For an account of the Emperor's code, which follows the Gospel's adage: "He Who Knows Much Shall Be Punished Much, But He Who Knows Little Shall Be Punished Little", see Norman Bentwich quoted in Sanford (1946, p. 85).
3. The 1968 peasant uprising in Gojjam was directed against the introduction of bourgeois relations in rural land ownership. The peasants rose up to defend the *rist* system. University students took the uprising as an example of class struggle, but failed to notice that it was a "reactionary" class struggle that tried to turn back the "wheel of history," the development of productive forces. For the peasants of Gojjam, the Land Tax Reform of 1967 was too radical; for the students it was too conservative. And yet, the students sided with the peasants against the state in the name of progress and revolution! For a discussion of the Gojjam peasant rebellion, see Schwab (*CJAS*, 4, 2, 1970)
4. For an excellent discussion of the overall conditions of peasants in *rist* regions, see Pausewang, in Hess ed. (1979, p. 707).
5. Gojjam and Begemidir, provinces with the least Muslim population, had the least percentage, just 0.5%, of men having more than one wife. On the other hand Muslim-dominated provinces like Bale had 25.5% of men with two or more wives. See Table II. 2 of the Central Statistical Office, *Statistical Bulletin*, (Jan. 1974, p. 17).
6. For a discussion of agrarian capitalism in Ethiopia, see Stahl (1974).
7. Shack quotes a comment on the Gurages made by Cecchi, who pondered: "might they not descend from Jewish immigrants in Ethiopia? In habits and moral traits they resemble the Jews of the European ghettos too; cunning, shrewd in business, very covetous of money, somewhat miserly" (1966, p. 77).
8. There is nothing Ethiopian in the changing of names as a reflection of the "civilizing process" of global capitalism. It is a global phenomenon that people adopt Western names to look more modern and "civilized," or take "ancestral" names to feel "authentic" to their origins. Black nationalists change their European names into African names so that they make contact with the spirit of their African ancestors. Hence Stokley Carmichael became Kwame Toure.
9. On the national origins of foreign capital investment in Ethiopia, see Duri Mohammed, (*JES*, 7, 2, p. 76).
10. For the history of Ethiopian coffee, see Winid, (*African Bulletin*,

10, 1969). For the role of coffee in Ethiopia's economy, see Teketel Haile Mariam (1973).

11. For peripheral capitalism in Africa, see Amin, (*JMAS*, 10, 4, 1972).

EPILOGUE

1. For an account of Haile Selassie the man, see Marcus (1987); Schwab (1979); Thesiger (1987). See also Haile Selassie's biography (1976).
2. For analysis of the Ethiopian revolution, see Marina and David Ottaway (1978); Fred and Molyneux Halliday (1981); Clapham (1988); Harbeson (1988); Andargachew Tiruneh (1993); and Keller (1988).

Bibliography

Abdel-Malek, Anouar. "The renaissance of Egypt, 1805-81." In J. F. Ade Ajayi (ed.), UNESCO, *General History of Africa, Vol. VI.: Africa in the Nineteenth Century until the 1880s*. Berkeley: Univ. of California Press, 1989, 325-355.

——. *Social Dialectics, Vol. I. Civilizations and Social Theory*. Albany: State Univ. of New York Press, 1981a.

——. *Social Dialectics, Vol. II. Nation and Revolution*. Albany: State Univ. of New York Press, 1981b.

Abir, Mordechai. "The Emergence and Consolidation of the Monarchies of Enarea and Jimma in the First Half of the 19th Century." *Journal of African History*, 6, no. 2 (1965):205-219.

——. *Ethiopia and the Red Sea: The Rise and Decline of the Solomonic Dynasty and Muslim-European Rivalry in the Region*. London: Frank Cass; Totowa, NJ: Biblio Distribution Centre, 1980.

——. *Ethiopia, The Era of the princes: The Challenge of Islam and the Reunification of the Christian Empire 1769-1855*. New York, Washington: Praeger Publishers, 1970.

——. "Trade and Christian-Muslim Relations in Post-Medieval Ethiopia." In Robert Hess (ed)., *Proceedings of the Fifth International Conference on Ethiopian Studies*, Chicago: Univ. of Illinois at Chicago Circle, 1979.

Addis Hiwet. "Ethiopia: From Autocracy to Revolution. " London, *Review of African Political Economy*, Occasional Publication, 1 (1975).

Ahmad, Abd El-Samei Muhammad. "Fetha Nagasht." Ph.D. diss., Cairo: Department of Oriental Languages, Cairo Univ. Press, 1965.

Ajayi, J. F. A. "West Africa in the Anti-Slave Trade Era." In John E. Flint (ed.), *The Cambridge History of Africa, Vol. 5: from c.1790 to c.1870*. Cambridge Univ. Press, 1976, 200-221.

Akalou Wolde Michael. "The Impermanency of Royal Capitals in Ethiopia." *Yearbook of the Association of Pacific Coast Geographers*, 28 (1966).

Akpan, M. B. "Black Imperialism: Americo-Liberian Rule Over the African Peoples of Liberia, 1841-1964." *Canadian Journal of African Studies*, 7, no. 2 (1973):217-236.

——. "Liberia and Ethiopia, 1880-1914: the survival of two African states." In A. Adu Boahen (ed.), UNESCO, *General History of Africa, Vol. VII.: Africa under Colonial Domination 1880-1935*. Berkeley: Univ. of California Press, 1985, 249-282.

Allen, W. E. D. *Guerrilla War in Abyssinia*. London: Penguin, 1943.

Almedia, Manoel de. "The History of High Ethiopia or Abassia." In C. F. Beckingham and G. W. B. Huntingford (eds.), *Some Records of Ethiopia 1593-1646*. Kraus Reprint Limited, 1967.

Alvarez, Francisco. *Narrative of the Portuguese Embassy to Abyssinia*. London: Hakluyt Society, 1881.

Amin, Samir. *Class and Nation: Historically and in the Current Crisis*. New York and London: Monthly Review Press, 1980.

——. "Underdevelopment and Dependence in Black Africa — Origins and Contemporary Forms." *Journal of Modern African Studies*, 10, no. 4 (1972):503-524.

Andargachew Tiruneh. *The Ethiopian Revolution, 1974 1987: from an aristocratic to a totalitarian autocracy*. Cambridge: Cambridge Univ. Press, 1993.

Anderson, James (ed.). *The Rise of the Modern State*. Atlantic Highlands, NJ.: Humanities Press, 1986.

Anderson, Benedict. *Imagined Communities: Reflections on the Origins and Spread of Nationalism*. London: Verso, 1991.

Anderson, Perry. *Lineages of the Absolutist State*. London: Verso, 1979.

Appiah, Kwame A. *In My Father's House: Africa in the Philosophy of Culture*. New York, Oxford: Oxford Univ. press, 1992.

Asafa Jalata. *Oromia & Ethiopia: State Formation and Ethnonational Conflict, 1868-1992*. Boulder & London: Lynne Reinner Publishers, 1993.

Asante, Molefi K. *Kemet, Afrocentricty and Knowledge*. Trenton, NJ.: Africa World Press, 1990.

Asante, S. K. *Pan-African Protest: West Africa and the Italo-Ethiopian Crisis, 1934-1941*. London: Longman, 1977.

Ashton, Robert. *The English Civil War: Conservatism and Revolution, 1603-1649*. London: Weidenfeld and Nicolson, 1978.

Asma Giyorgis. *History of the Galla and the Kingdom of S[h]awa.* Translated and Edited by Bairu Tafla. Stuttgart: Franzsteiner Verlag Wiesbaden Gmbh, 1987.

Assefa Bequele and Eshetu Chole. *A Profile of the Ethiopian Economy.* Oxford, etc.: Oxford Univ. Press, 1969.

Aston, T. H. (ed.). *The Brenner Debate: Agrarian Class Structure and Economic Development in Pre-Industrial Europe.* Cambridge, New York: Cambridge Univ. Press, 1985.

Austen, Ralph A. "The Islamic Red Sea Slave Trade: An Effort at Quantification." In Robert Hess (ed)., *Proceedings of the Fifth International Conference on Ethiopian Studies.* Chicago: Univ. of Illinois at Chicago Circle, 1979.

Badoglio, Pietro. *The War in Abyssinia.* Methuen, 1937.

Baer, Gabriel. "Slavery in Nineteenth-Century Egypt." *Journal of African History,* 8, no. 3 (1967):417-441.

Bahrey. "History of the Galla." In C. F. Beckingham and G. W. B. Huntingford (eds.), *Some Records of Ethiopia, 1593-1646.* Kraus Reprint Limited, 1967.

Bahrey, Almeida, Huntingford & Beckingham. *History of the Galla (Oromo) of Ethiopia, With Ethnology and History of South West Ethiopia.* Oakland, CA: African Sun Publishing, 1993.

Bahru Zewde. "Economic Origins of the Absolutist State in Ethiopia (1916-1935)." *Journal of Ethiopian Studies,* 17 (1984):1-29.

——. *A History of Modern Ethiopia, 1855-1974.* Athens, OH: Ohio Univ. Press, 1991.

——. "Relations Between Ethiopia and the Sudan on the Western Ethiopian Frontier 1898-1935." Ph. D. diss., Univ. of London, 1976.

Bairu Tafla (ed.). *A Chronicle of Emperor Yohannes IV (1872-89).* Wiesbaden: Steiner, 1977.

——. "Marriage as a Political Device: An Appraisal of a Socio-Political Aspect of the Menelik Periods 1889-1916." *Journal of Ethiopian Studies,* 10, no. 1 (1972):13-22.

Baladacci, A. "Italian Colonial Expansion: Its Origins, Progress, and Difficulties." *United Empire,* 2 (1911).

Balibar, Etienne, and Immanuel Wallerstein. *Race, Nation, Class: Ambiguous Identities.* London & New York: Verso, 1991.

Balsuik, Randi R. *Haile Selassie's Students: The Intellectual and Social Background to Revolution, 1952-1977.* East Lansing, MI.: African Studies Center, Michigan State Univ., 1985.

Baravelli, G. C. *The Last Stronghold of Slavery: What Abyssinia Is.*

Rome, 1935.

Barclay, Glen St. John. *The Rise and Fall of the New Roman Empire: Italy's Bid for World Power, 1890-1943*. London: Sidgwick & Jackson, 1973.

Barrow, G. W. S. *Feudal Britain: The Completion of the Medieval Kingdoms 1066-1314*. London: Edward Arnold, 1956.

Batran, A. "The nineteenth-century Islamic revolutions in West Africa." In J. F. Ade Ajayi (ed.), UNESCO, *General History of Africa, Vol. VI.: Africa in the Nineteenth Century until the 1880s*. Berkeley: Univ. of California Press, 1989, 537-554.

Baum, James E. *Savage Abyssinia*. New York: J. H. Sears & Company, Int. Publishers, 1927.

Beachey, R. W. (ed.). *Collection of Documents on the Slave Trade of Eastern Africa*. London: Rex Collings, 1976.

Beauregard, Erving E. "Menelik II: Another Look." *TransAfrican Journal of History*, 5, no. 2 (1976):21-31.

Beckingham, C. F., and G. W. B. Huntingford (eds.). *Francisco Alvarez: The Prester John of the Indies*. In two volumes. Cambridge: Cambridge Univ. Press, 1961.

Beke, Charles T. *Letters on the Commerce and Politics of Abessinia and Other Parts of Eastern Africa*. London: 1852.

Bender, M. L. (ed.). *Language in Ethiopia*. London: Oxford Univ. Press, 1976a.

——. *The Non-Semitic Languages of Ethiopia*. East Lansing: African Studies Center, Michigan State Univ., 1976b.

Bennett, Norman R. *Arab Versus European: Diplomacy and War in Nineteenth-Century East Central Africa*. New York; London: Africana Publishing Co., 1986.

Bent, James T. *The Sacred City of Ethiopians*. London: Longmans, Green, And Co., 1893.

Berkeley, G. F. H. *The Campaign of Adowa and the Rise of Menelik*. New York: Negro Univ. Press, 1969.

Berlin, Isaiah. *Four Essays on Liberty*. Chicago: Univ. of Chicago Press, 1960.

Bernal, Martin. *Black Athena: The Afroasiatic Roots of Classical Civilization, Vol. I: The Fabrication of Ancient Greece, 1785-1985*. New Brunswick, NJ.: Rutgers Univ. Press, 1989.

Bettelheim, Charles. *Economic Calculation and Forms of Property*. New York and London: Monthly Review Press, 1975.

Bloch, Marc L. *Feudal Society*. Chicago, London, etc.: Univ. of Chicago Press; Routledge & Kegan Paul Ltd., 1961.

——. *French Rural History: An Essay on its Basic Characteristics.* Berkeley: Univ. of California Press, 1966.

——. *The Historian's Craft.* New York: Vintage Books, 1953.

Boahen, Albert A. "New trends and processes in Africa in the nineteenth century." In J. F. Ade Ajayi (ed.), UNESCO, *General History of Africa, Vol. VI.: Africa in the Nineteenth Century until the 1880s.* Berkeley: Univ. of California Press, 1989, 40-63.

——. *Topics in West African History.* Longman, 1986.

Bondestam, Lars. "Notes on Multinational Corporations in Ethiopia." *The African Review*, 5 (1975).

——. "People and Capitalism in the North-Eastern Lowlands of Ethiopia." *Journal of Modern African Studies*, 12, no. 3 (1974):423-439.

Bosworth, R. J. B. *Italy, the Least of the Great Powers: Italian Foreign Policy Before the First World War.* Cambridge, New York: Cambridge Univ. Press, 1979.

Braudel, Fernand. *The Mediterranean and the Mediterranean World in the Age of Philip II.* In two volumes. New York: Harper & Row, 1972.

——. *Civilization & Capitalism 15th-18th Century, Vol. 2: The Wheels of Commerce.* New York: Harper & Row Publishers, 1979.

Brogger, Jan. *Belief and Experience Among the Sidamo: A Case Study Towards and Anthropology of Knowledge.* Norwegian Univ. Press, 1986.

Brown, Reginald A. *The Origins of English Feudalism.* London: Allen & Unwin; New York: Barnes and Noble, 1973.

Buckland, W. W. *The Roman Law of Slavery: The Condition of the Slave in Private Law From Augustus to Justinian.* New York: AMS Press, 1969.

Budge, E. A. Wallis. *The History of Ethiopia, Nubia & Abyssinia.* In two volumes. Osterhot Anthropological Publications, 1970.

——. *The Queen of Sheba and Her only Son Menyelek.* London: Oxford Univ. Press, 1932.

Bulatovich, A. *With the Troops of Menelik II.* Moscow: Academy of Sciences, 1971.

Burton, Richard F, Sir. *First Footsteps in East Africa, or an Exploration of Harar.* Two volumes in one. Edited by Isabel Burton. New York: Dover Publications, Inc., 1987.

Buxton, David. *Travels in Ethiopia.* New York and Washington: Praeger, 1967.

Byres, T. J. and Harbans Mukhia (eds.). *Feudalism and Non-European Societies*. London; Totowa, New Jersey: Frank Cass, 1985.
Caplan, Andrew S. "British Policy Towards Ethiopia, 1909-1919." Ph. D. diss., Univ. of London, 1971.
Caraman, Philip. *The Lost Empire: The Story of the Jesuits in Ethiopia 1555-1634*. London: Sidgwick & Jackson, 1985.
Caulk, Richard A. "Armies as Predators: Soldiers and Peasants in Ethiopia c. 1850-1935." *International Journal of African Historical Studies*, 11, no. 3 (1978):457-493.
——. "Bad Men of the Borders: Shum and Shefta in Northern Ethiopia in the Nineteenth Century." *International Journal of African Historical Studies*, 17, no. 2 (1984):201-227.
——. "'Black Snake, White Snake': Bahta Hagos and His Revolt Against Italian Overrule in Eritrea, 1894." In Donald Crummey (ed.), *Banditry, Rebellion, and Social Protest in Africa*. London: J. Currey; Portsmouth, N.H.: Heinemann, 1986.
——. "Firearms and Princely Power in Ethiopia in the 19th Century." *Journal of African History*. 13, 4 (1972):609-630.
——. "The Occupation of Harar: January 1887." *Journal of Ethiopian Studies*, 9, no. 2 (1971):1-20.
——. "The Origins and Development of the Foreign Policy of Menelik II, 1865-1896." Ph.D. diss., Univ. of London, 1966.
——. "Religion and State in Nineteenth Century Ethiopia." *Journal of Ethiopian Studies*, 10, no. 1 (1972):23-42.
——. "Territorial Competition and the Battle of Embabo." *Journal of Ethiopian Studies*, 13, no. 1 (1975):65-88.
——. "Yohannes IV, the Mahdists, and the Colonial Partition of North-East Africa." *TransAfrican Journal of History*, 1, no. 2 (1971).
Central Statistical Office. *Statistical Bulletin*. Addis Ababa, January, 1974.
Cerulli, Enrico. *Peoples of South-West Ethiopia and Its Borderland*. London: International African Institute, 1956.
Christopher, John B. *Ethiopia: The Jibuti Railway and the Powers, 1899-1906*. Ph. D. diss., Harvard Univ., 1942.
Cipolla, Carlo M. *Before the Industrial Revolution—European Society and Economy, 1000-1700*. New York: W. W. Norton & Company, Inc., 1976.
Clapham, Christopher. "Feudalism, Modernization, and the Ethiopian Monarchy." *Conference on Ethiopian Feudalism*, Addis Ababa: Addis Ababa Univ. Press, 1976.

——. *Haile Selassie's Government*. New York: Praeger, 1969.
——. *Transformation and Continuity in Revolutionary Ethiopia*. Cambridge Univ. Press, 1988.
Clark, Kenneth. *Civilization: A Personal View*. New York: Harper & Row, 1969.
Cohen, John M. "Peasants and Feudalism in Africa: The Case of Ethiopia." *Canadian Journal of African Studies*, 8, no. 1 (1974):155-157.
Cohen, John M. and Dov Weintraub. *Land and Peasants in Imperial Ethiopia: The Social Background to a Revolution*. Assen: The Netherlands: Van Gorcum and Co., 1975.
Colin, Legum. *Ethiopia: The Fall of Haile Selassie's Empire*. London: Rex Collins, 1975
Connah, Graham. *African civilizations: Precolonial cities and states in tropical Africa: an archaeological perspective*. Cambrige, etc.: Cambridge Univ. Press, 1991.
Consolidated Laws of Ethiopia. Addis Ababa: Haile Selassie I Univ. Press, 1972.
Cooper, Frederick. "Africa and the World Economy." *African Studies Review*, 24, (June/Sept. 1981):1-86.
——. *Plantation Slavery on the East Coast of Africa*. New Haven and London: Yale Univ. Press, 1977.
Coquery-Vidrovitch, Catherine. *Africa: Endurance and Change South of the Sahara*. Translated by David Maisel. Berkeley, Los Angeles, London: Univ. of California Press, 1988.
Coulborn, Rushton (ed.). *Feudalism in History*. Hamden, Connecticut: Archon Books, 1965.
Critchley, John S. *Feudalism*. London, Boston: Allen & Unwin, 1978.
Croce, Benedetto. *A History of Italy 1871-1915*. Oxford: Clarendon Press, 1929.
Crummey, Donald. "Abyssinian Feudalism." *Past and Present*, 89, (1980):115-138.
——. "Banditry and Resistance: Noble and Peasant in Nineteenth-Century Ethiopia." In Donald Crummey (ed.), *Banditry Rebellion, and Social Protest in Africa*, London: J. Currey; Portsmouth, N.H.: Heinemann, 1986.
——. "Family and Property Amongst the Amhara Nobility." *Journal of African History*, 24, no. 2 (1983):207-220.
——. "Gondarine *Rim* Land Sales: An Introductory Description and Analysis." In Robert Hess (ed.), *Proceedings of the Fifth International Conference on Ethiopian Studies*, Chicago: Univ.

of Illinois at Chicago Circle, 1979.
——. *Priests and Politicians: Protestant and Catholic Missions in Orthodox Ethiopia, 1830-1868*. Oxford: Clarendon Press, 1972.
——. "Women and Landed Property in Gondarine Ethiopia." *International Journal of African Historical Studies*, 14, no. 3 (1981):444-465.
Cutler, Allan H., and E. C. Cutler. *The Jew As Ally of the Muslim: Medieval Roots of Anti-Semitism*. Notre Dame, Indiana: Univ. of Notre Dame Press, 1986.
Darkwah, R. H. *Menelik of Ethiopia*. London: Heinemann, 1972.
——. "The Rise of the Kingdom of Shoa, 1813-1889." Ph.D. diss., Univ. of London, 1966.
——. *Shewa, Menelik and the Ethiopian Empire, 1813-1889*. London: Heinemann, 1975.
Darley, Major H. *Slaves and Ivory in Abyssinia*. New York: Negro Univ. Press, 1969.
Davidson, Basil. *The Black Man's Burden: Africa and the Curse of the Nation-State*. New York: Times Books, 1992.
Denman, D. R. *Origins of Ownership: A Brief History of Land Ownership and Tenure in England from Earliest Times to the Modern Era*. London: George Allen & Unwin Ltd., 1958.
de Ste. Croix, G. E. M. *The Class Struggles in the Ancient Greek World from the Archaic Age to the Arab Conquests*. London: Duckworth, 1981.
del Boca, Angelo. *The Ethiopian War, 1935-1941*. Chicago: Univ. of Chicago Press, 1969.
Devens, Monica S. "An Annotated Bibliography of the Works of Wolf Leslau." In Stanislav Segert and Andras J. E. Bodrogligeti eds., *Ethiopian Studies*. (Dedicated to Wolf Leslau.) Weisbaden: Otto Harrassowitz, 1983, 1-37.
Dillman, August. *Ethiopic Grammar*. Amsterdam: Philo Press, 1974.
Diop, Chiekh Anta. *The Cultural Unity of Black Africa: The Domains of Patriarchy and Matriarchy in Classical Antiquity*. Chicago: Third World Press, 1990.
Donham, Donald L. and Wendy James, (eds.). *The Southern Marches of Imperial Ethiopia*. Cambridge, etc.: Cambridge Univ. Press, 1986.
Donzel, E. J. V. (ed.). *Foreign Relations of Ethiopia, 1642-1700: Documents Relating to the Journeys of Khodja Murad*. Istanbul: Nederlands Historisch-Archaeologisch Institut, 1979.
Doyle, William. *The Ancien Regime*. Basingstoke, Hampshire:

Macmillan, 1986.
Drake, St. Claire. *Black Folk Here and There: An Esaay in History and Anthropolgy*. In two volumes. Vol. 2. Los Angeles: UCLA, Center for Afro-American Studies, 1990.
Duby, Georges. *The Three Orders: Feudal Society Imagined*. Chicago and London: Univ. of Chicago Press, 1980.
Dugan, James and Laurence Lafore. *Days of Emperor and Clown: The Italo-Ethiopian War 1935-1936*. Garden City, NY: Doubleday, 1973.
Dufton, Henry. *Narrative of a Journey Through Abyssinia in 1862-3*. Westport: Conn.: Negro Univ. Press, 1970. (orig. published in 1867).
Duri Mohammed. "Industrialization and Income Distribution in Ethiopia." In J. F. Rweyemamu (ed.), *Industrialization and Income Distribution in Africa*. Dakar: Codesira, 1980.
——. "Private Foreign Investment in Ethiopia (1950-1968)." *Journal of Ethiopian Studies*. 7, no. 2 (1969):53-78.
Dye, William M. *Moslem Egypt and Christian Abyssinia*. New York: Negro Univ. Press, 1969.
Edwards, Jon R. "Slavery, the Slave Trade and the Economic Reorganization of Ethiopia." *African Economic History*, 11 (1982):3-14.
Ehret, Christopher. "On the Antiquity of Agriculture in Ethiopia." *Journal of African History*, 20, no. 2 (1979):161-177.
Elbashir, Ahmed E. *The United States, Slavery and the Slave Trade in the Nile Valley*. Lanham, New York and London: Univ. Press of America, 1983.
Elias, Norbert. *The Civilizing Process, Vol. I: The History of Manners*. New York: Urizen Books, 1978.
——. *The Civilizing Process, Vol: II. Power and Civility*. New York: Pantheon Books, 1982.
Ellis, Gene. "The Feudal Paradigm as a Hindrance to
Understanding Ethiopia." *Journal of Modern African Studies*, 14, no. 2 (1976):275-295.
Engels, Frederick. "The Origin of the Family, Private Property and the State." In Marx & Engels, *Selected Works*. In one volume. New York: International Publishers, 1968.
Ephraim Isaac. *The Ethiopian Church*. Boston: H. N. Sawyer, 1967.
——. "Social Structure of the Ethiopian Church." *Ethiopia Observer*, 14, no. 4 (1971).
——. "A Study of Mashafa Berhan and the Question of Hebraic-Jewish

Molding of Ethiopian Culture." Ph.D. diss., Harvard Univ., 1969.
Erlich, Haggai. *Ethiopia and the Challenge of Independence*. Boulder, Colorado: Lynne Rienner Publishers, 1986.
——. "A Political Biography of Ras Alula, 1875-1897." Ph.D. diss., Univ. of London, 1973.
Farrant, Leda. *Tippu Tip and the East African Slave Trade*. New York: St. Martin's Press, 1975.
Fernyhough, Timothy. "Social Mobility and Dissident Elites in Northern Ethiopia: The Role of Banditry, 1900-69." In Donald Crummey (ed.), *Banditry, Rebellion, and Social Protest in Africa*. London: J. Currey; Portsworth, NH: Heinemann, 1986.
Finer, Samuel. "State-and Nation-Building in Western Europe: The Role of the Military." In Charles Tilly (ed.), *The Formation of National States in Western Europe*. Princeton, NJ: Princeton Univ. Press, 1975, 84-163.
Finley, Moses I. "Slavery." *International Encyclopedia of the Social Sciences*, 14 (1968). The Macmillan Co. and the Free Press.
Fisch, Jorg. "Africa as *terra nullius*: The Berlin Conference and International Law." In Stig Forster et al. eds., *Bismarck, Europe, and Africa: The Berlin African Conference 1884-1885 and the Onset of Partition*. London: (German Historical Institute). Oxford Univ. Press, 1988, 347-375.
Fisher, Allan G. B. and Humphrey J. Fisher. *Slavery and Muslim Society in Africa: The Institution in Saharan and Sudanic Africa and the Trans-Saharan Trade*. London: C. Hurst & Co., 1970.
Freund, Bill. *The Making of Contemporary Africa: The Development of African Society Since 1800*. Bloomington: Indiana Univ. Press, 1984.
Gamst, Frederick C. "Peasantries and Elites without Urbanism: The Civilization of Ethiopia." *Comparative Studies in Society and History*, 12, no. 4 (1970):373-392
——. *The Qemant: A Pagan-Hebraic Peasantry of Ethiopia*. New York: Holt, Rinehart and Winston, 1969.
Garretson, Peter P. "A History of Addis Ababa from Its Foundation in 1886 to 1910." Ph.D. diss., Univ. of London, 1974.
——. "The Naggadras, Trade, and Selected Towns in Nineteenth and Early Twentieth Century Ethiopia." *International Journal of African Historical Studies*, 12, no. 3 (1979):416-439.
——. "Vicious Cycles: Ivory, Slaves, and Arms on the New Maji Frontier." In Donald Donham and Wendy James (eds.), *The Southern Marches of Imperial Ethiopia*. Cambridge, etc.:

Cambridge Univ. Press, 1986, 196-218.
Gebre Wold Ingida Work. "Ethiopia's Traditional System of Land Tenure and Taxation." Translated by Mengesha Gessesse. *Ethiopia Observer*, 5, no. 4 (1962):302-339.
Gebru Tareke. *Ethiopia: Power and Protest: Peasant revolts in the twentieth century*. Cambridge, etc.: Cambridge Univ. Press, 1991.
——. "Rural Protest in Ethiopia, 1941-1970: A Study of Three Rebellions." Ph.D. diss., Syracuse Univ., 1977.
Gellner, Ernest. *Nations and Nationalism*. Ithaca, NY.: Cornell Univ. Press, 1992.
Geshekter, Charles L. "Anti-Colonialism and Class Formation: The Eastern Horn of Africa Before 1950." *International Journal of African Historical Studies*, 18, no. 1 (1985):1-32.
Getachew Haile. "The Forty-Nine Hour Sabbath of the Ethiopian Church." *Journal of Semitic Studies*, 33, no. 2 (Autumn 1988):233-254.
Getahun Dilebo. "Emperor Menelik's Ethiopia, 1865-1916: National Unification or Amhara Communal Domination." Ph.D. diss., Howard Univ., 1974 (in microfilm).
Gibbon, Edward. *The Decline and Fall of the Roman Empire*. In three volumes. New York: Modern Library, 1977.
Gilkes, Patrick. *The Dying Lion. Feudalism and Modernization in Ethiopia*. New York: St. Martin's Press, 1975.
Gleichen, C. *With the Mission to Menelik, 1897*. London: Edward Arnold, 1898.
Goody, Jack. *Technology, Tradition, and the State in Africa*. Oxford Univ. Press, 1971.
Greenfield, Richard. *Ethiopia: A New Political History*. New York: Praeger, 1965.
Grey, Robert D. "Education and Politics in Ethiopia." Ph.D. diss., Yale Univ., 1970 (in microfilm).
Guy, Jeff. *The Destruction of the Zulu Kingdom: The Civil War in Zululand, 1879-1884*. London: Longman, 1979.
Gyenge, Zoltan. *Ethiopia on the Road of Non-Capitalist Development*. Budapest, 1976.
Haberland, Eike. "Hiob Ludolf, Father of Ethiopian Studies in Europe." In *Procedings of the Third International Conference on Ethiopian Studies, 1966, Vol. I*. Addis Ababa: Institute of Ethiopian Studies, Haile Selassie I Univ. Press, 1969, 131-136.
——. "The Horn of Africa." In B. A. Ogot (ed.), UNESCO, *General History of Africa, Vol. V.: Africa from the Sixteenth to the*

Eighteenth Century. Berkeley: Univ. of California Press, 1992, 703-749.

——. "The Influence of the Christian Empire on Southern Ethiopia." *Journal of Semitic Studies*, 9, no. 1 (Spring 1964):235-238.

——. "Special Castes in Ethiopia." In Robert Hess ed., *Proceedings of the Fifth International Conference on Ethiopian Studies*, Chicago: Univ. of Illinois at Chicago Circle, 1979.

Haile Kiros Asmerom. *Emergence, Expansion, and Decline of Patrimonial Bureaucracy in Ethiopia 1907-1974: An Attempt at Historical Interpretation*. 1978.

Haile Selassie I. *My Life and Ethiopia's Progress 1892-1937*. Translated and annotated by Edward Ullendorff. Oxford Univ. Press, 1976.

Hailu Habtu. "The Fallacy of the Triple Heritage Thesis: A Critique." *Issue*, 13 (1984):26-29.

Halldin, Viveca. *Swedes in Haile Selassie's Ethiopia, 1924-1952: A Study in Early Development and Co-Operation*. Uppsala; Stockholm: Almquist & Wiksell International Distributors, 1977.

Halliday, Fred and Maxine Molyneux. *The Ethiopian Revolution*. London: New Left Books, 1981.

Hallpike, C. R. *The Konso of Ethiopia: A Study of the Values of a Cushitic People*. Oxford: Clarendon Press, 1972.

——. "The Status of Craftsmen Among the Konso of South-West Ethiopia." *Africa*, 38, no. 3 (July 1968).

Hamilton, David N. "Ethiopia's Frontiers: The Boundary Agreements and Their Demarcation, 1896-1956." Ph.D. diss., Oxford Univ., 1974.

Hammerschmidt, Ernst. "Jewish Elements in the Cult of the Ethiopian Church." *Journal of Ethiopian Studies*, 3 no. 2 (1965):1-12.

Hancock, Graham. *The Sign and the Seal: The Quest for the Lost Ark of the Covenant*. New York: Crown Publishers, Inc., 1992.

Harbeson, John W. "Afar Pastoralists and Ethiopian Rural Development." *Rural Africana*, 28 (1975).

——. *The Ethiopian Transformation. The Quest for the Post-Imperial State*. Boulder & London: Westview Press, 1988.

Harris, Brice, Jr. *The United States and the Italo-Ethiopian Crisis*. Stanford: Stanford Univ. Press, 1964.

Harris, W. C. *The Highlands of Ethiopia*. In three volumes. London: Longman, Brown, Green, and Longmans, 1844.

Hegel, Georg W. F. *The Phenomenology of Spirit*. Translated by A. V. Miller. Oxford, etc.: Oxford Univ. Press, 1977.

——. *The Philosophy of History*. Translated by J. Sibree. New York: Dover Publications, 1956.

Hellie, Richard. *Slavery in Russia, 1450-1725*. Chicago: Univ. of Chicago Press, 1982.

Herlihy, David (ed.). *The History of Feudalism*. New York: Walker, 1971.

Herskovits, Melville. *Dahomey: An Ancient African Kingdom*. In two volumes. New York: J. J. Augustin, 1938.

Hertzron, Robert. *Ethiopian Semitic: Studies in Classification*. Manchester: Manchester Univ. Press, 1975.

Hess, Robert L. *Ethiopia: The Modernization of Autocracy*. Ithaca and London: Cornell Univ. Press, 1970.

Hill, Christopher. "Science and Magic." In *Collected Essays of Christopher Hill*. In three volumes. Vol. Three. Amherst: Univ. of Massachusetts Press, 1986.

Hilton, Rodney H. (ed.). *The Transition from Feudalism to Capitalism*. London: Verso, 1978.

Hiskett, Mervyn. *The Development of Islam in West Africa*. London and New York: Longman, 1984.

——. "The Nineteenth Century Jihads in West Africa." In John E. Flint ed. *The Cambridge History of Africa, Vol. 5: from c. 1790 to c. 1870*. Cambridge Univ. Press, 1976, 125-169.

Hoben, Allan. "Family, Land, and Class in Northwest Europe and Northern Highland Ethiopia." In Harold Marcus (ed.), *Proceedings of the First United States Confernce on Ethiopian Studies, 1973*. East Lansing, MI.: Michigan State Univ., African Studies Center, 1975, 157-170.

——. *Land Tenure Among the Amhara of Ethiopia: The Dynamic of Cognatic Descent*. Chicago: Univ. of Chicago Press, 1973.

——. "The Role of Ambilian Descent Groups in Gojjam Amhara Social Organization." Ph.D. diss., Univ. of California at Berkeley, 1963.

——. "Social Stratification in Traditional Amhara Society." In Arthur Tudena and Leonard Plotnicov (eds.). *Social Stratification in Africa*. New York: The Free Press, 1970, 187-224.

Hobsbawm, Eric and Terence Ranger eds. *The Invention of Tradition*. Cambridge, etc: Cambridge Univ. Press, 1983.

Hodgkin, Thomas. *Nationalism in Colonial Africa*. New York: New York Univ. Press, 1957.

Holt, Edgar. *Risorgimento: The Making of Italy 1815-1870*. New York: Macmillan, 1970.

Holt, P. M. *The Mahdist State in the Sudan 1881-1898: A Study of Its Origins, Development and Overthrow*. Oxford: Clarendon Press, 1958.

Hopkins, Anthony G. *An Economic History of West Africa*. New York: Columbia Univ. Press, 1973.

Hopkins, Simon. "Bibliography of the Writings of Professor Edward Ullendorff." *Journal of Semitic Studies*, XXXIV, no. 2 (Autumn 1989):253-289.

Horvath, Ronald J. "The Wandering Capitals of Ethiopia." *Journal of African History*, 10, no. 2 (1969):205-219.

Howard, W. E. H. *Public Administration in Ethiopia. A Study in Retrospect and Prospect*. Groningen, Netherlands: J. B. Wolters, 1956.

Huntingford, George W. B. *The Historical Geography of Ethiopia From the First Century AD to 1704*. Edited by Richard Pankhurst. Oxford: Oxford Univ. Press, 1989.

——. *The Galla of Ethiopia: The Kingdoms of Kafa and Janjero*. London: Hazell Watson and Viney, Ltd., 1955.

——. Translated and Edited. *The Land Charters of Northern Ethiopia*. Addis Ababa: Commercial Printing Press, 1965.

Ibn Khaldun. *The Muqaddimah*. In three volumes. Translated and edited by Franz Rosenthal. Princeton, NJ.: Princeton Univ. Press, 1958.

Ibrahim, H. A. "African initiatives and resistance in North-East Africa." In A. Adu Boahen (ed.), UNESCO, *General History of Africa, Vol. VII.: Africa under Colonial Domination 1880-1935*. Berkeley: Univ. of Californa Press, 1985, 63-86.

——. "The Sudan in the nineteenth century." In J. F. Ade Ajayi (ed.), UNESCO, *General History of Africa. Vol. VI.: Africa in the Nineteenth Century until the 1880s*. Berkeley: Univ. of California Press, 1989, 356-375.

Iliffe, John. *The African Poor: A history*. Cambridge: Cambridge Univ. Press, 1989.

Imbakom Kalewold. *Traditional Ethiopian Church Education*. New York: Columbia Univ., Teachers College Press, 1970.

Inalcik, Halil. "Servile Labor in the Ottoman Empire." In *Studies in Ottoman Social and Economic History*. London: Variorum Reprints, 1985.

Jesman, Czeslaw. *The Ethiopian Paradox*. New York: Oxford Univ. Press, 1963.

Johanson, Donald and Maitland Edey. *Lucy: The Beginnings of*

Humankind. New York: Simon and Schuster, 1981.
Jones, A. H. M. and Elizabeth Monroe. *A History of Abyssinia*. New York: Negro Univ. Press, 1969.
Johnston, Charles. *Travels in Southern Abyssinia Through the Country of Adals to the Kingdom of Shoa During the Years 1842-43*. London, 1844.
Johnston, H. A. S. *The Fulani Empire of Sokoto*. London: Oxford Univ. Press, 1967.
July, Robert W. *A History of the African People*. Prospects Heights, Ill.: Waveland Press, 1992.
Kapuscinski, Ryszard. *The Emperor: Downfall of an Autocrat*. Translated from the Polish by William R. Brand and Katarzyna Mroczkowska-Brand. New York: Vintage, 1984
Kautsky, John. *The Politics of Aristocratic Empires*. Chapel Hill: The Univ. of North Carolina Press, 1982.
Kazancigil, Ali (ed.) *The State in Global Perspective*. Gower/Unesco, 1986.
Kebede Ashenafi. "The Music of Ethiopia: Its Development and Cultural Setting." Ph.D. diss., Wesleyan Univ., 1971.
Keefer, Edward C. "Great Britain and Ethiopia, 1897-1910: Competition for Empire." *International Journal of African Historical Studies*, 6, no. 3 (1973):468-474.
Keller, Edmond. *Revolutionary Ethiopia: From Empire to People's Republic*. Bloomington and Indianapolis: Indiana Univ. Press, 1988.
Krige, Eileen J. *African Techniques of Domination and State Formation: Their Relevance Today*. Johannesburg: Witwatersrand Univ. Press, 1980.
Kwamena-Poh M. et al. *African History in Maps*. Longman, 1991.
Kobishanov, Yuri. *Axum*. Philadelphia: Univ. of pennsylvania Press, 1979.
——. "Axum: political system, economics and culture, first to fourth century." In G. Mokhtar (ed.), UNESCO, *General History of Africa, Vol. II. Ancient Civilzations of Africa*. Berkeley: Univ. of California Press, 1981, 381-399.
Kuper, Hilda. *An African Arsitocracy: Rank Among the Swazi of Bechuanaland*. London: Oxford Univ. Press, 1947.
Laketch Dirasse. "The Socio-Economic Position of Women in Addis Ababa: The Case of Prostitution." Ph. D. diss., Boston Univ., 1978.
Lange, Werner J. *History of the Southern Gonga (Southwestern*

Ethiopia). Wiesbaden: Stirner, 1982.
Lapidus, Ira M. *A History of Islamic Societies*. Cambrige, etc.: Cambridge Univ. Press, 1990.
Last, Murray. *The Sokoto Caliphate*. New York: The Humanities Press, 1967.
——. "The Sokoto caliphate and Borno." In J. F. Ade Ajayi (ed.), UNESCO, *General History of Africa, Vol. VI.: Africa in the Nineteenth Century until the 1880s*. Berkeley: Univ. of California Press, 1989, 555-599.
Lefebvre, Georges. *The Great Fear of 1789; Rural Panic in Revolutionary France*. New York: Pantheon Books, 1973.
Legassick, Martin. "Firearms, Horses and Samorian Army Organization 1870-1898." *Journal of African History*, 7, no. 1 (1966):95-115.
Legesse Lemma. "Political Economy of Ethiopia, 1875-1974." Ph.D. diss., Univ. of Notre Dame, 1979.
Le Goff, Jacques. "The Town as an Agent of Civilizations, 1200-1500." In Carlo Cipolla ed., *Fontana Economic History of Europe, Vol. I.: The Middle Ages*. London and Glasgow: Fontana, 1972.
Legum, Colin. *Ethiopia: The Fall of Haile Selassie's Empire*. London: Rex Collins, 1975.
Lerner, Daniel. *The Passing of Traditional Society: Modernizing the Middle East*. New York: The Free Press; London:Collier-Macmillan, Ltd. 1965
Leslau, Wolf. *An Annotated Bibliography of the Semitic Languages of Ethiopia*. (Bibliographies of the Near East I). The Hague: Mouton, 1965.
——. *Arabic Loanwords in Ethiopian Semitic*. Weisbaden: Otto Harrassowitz, 1990.
——. *English-Amharic Context Dictionary*. Weisbaden: Otto Harrassowitz, 1973.
——. *Etymological Dictionary of Gurage (Ethiopic)*. In three volumes. Weisbaden: Otto Harrassowitz, 1979.
Levine, Donald M. "The Concept of Masculinity in Ethiopian Culture." *International Journal of Social Psychiatry*, 12, no. 1 (1966):17-23.
——. *Greater Ethiopia: The Evolution of a Multiethnic Society*. Chicago and London: The Univ. of Chicago Press, 1974.
——. "Menelik and Oedipus: Further Observations on the Ethiopian National Epic." In Harold Marcus (ed.), *Proceedings of the First United States Conference on Ethiopian Studies, 1973*. East

Lansing, MI.: Michigan State Univ., 1975, 11-23.
——. *Wax and Gold. Tradition and Innovation in Ethiopian Culture.* Chicago and London: The Univ. of Chicago Press, 1967.
Lewis, Bernard. *The Arabs in History.* London: Hutchinson & Co., Ltd., 1968.
——. *Race and Color in Islam.* Harper and Row, 1971.
Lewis, David L. *The Race to Fashoda. European Colonialism and African Resistance in the Scramble for Africa.* New York: Weidenfeld & Nicholson, 1987.
Lewis, H. S. *A Galla Monarchy: Jimma Abba Jifar, 1830-1932.* Madison: Univ. of Wisconsin Press, 1965.
Lewis, I. M. *A Modern History of Somalia.* Boulder: Westview, 1987.
——. ed. *Nationalism and Self Determination in the Horn of Africa.* London: Ithaca Press, 1983.
——. *Peoples of the Horn of Africa: Somali, Afar and Saho.* London: International African Institute, 1969.
Lipsky, George A. *Ethiopia: Its People, Its Society, Its Culture.* New Haven: Hraf Press, 1967.
Lobo, Jerome. *A Voyage to Abyssinia.* New York: AMS Press, 1978.
Lord, Edith. *Cultural Patterns of Ethiopia: Queen of Sheba's Heirs.* Washington, D. C.: Acropolis Books, 1970.
Lovejoy, Paul E. "Plantations in the Economy of the Sokoto Caliphate." *Journal of African History*, 19, no. 3 (1978):341-368.
——. *Transforamtions in Slavery. A History of Slavery in Africa.* London: Cambridge Univ. Press, 1983.
Lundstrom, K. J. *Communal-Individual Land Ownership in Northern Ethiopia.* Uppsala, 1974.
Machiavelli, Niccolo. "The Prince." In *The Prince and the Discourses.* New York: The Modern Library, 1950.
Mahteme Sellassie Wolde Maskal. "The Land System of Ethiopia." *Ethiopia Observer*, 1, no. 9 (1957).
Maitland, F. W. *Domesday Book and Beyond. Three Essays in the Early History of England.* Cambridge Univ. Press, 1987.
Major Asseged. "Ethiopia: Revolution and War, 1974-1978." Ph.D. diss., Univ. of Denver, 1982.
Mantel-Niecko, Joanna. *The Role of Land Tenure in the System of Ethiopian Imperial Government in Modern Times.* Warsaw, 1980.
Maquet, Jacques J. *Power and Society in Africa.* BAS Printers, 1971.
Maravall, J.A. "The Origins of the Modern State." *Journal of World History*, 6, no. 4 (1961).

Marcus, Harold. "The Black Men Who Turned White." *Archiv Orientalni*, 39 (1971).
——. *Ethiopia, Great Britain, and the United States, 1941-1974: The Politics of Empire*. Berkeley: Univ. of California Press, 1983.
——. "The Foreign Policy of the Emperor Menelik 1896-1898, A Rejoinder." *Journal of African History*, 7, no. 1 (1966):117-122.
——. *Haile Selassie I: The Formative Years, 1892-1936*. Berkeley: Univ. of California Press, 1987.
——. "The Infrastructure of the Italo-Ethiopian Crisis: Haile Selassie, The Solomonic Empire, and the World Economy, 1916-1936." In Robert Hess ed., *Proceedings of the Fifth International Conference on Ethiopian Studies*, Chicago: Univ. of Illinois at Chicago Circle, 1979.
——. *The Life and Times of Menelik II: Ethiopia 1844-1913*. Oxford: Clarendon, 1975.
——. "The Organization of Menelik II's Palace and Imperial Hospitality (After 1896)." *Rural Africana*. East Lansing: African Studies Center (Spring, 1970).
——. "A Preliminary History of the Tripartite Treaty of December 13, 1906." *Journal of Ethiopian Studies*, 2, no. 2 (1964):21-40.
Markakis, John. *Ethiopia: Anatomy of a Traditional Polity*. Oxford: Clarendon Press, 1974.
——. "An Interpretation of Political Tradition in Ethiopia." *Presence Africaine*, 66 (1968):79-97.
——. *National and Class Conflict in the Horn of Africa*. Cambridge Univ. Press, 1987.
——. "Social Formation and Political Adaptation in Ethiopia." *Journal of Modern African Studies*, 11, no. 3 (1973):361-381.
——. and Nega Ayele. *Class and Revolution in Ethiopia*. Nottingham: Spokesman, 1978.
Marsot, Afaf Lutfi Al-Sayyid. *Egypt in the Reign of Muhammad Ali*. Cambridge Univ. Press, 1984.
Marx, Karl. "Critique of the Gotha Programme." In Marx and Engels, *Selected Works*. New York: International Publishers, 1968.
____. *Grundrisse*. Middlesex, England: Penguin Books, Ltd., Harmondsworth, 1973.
____. "The Poverty of Philosophy." In Marx and Engels, *Collected Works, Vol. 6*. New York: International Publishers, 1976.
____. *Theories of Surplus Value*. In Three Parts. Part 2. Moscow: Progress Publishers, 1977.
Mathew, David. *Ethiopia: The Study of a Polity, 1540-1935*. London:

Eyre and Spottiswoode, 1974.
Matthew, A. F. "Slavery in Abyssinia." *The Church Overseas*, 6 (1933).
Mazrui, Ali A. *The Africans: A Triple Heritage*. Boston, Toronto: Little Brown & Company, 1986.
——. "The Semitic Impact on Black Africa: Arab and Jewish Cultural Influences." *Issue*, 13 (1984):3-8.
McCann, James. "'Children of the House': Slavery and Its Suppression in Lasta, Northern Ethiopia, 1916-1935." In Suzanne Meirs and Richard Roberts eds., *The End of Slavery in Africa*. Madison, WI: Univ. of Wisconsin Press, 1988, 332-361.
——. *From Poverty to Famine in Northeast Ethiopia. A Rural History 1900-1935*. Philadelphia: Univ. of Pennsylvania Press, 1987.
McClellan, Charles. "Perspectives on the *Neftenya-Gabbar* System: The Darasa, Ethiopia." *Africa* (Roma), 33, no. 3 (1978).
——. "State Transformations and Social Reconstitution in Ethiopia: The Allure of the South." *Interntional Journal of African Historical Studies*, 17, no. 4 (1984):657-675.
Meirs, Suzanne. "Britain and the suppression of Slavery In Ethiopia." In Taddesse Beyene ed., *Proceedings of the Eighth International Conference on Ethiopian Studies, Vol. 2*. Addis Ababa: Addis Ababa Univ. Press, 1989, 253-266.
Meirs, Suzanne and Igor Kopytoff (eds.). *Slavery in Africa. Historical and Anthropological Perspectives*. Madison: Univ. of Wisconsin Press, 1977.
Merid Wolde Aregay. "A Reappraisl of the impact of Firearms in the History of Warfare in Ethiopia (c. 1500-1800)." *Journal of Ethiopian Studies*, 14 (1980):89-122.
——. "Society and Technology in Ethiopia, 1500-1800." *Journal of Ethiopian Studies*, 17 (1984):127-147.
——. "Southern Ethiopia and the Christian Kingdom 1508-1708, with Special Reference to the Galla Migrations and Their Consequences." Ph. D. diss., Univ. of London, 1971 (in microfilm).
Mesfin Wolde Mariam. *An Introductory Geography of Ethiopia*. Addis Ababa: Berhanena Selam Press, 1972.
——. *Rural Vulnerability to Famine in Ethiopia 1958-1977*. Vikas Publishing House Pvt. Ltd. in Association with Addis Ababa Univ., 1984.
Messing, Simon D. *Highland Plateau Amhara of Ethiopia*. In three volumes. Edited by M. Lionel Bender. New Haven: Human

Relations Area File, 1985.
Mies, Maria. *Patriarchy and Accumulation on a World Scale*. London: Zed Press, 1984.
Mockler, Anthony. *Haile Selassie's War*. New York: Random House, 1984.
Mohammed Hassen. *The Oromo of Ethiopia: A History, 1570-1860*. Cambridge, etc.: Cambridge Univ. Press, 1990.
Montesquieu, Baron De. *The Spririt of the Laws*. Two volumes in One. New York: Hafner Press, 1949.
Moore, Barrington. *Social Origins of Dictatorship and Democracy: Lord and Peasant in the Making of the Modern World*. Boston: Beacon Press, 1966.
Mosley, Leonard. *Haile Selassie: The Conquering Lion*. Englewood Cliffs, NJ: Prentice-Hall, 1964.
Mudimbe, V. Y. *The Invention of Africa: Gnosis, Philosophy, and the Order of Knowledge*. Bloomington and Indianapolis: Indiana Univ. Press, 1988.
Mulatu Wubneh and Yohannes Abate. *Ethiopia: Transition and Development in the Horn of Africa*. Boulder, CO.: Westview Press; London: Avebury, 1988.
Munro-Hay, S. C. *Aksum*. Edinburgh: Edinburgh Univ. Press, 1991.
Murdock, George P. *Africa: Its Peoples and Their Culture History*. McGraw Hill, 1959
Murphy, Dervla. *In Ethiopia with a Mule*. London: John Murray, 1968.
The National Archives and Records Service. *Records of the Department of State Relating to Internal Affairs of Ethiopia (Abyssinia) 1910-1929*. Washington, D. C.: 1962 (in microfilm).
Ngcongco, L. D. "The Mfecane and the rise of new African states." In J. F. Ade Ajayi (ed.), UNESCO, *General History of Africa, Vol. VI.: Africa in the Nineteenth Century until the 1880s*. Berkeley: Univ. of California Press, 1989, 90-123.
Norman, A. V. B. *The Medieval Soldier*. New York: Thomas Y. Crowell Co., 1971.
Oded, Arye. *Islam in Uganda. Islamization Through a Centralized State in Pre-colonial Africa*. New York and Toronto: John Wiley and Sons; Jerusalem: Israel Universities Press, 1974.
Oliver, Roland. *The African Experience: Major Themes in African History from Earliest Times to the Present*. New York: Harper Collins, 1991.
Oliver, Roland and J. D. Fage. *A Short History of Africa*. Penguin

Books, 1970.
Orent, Amnon. "Refocusing on the History of Kafa Prior to 1897: A Discussion of Political Processes." *African Historical Studies*, 3, no. 2 (1970).
Oriental Documents IX: *Letters from Ethiopian Rulers (Early Mid-Nineteenth Century)*. Oxford Univ. Press, 1985.
Ottaway, Marina and David Ottaway. *Ethiopia: Empire in Revolution*. New York: Africana Publishing Co., 1978.
Pankhurst, Richard K. P. "The Advent of the Maria Theresa Dollar in Ethiopia, Its Effect on Taxation and Wealth Accumulation, and Other Economic, Political and Cultural Implications." *North East African Studies* [formerly *Ethiopianist Notes*], 1, no. 3 (1979-1980):19-48.
——. "The `Banyan' or Indian Presence at Massawa, the Dahlak Islands and the Horn of Africa." *Journal of Ethiopian Studies*, 12, no. 1 (1974):185-212.
——. *Economic History of Ethiopia, 1800-1935*. Addis Ababa: Haile Selassie Univ. Press, 1968.
——. "Economic Verdict on the Italian Occupation of Ethiopia, 1936-41." *Ethiopia Observer*, 14, no 1 (1971):68-82.
——. "The Emperor Theodore and the Question of Foreign Artisans in Ethiopia." *Boston Univ. Papers in African History*, vol. 2, Boston: Boston Univ. Press, 1966.
——. "An Inquiry into the Penetration of Fire-Arms into Southern Ethiopia in the 19th Century Prior to the Reign of Menelik." *Ethiopia Observer*, 12, no. 2 (1968):128-136.
——. "Ethiopia and Somaila." In J. F. Ade Ajayi (ed.), UNESCO, *General History of Africa, Vol. VI.: Africa in the Nineteenth Century until the 1880s*. Berkeley: Univ. of California Press, 1989, 376-411.
——. "Ethiopia and the Red Sea and the Gulf of Aden Ports in the Nineteenth and Twentieth Centuries." *Ethiopia Observer*, 8, no. 1, (1964):36-104.
——. "The Ethiopian Army in Former Times." *Ethiopia Observer*, 7, no. 2 (1963):118-142.
——. "The Ethiopian Patriots and the Collapse of Italian Rule in East Africa, 1940-1941." *Ethiopia Observer*, 12, no. 2 (1969):92-127.
——. (ed.). *The Ethiopian Royal Chronicles*. Oxford Univ. Press, 1967.
——. "Ethiopian Slave Reminiscences of the Nineteenth Century." *TransAfrican Journal of History*, 5, no. 1 (1976):98-110.

——. "The Ethiopian Slave Trade in the Nineteenth and Early Twentieth Century: A Statistical Inquiry." *Journal of Semitic Studies*, 9, no. 1 (1964):220-228.

——. "The History of Fire-Arms in Ethiopia Prior to the Nineteenth Century." *Ethiopia Observer*, 11, no. 2 (1967):202-25.

——. "The History of Bareya, Sanquella and Other Ethiopian Slaves From the Borderlands of the Sudan." In *Conference on Ethiopian Feudalism*. Addis Ababa: Addis Ababa Univ. Press, 1976.

——. *History of Ethiopian Towns From the Middle Ages to the Early Nineteenth Century*. Stuttgart: Franz Steiner Verlag GMBH, 1982.

——. *History of Ethiopian Towns From the Mid-Nineteenth Century to 1935*. Stuttgart: Franz Steiner Verlag Weisbaden GMBH, 1985.

——. "The History of Prostitution in Ethiopia." *Journal of Ethiopian Studies*, 12, no. 2 (1974):159-178.

——. "Indian Trade with Ethiopia, the Gulf of Aden and the Horn of Africa in the Nineteenth and Early Twentieth Centuries." *Cahiers d'Etudes Africaines*, 14, no. 3 (1974):453-497.

——. *An Introduction to the Medical History of Ethiopia*. Trenton, NJ: Red Sea Press, 1991.

——. "Linguistic and Cultural Data on Penetration of Fire-Arms into Ethiopia." *Journal of Ethiopian Studies*, 9, no. 1 (1971):47-82.

——. "Menelik and the Utilization of Foreign Skills in Ethiopia." *Journal of Ethiopian Studies*, 5, no. 1 (1967):29-86.

——. "A Page of Ethiopian History: Italian Settlement Plans During the Fascist Occupation of 1936-1941." *Ethiopia Observer*, 13, no. 2 (1970).

——. "The Role of Fire-Arms in Ethiopian Culture (16th. to 20th Centuries)." *Journal des Africanistes*, XLVIII, no. 2:131-44.

——. "The Role of Foreigners in 19th Century Ethiopia, Prior to the Rise of Menelik." *Boston Univ. Papers in African History*, 2 (1966).

——. *A Social History of Ethiopia: The Northern and Central Highlands from Early Medieval Times to the Rise of Emperor Tewodros II*. Trenton, NJ.: Red Sea Press, 1992.

——. "Some Factors Depressing the Strandard of Living of Peasants in Traditional Ethiopia." *Journal of Ethiopian Studies*, 4, no. 2 (1966):45-98.

——. *State and Land in Ethiopian History*. Nairobi: Oxford Univ. Press, 1966.

——. "The Tents of the Ethiopian Court." *Azania*, 18, (1983):181-95.
——. "The Trade of Central Ethiopia in the Nineteenth and Early Twentieth Centuries." *Journal of Ethiopian Studies*, 2, no. 2 (1964):41-91.
——. "The Trade of Northern Ethiopia in the Nineteenth and Early Twentieth Centuries." *Journal of Ethiopian Studies*, 2, no. 1 (1964):49-159.
——. "The Trade of Southern and Western Ethiopia and Indian Ocean Ports in the Nineteenth and Early Twentieth Centuries." *Journal of Ethiopian Studies*, 3, no. 2 (1965):37-74.
——. *Travellers in Ethiopia*. Edited by Richard Pankhurst. London: Oxford Univ. Press, 1965.
——. "Tribute, Taxation and Government Revenues in Nineteenth and Early Twentieth Century Ethiopia: Part I." *Journal of Ethiopian Studies*, 5, no. 2 (1967):37-87.
——. "Tribute, Taxation and Government Revenues in Nineteenth and Early Twentieth Century Ethiopia: Part II." *Journal of Ethiopian Studies*, 6, no. 1 (1968):21-72.
——. "Tribute, Taxation and Government Revenues in Nineteenth and Early Twentieth Century Ethiopia: Part III." *Journal of Ethiopian Studies*, 6, no. 2 (1968):93-118.
Parkyns, Mansfield. *Life in Abyssinia*. London: Frank Cass, 1966.
Parsons, Neil. *A New History of Southern Africa*. New York: Holmes & Meier, 1986.
Patterson, Orlando. *Slavery and Social Death*. Cambridge, MA: Harvard Univ. Press, 1982.
——. *Freedom: Volume I: Freedom in the Making of Western Culture*: New York: Basic Books, 1991
Paulos Tzadua. Translator. *The Fetha Negast: The Law of Kings*. Addis Ababa: Central Printing Press, 1968.
Pausewang, Siegfried. "Land, Market, and Rural Society (Rural Ethiopia 1840-1976." In Robert Hess ed., *Proceedings of the Fifth International Conference on Ethiopian Studies*, Chicago: Univ. of Illinois at Chicago Circle, 1979.
Pearce, Nathaniel. *The Life and Adventures of Nathaniel Pearce*. Edited by J. J. Hallis. London, 1831.
Penzer, N.M. *The Harem*. London: Spring Books, 1965.
Perham, Margery. *The Government of Ethiopia*. London: Faber and Faber Limited, 1969.
Pirenne, Henri. *Mohammed and Charlemagne*. London: G. Allen &

Unwin, Ltd., 1939.
Pflanze, Otto. "Nationalism in Europe, 1848-1871." *Review of Politics*, 28, no. 2 (1966):129-143.
Plowden, Walter C. *Travels in Abyssinia and the Galla Country with an Account of a Mission to Ras Ali in 1848*. Farnborough, Hants: Gregg International Publishers, Ltd., 1972.
Polanyi, Karl A. *Dahomey and the Slave Trade, An Analysis of an Archaic Economy*. Seattle and London: Univ. of Washington Press, 1966.
——. *Primitive, Archaic, and Modern Economies*. Edited by George Dalton. Boston: Beacon Press, 1971.
Portal, G. H. *My Mission to Abyssinia*. London: Edward Arnold, 1892.
Pratt, Mary L. "Scrathces on the Face of the Country: or What Mr. Barrow Saw in the Land of the Bushman." In Henry L. Gates (ed.), *Race, Writing, and Difference*. Chicago and London: Univ. of Chicago Press, 1986, 138-162.
——. *Imperial Eyes: Travel Writing and Transculturation*. London and New York: Routledge, 1992.
Quirin, James. "The Beta Israel (Felasha) in Ethiopian History." Ph. D. Diss., Univ. of Minnesota, 1977.
——. *The Evolution of Ethiopian Jews: A history of the Beta Israel (Falasha) to 1920*. Philadelphia: Univ. of Pennsylvania Press, 1992.
——. "The Process of Caste Formation in Ethiopia: A Study of the Beta Israel (Felasha), 1270-1868." *International Journal of African Historical Studies*, 12, no. 2 (1979):235-258.
Redden, Kenneth, R. *The Legal System of Ethiopia*. Charlottesville, Virginia: The Michie Company, 1968.
Reminick, Ronald A. "The Manze Amhara of Ethiopia: A Study of Authority, Masculinity, and Sociality." Ph.D. diss., Univ. of Chicago, 1973.
Renan, Ernest. "What is a Nation?". Translated and Annotated by Martin Thom. In Homi Bhabha ed., *Nation and Narration*. London and New York: Routledge, 1990.
Rennell Rodd, Sir James. *Social and Diplomatic Memoirs, 1894-1901: Egypt and Abyssinia*. Vol. II. London: Edward Arnold and Co., 1923.
Rey, Charles F. *The Real Abyssinia*. New York: Negro Universities Press, 1969.
——. *Unconquered Abyssinia As It Is Today*. London: Seeley, Service

& Co. Limited, 1923.
Ricci, L. "The Organization of the State and Social Structures in Ethiopia." In P. J. McEwan (ed.), *Twentieth Century Africa*. New York: Oxford Univ. Press, 1968.
Ritter, E. A. *Shaka Zulu: The Rise of the Zulu Empire*. London: Allen & Lane, 1935.
Robbins, Jerrold. "The Americans in Ethiopia." *American Mercury*, 29 (1933).
Roberts, A. D. "The Sub-Imperialism of Buganda." *Journal of African History*. 3, no. 3 (1962):435-50.
Robertson, A. J. Translator and Editor. *Anglo-Saxon Charters*. Holmes Beach, Florida: WMW Gaunt & Sons, Inc., 1986.
Roehl, Richard. "Patterns and Structure of Demand 1000-1500." In Carlo Cipolla (ed.), *The Fontana Economic History of Europe, Vol. I: The Middle Ages*. London and Glasgow: Fontana, 1972
Rosenfeld, Chris Prouty. *A Chronology of Menelik II of Ethiopia, 1844-1913: Emperor of Ethiopia, 1889-1913*. East Lansing, MI.: African Studies Center, 1976.
——. *Empress Taytu and Menelik II: Ethiopia, 1883-1910*. Trenton, N. J.: Red Sea Press, 1986.
Rotberg, Robert I. *The Founder: Cecil Rhodes and the Pursuit of Power*. New York; Oxford: Oxford Univ. Press, 1988.
Rotberg, Robert I and Ali A. Mazrui (eds.). *Protest and Power in Black Africa*. New York: Oxford Univ. Press, 1970.
Rubenson, Sven. *King of Kings Tewodros of Ethiopia*. Addis Ababa and Nairobi. Published by Haile Selassie I Univ. Press, in association with Oxford Univ. Press, 1966.
——. "The Lion of the Tribe of Judah: Christian Symbol and/or Imperial Title." *Journal of Ethiopian Studies*, 3, no. 2 (1965):75-85.
——. *The Survival of Ethiopian Independence*. Heinemann, in association with Esselete Studium & Addis Ababa Univ. Press, 1976.
Said, Edward. *Orientalism*. New York: Random House, 1979.
Salim, Ahmed Idha (ed.). *State Formation in Eastern Africa*. New York: St. Martin's Press, 1985.
Salt, Henry. *A Voyage to Abyssinia and Travels into the Interior of that Country*. London: Frank Cass, 1967.
Sanceau, Elaine. *The Land of Prester John: A Chronicle of Portuguese Exploration*. New York: 1944.
Sanderson, G. N. "The Foreign Policy of the Negus Menelik, 1896-1898." *Journal of African History*, 5, 1 (1964):87-97.

Sandford, Christine. *Ethiopia Under Haile Selassie*. London: Dent, 1946.
Sbacchi, Alberto. *Ethiopia Under Mussolini: Fascism and the Colonial Experience*. London: Zed Press, 1985.
——. "Italian Colonialism in Ethiopia 1936-1940." Ph.D. diss., Univ. of Illinois at Chicago-Circle, 1975. (in microfilm)
——. "Italy and the Treatment of the Ethiopian Aristocracy, 1937-1940." *International Journal of African Historical Studies*, 10, no. 2 (1977):209-241.
Scaetta, H. "Geography, Ethiopia's Ally." *Foreign Affairs*, 14, no. 1, October (1935).
Schaefer, Ludwig F. (ed.). *The Ethiopian Crisis: Touchstone of Appeasement*. D. C. Heath and Company, 1961.
Schama, Simon. *Citizens: A Chronicle of the French Revolution*. New York: Random House, 1989.
Schumpeter, Joseph A. *Capitalism, Socialism and Democracy*. New York: Harper and Row, 1950.
Schwab, Peter. *Decision-Making in Ethiopia: A Study of the Political Process*. Rutherford, etc.: Fairleigh Dickinson Univ. Press, 1972.
——. *Ethiopia: Politics, Economics and Society*. London: Frances Pinter Publishers, 1985.
——. *Haile Selassie I: Ethiopia's Lion of Judah*. Chicago: Nelson-Hall, 1979.
——. "Rebellion in Gojam Province, Ethiopia." *Canadian Journal of African Studies*, 4, no. 2 (1970):249-256.
Sedler, Robert A. "The Chilot Jursidiction of the Emperor of Ethiopia." *Journal of African Law*, 8, no. 2 (1964).
Seifu Metaferia. *Ya Barya sim ba Amaraw bahil*. (In Amharic.) *Journal of Ethiopian Studies*, 10, no. 2 (1972):127-200.
Seligman, C. G. *Races of Africa*. London: Oxford Univ. Press, 1959.
Sergew Hable Sellassie. *Ancient and Medieval Ethiopian History to 1270*. Addis Ababa: United Printers, 1972.
——. "Church and State in the Aksumite Period." In *Procedings of the Third International Conference on Ethiopian Studies, 1966*. Addis Ababa: Institute of Ethiopian Studies, Haile Selassie I Univ., 1969, 5-8.
——. "The Problem of Gudit." *Journal of Ethiopian Studies*, 10, no. 1 (1972):113-124.
Serjeant, R. B. "South Arabia and Ethiopia: African Elements in the South Arabian Population." In *Procedings of the Third International Conference on Ethiopian Studies, 1966*. Addis

Ababa: Institute of Ethiopian Studies, Haile Selassie I Univ., 1969, 25-33.

Shack, William A. *The Central Ethiopians: Amhara, Tigrina and Related Peoples*. London: International African Institute, 1974.

——. *The Gurage: A People of the Enset Culture*. Oxford Univ. Press, 1966.

——. "Notes on Occupational Castes Among the Gurage of South-West Ethiopia." *Man*, LXIV, March-April (1964).

——. "Occupational Prestige, Status and Social Change in Modern Ethiopia." *Africa*, 46, no. 2 (1976).

Sheik-`Abdi, `Abdi. *Divine Madness: Mohammed `Abdulle Hassan (1856-1920*. London, and Atlantic Highlands, NJ: Zed Books Ltd., 1993.

Shelemay, Kay K. "The Music of the Lalibeloc: Musical Mendicants in Ethiopia." *Journal of African Studies*, 9, no. 3 (1982):128-138.

Sheriff, Abdul. *Slaves, Spices & Ivory in Zanzibar: Integration of an East African Commercial Empire into the World Economy, 1770-1873*. Athens, OH: Ohio Univ. Press, 1987.

Shinn, David. "A Survey of American-Ethiopian Relations Prior to the Italian Occupation of Ethiopia." *Ethiopia Observer*, 14, no. 4 (1971).

Simmel, Georg. *The Philosophy of Money*. Translated by Tom Bottomre and David Frisby. London; Boston: Routledge & Kegan Paul, 1978.

——. *The Sociology of Georg Simmel*. Translated, EDited, and with an Introduction by Kurt H. Wolff. New York: The Free Press, 1969.

Simoons, Frederick J. *Northwest Ethiopia: Peoples and Economy*. Madison: The Univ. of Wisconsin Press, 1960.

Skinner, Robert P. *Abyssinia of Today: An Account of the First Mission Sent by the American Government to the Court of the King of Kings, 1903-1904*. New York: Negro Univ. Press, 1969.

Skocpol, Theda. *States and Social Revolution: A Comparative Analysis of France, Russia, and China*. Cambridge, New York: Cambridge Univ. Press, 1979.

Smith, R. E. F. "Drink in Old Russia." In Eric Hobsbawm (ed.), *Peasants in History, Essays in honor of Daniel Thorner*. Oxford Univ. Press, 1980.

Sorenson, John. *Imagining Ethiopia: Struggles for History and Identity in the Horn of Africa*. New Brunswick, NJ.: Rutgers Univ. Press, 1993.

Spencer, John H. *Ethiopia at Bay: A Personal Account of the Haile Selassie Years*. Algonac, MI.: Reference Publications, Inc. 1984.
Stahl, Michael. *Ethiopia: Political Contradictions in Agricultural Development*. Uppsala: Scandinavian Institute of African Studies, 1974.
Stavrianos, L. S. *Global Rift: The Third World Comes of Age*. New York: William Morrow, 1981.
Steer, George L. *Caesar in Abyssinia*. London: Hodder and Stoughton, 1936.
——. *Sealed and Delivered: A Book on the Abyssinian Campaign*. London: Hodder and Stoughton Limited, 1942.
Steffanson, Borg G. and Ronald K. Starrett (eds.). *Documents on Ethiopian Politics*. In four volumes. Salisbury, North Carolina: Documentary Publications, 1976.
Sterns, Henry A. *Wanderings Among the Falashas in Abyssinia with a Description of the Country and its Various Inhabitants*. London: Frank Cass, 1968.
Stitz, Volker. "Distribution and Foundation of Churches in Ethiopia." *Journal of Ethiopian Studies*, 13, no. 1 (1975):11-36.
Sumner, Claude. *Ethiopian Philosophy*. In three volumes. Vol. II. Addis Ababa: Addis Ababa Univ. Press, 1974
Taddesse Tamrat. *Church and State in Ethiopia, 1270-1527*. Oxford: Clarendon Press, 1972.
——."Hagiographers and the Reconstruction of the Medieval Ethiopian History." *Rural Africana*, 10 (1970).
——. "A Short Note on the Traditions of Pagan Resistance to the Ethiopian Church (14th and 15th Centuries)." *Journal of Ethiopian Studies*, 10, no. 1 (1972):137-150.
——. "The Horn of Africa: The Solomonids in Ethiopia and the States of the Horn of Africa." In D. T. Niane (ed.). UNESCO, *General History of Africa, Vol. IV: Africa From the Twelth to the Sixteenth Century*. Berkeley: Univ. of California Press, 1984, 423-454.
Tekalign Wolde Mariam. "The Slave Trade in the Economy of Jimma." In Tadesse Beyene ed., *Proceedings of the Eighth International Conference on Ethiopian Studies, Vol. 2*. Addis Ababa: Addis Ababa Univ. Press, 1989, 309-318.
Teketel Haile-Mariam. "The Production, Marketing, and Economic Impact of Coffee in Ethiopia." Ph. D. diss., Stanford Univ., 1973.
Teklehaimanot Teferi. "The Ethiopian Feudal Army and Its Wars, 1868-1936." Ph.D. diss., Kansas State Univ., 1972 (in microfilm).

Tekle Tsadik Mekouria. *Atse Menelikena Yaityopia Andenat*. (In Amharic). Addis Ababa: Kuraz Publishers, 1983 (Eth. calendar).
——. *Atse Tewodrosna Yaityopia Andenat*. (In Amharic). Addis Ababa: Kuraz Publishers, 1981 (Eth. calendar).
——. *Atse Yohanessna Yaityopia Andenat*. (In Amharic). Addis Ababa: Kuraz Publishers, 1982 (Eth. calendar).
——. "Christian Aksum." In G. Mokhtar (ed.), UNESCO, *General History of Africa, Vol. II. Ancient Civilzations of Africa*. Berkeley: Univ. of California Press, 1981, 401-422.
Temperly, H. *England and the Near East: The Crimea*. Longman, 1936.
Terrefe Woldetsadik. "The Unification of Ethiopia (1880-1935) Wallaga." *Journal of Ethiopian Studies*, 6, no. 1 (1968).
Teshale Tibebu. "On the Question of Feudalism, Absolutism, and the Bourgeois Revolution." *Review*, 13, no. 1 (Winter, 1990):49-151.
Tessema Ta'a. "The Political Economy of Western Central Ethiopia: From the Mid-16th to the Early-20th Centuries." Ph.D. diss., Michigan State Univ., East Lansing, 1986.
Thesiger, Wilfred. *The Life of My Choice*. W. Collins Sons and Co., Ltd., 1987.
Thompson, Leonard. *A History of South Africa*. New Haven and London: Yale Univ. Press, 1990.
Tilly, Charles. "Reflections on the History of European State-Making." In Charles Tilly (ed.), *The Formation of National States in Western Europe*. Princeton, NJ: Princeton Univ. Press, 1975, 3-83.
Toledano, Ehud R. *The Ottoman Slave Trade and Its Suppression, 1840-1890*. Princeton, NJ: Princeton Univ. Press, 1982.
Tonkin, Thelma. *Ethiopia With Love*. London: Hodder and Stoughton, 1972.
Toynbee, Arnold J. *Between Niger and Nile*. London: Oxford Univ. Press, 1965.
——. *A Study of History: Vol. II*. New York: Oxford Univ. Press, 1962.
Trevor-Roper, Hugh R. *The European Witch-Craze of the Sixteenth and Seventeenth Centuries, and Other Essays*. New York: Harper and Row, 1969.
Trimingham, John S. *The Christian Church and Missions in Ethiopia (including Eritrea and the Somalilands)*. World Dominion Press, 1950.
——. *A History of Islam in West Africa*. Oxford Univ. Press, 1962.
——. *Islam in East Africa*. Oxford: Clarendon Press, 1964.

——. *Islam in Ethiopia*. New York: Barnes and Noble, Inc., 1965.

Triulzi, Alessandro. *Salt, Gold and Legitimacy: Prelude to the History of a No-man's Land: Bela Shangul, Wallaga, Ethiopia (ca. 1800-1898)*. Napoli, 1981.

Tsehai Berhane Selassie. "The Political and Military Traditions of the Ethiopian Peasantry (1800-1941)." Ph.D. diss., Saint Anne's College, Oxford Univ., 1980.

Tsukahira, Toshio G. *Feudal Control in Tokugawa Japan: The Sankin Kotai System*. Cambridge, MA: Harvard Univ. Press, 1966.

Tubiana, Joseph (ed.). *Modern Ethiopia from the Accession of Menelik II to the Present*. Rotterdam: 1980.

Udovitch, Abraham L. (ed.). *The Islamic Middle East, 700-1900: Studies in Economic and Social History*. Princeton, NJ: Darwin Press, Inc., 1981.

Ullendorf, Edward. *The Ethiopians*. London: Oxford Univ. Press, 1960.

——. "Hebraic-Jewish Elements in Abyssinian (monophyste) Christianity." *Journal of Semitic Studies*, 1, no. 3 (July 1956):216-256.

——. *The Two Zions: Reminiscences of Jerusalem and Ethiopia*. Oxford; New York: Oxford Univ. Press, 1988.

Vansina, Jan. "Population movements and emergence of new socio-political forms in Africa." In B. A. Ogot (ed.), UNESCO, *General History of Africa, Vol. V.: Africa from the Sixteenth to the Eighteenth Century*. Berkeley: Univ. of California Press, 1992, 46-73.

Veblen, Thorstein. *The Theory of the Leisure Class: An Economic Study of Institutions*. New York: Viking Press, 1945.

Verlinden, Charles. *The Beginnings of Modern Colonization*. Translated by Yvonne Freccero. Ithaca and New York: Cornell Univ. Press, 1970.

Villari, Luigi. *Italian Foreign Policy Under Mussolini*. New York: 1956.

Vivian, Herbert. *Abyssinia Through the Lion-Land to the Court of the Lion of Judah*. New York: Negro Universities Press, 1969.

Wadhawan, G. N. "Indians in Ethiopia." *Ethiopia Observer*, 4, no. 10 (1960).

Waldron, Sidney R. "Harer: The Muslim City in Ethiopia." In Robert Hess (ed.), *Proceedings of the Fifth International Conference on Ethiopian Studies*. Chicago: Univ. of Illinois at Chicago Circle, 1979, 239-57.

Wallerstein, Immanuel. "Africa and the world economy." In J. F. Ade Ajayi (ed.), UNESCO, *General History of Africa, Vol. VI.: Africa in the Nineteenth Century until the 1880s*. Berkeley: Univ. of California Press, 1989, 23-39.

——. *Historical Capitalism*. London: Verso, 1992.

——. *The Modern World-System, Vol. I. Capitalist Agriculture and the Origins of the European World-Economy in the Sixteenth Century*. New York, San Francisco, London: Academic Press, 1974.

——. *The Modern World-System, Vol. II. Mercantilism and the Consolidation of the European World-Economy, 1600-1750*. New York and London: Academic Press, 1980.

——. *The Modern World-System, Vol. III. The Second Era of Great Expansion of the Capitalist World-Economy, 1730-1840's*. New York and London: Academic Press, 1989.

——. "Peripheralization of Southern Africa: Changes in Household Structure and Labor-Force Formation." In Immanuel Wallerstein, *Africa and the Modern World*. Trenton, NJ.: Africa World Press, 1986.

——. "The Three Stages of Africa's Involvement in the World-Economy." In Peter C. W. Gutkind and I. Wallerstein (eds.), *Political Economy of Contemporary Africa*. Beverly Hills: Sage Publications, 1985, 35-63.

Walz, Terence. *Trade Between Egypt and Bilad As-Sudan*. Cairo: Instit Francais D'Archchelogie Orientale Du Caire, 1978.

Watson, James L. (ed). *Asian and African Systems of Slavery*. Oxford: Basil Blackwell, 1980.

Waugh, Evelyn. *Waugh in Abyssinia*. London: Methuen, 1984.

Weber, Eugen. *Peasants into Frenchmen: The Modernization of Rural France, 1870-1914*. Stanford: Stanford Univ. Press, 1976.

Weber, Max. *The Agrarian Sociology of Ancient Civilizations*. London: New Left Books, 1976.

——. *Economy and Society*. Vols. I and II. Berkeley: Univ. of California Press, 1978.

——. "Politics as a Vocation." In R. Bendix (ed.), *From Max Weber: Essays in Sociology*. New York: Oxford Univ. Press, 1974.

——. *The Sociology of Religion*. Boston: Beacon Press, 1964.

Webster, James B. and Albert A. Boahen. *The Revolutionary Years: West Africa since 1800*. Longman, 1990.

Weissleder, Wolfgang. "The Political Ecology of Amhara Domination." Ph. D. diss., Univ. of Chicago, 1965.

Wilkinson, J. G. "Account of the Jimma Country." *Journal of the Royal Geographic Society*, 25 (1855).

Wilks, Ivor. *Asante in the Nineteenth Century: The Structure and Evolution of a Political Order*. Cambridge: Cambridge Univ. Press, 1989.

Williams, Chancellor. *The Destruction of Black Civilization: Great Issues of a Race from 4500 B.C. to 2000 A.D.*. Chicago: Third World Press, 1987.

Willis, John R. (ed.). *Slaves and Slavery in Muslim Africa, Vol. I: Islam and the Ideology of Enslavement*. London: Frank Cass, 1985.

Winid, J. B. "The History of Ethiopian Coffee." *African Bulletin*, Warsaw, 10 (1969).

Woolbert, Robert G. "Feudal Ethiopia and Her Armies." *Foreign Affairs*, 14, no. 1 (October 1935).

Wylde, Augustus B. *Modern Abyssinia*. Westport: Negro Universities Press, 1970.

Zewde Gebre Sellassie. *Yohannes IV of Ethiopia. A Political Biography*. Oxford: Clarendon Press, 1975.

Index